Routledge Revivals

A Second Book of Broadsheets

This book, together with *A Book of Broadsheets* makes up an anthology of the 1915 broadsheets distributed by *The Times* to members of H.M. Forces serving in the trenches of World War I. The volume contains a wide variety of rich literature from before the war and was designed to give soldiers entertainment. It includes extracts from the works of Francis Bacon, Rudyard Kipling, Sir Walter Raleigh, William Wordsworth and Charles Dickens.

A Second Book of Broadsheets

With an Introduction by Geoffrey Dawson

First published in 1928
by Methuen & Co. Ltd.

This edition first published in 2015 by Routledge
2 Park Square, Milton Park, Abingdon, Oxon, OX14 4RN
and by Routledge
711 Third Avenue, New York, NY 10017

Routledge is an imprint of the Taylor & Francis Group, an informa business

© 1928 Methuen & Co. Ltd.

All rights reserved. No part of this book may be reprinted or reproduced or utilised in any form or by any electronic, mechanical, or other means, now known or hereafter invented, including photocopying and recording, or in any information storage or retrieval system, without permission in writing from the publishers.

Publisher's Note
The publisher has gone to great lengths to ensure the quality of this reprint but points out that some imperfections in the original copies may be apparent.

Disclaimer
The publisher has made every effort to trace copyright holders and welcomes correspondence from those they have been unable to contact.

A Library of Congress record exists under LC control number: 30015321

ISBN 13: 978-1-138-90139-1 (hbk)
ISBN 13: 978-1-315-69777-2 (ebk)

A SECOND BOOK OF BROADSHEETS

WITH AN INTRODUCTION BY
GEOFFREY DAWSON
EDITOR OF 'THE TIMES'

METHUEN & CO. LTD.
36 ESSEX STREET W.C.
LONDON

First Published in 1929

PRINTED IN GREAT BRITAIN

CONTENTS

		PAGE
I.	FOUR POEMS ON THE WAR	1

1. 'FOR ALL WE HAVE AND ARE': Rudyard Kipling
   (From *Twenty Poems*, Methuen & Co. Ltd., by courtesy of the author)

2. INTO BATTLE: Julian Grenfell
   (By courtesy of Lady Desborough)

3. TO WOMEN: Laurence Binyon
   (By courtesy of the author and Messrs. Elkin Mathews & Marrot)

4. THE WIFE OF FLANDERS: G. K. Chesterton
   (By courtesy of the author and Messrs. Burns, Oates & Washbourne)

II. THREE ESSAYS BY FRANCIS BACON . 6
   1. OF DEATH
   2. OF REVENGE
   3. OF ADVERSITY

III. THE SONG OF DEBORAH 10
   (From *Judges v*)

IV. THE PASHA: A. W. Kinglake . . . 13
   (From *Eothen*)

V. INTIMATIONS OF IMMORTALITY: William Wordsworth 17
   (From *Ode on Intimations of Immortality from Recollections of Early Childhood*)

VI. A WORTHY COMMANDER: Sir Thomas Overbury 19
   (From *Characters*)

VII. THE SECRET OF HAPPINESS: Alexander Pope 21
   (From the *Essay on Man*)

		PAGE
VIII.	D'ARTAGNAN'S APPRENTICESHIP: Alexandre Dumas (From *The Three Musketeers*)	25
IX.	ELEGY WRITTEN IN A COUNTRY CHURCHYARD: Thomas Gray	31

X.	THE CITY AT NIGHT
	 1. THE POET
	     (Sonnet by William Wordsworth)
	 2. THE PHILOSOPHER
	     (From *Sartor Resartus*, by Thomas Carlyle)
	 3. THE CONSTABLE
	     (From Shakespeare's *Much Ado About Nothing*, iii, 3)
		35

XI.	BOB ACRES' DUEL: Richard Brinsley Sheridan (From *The Rivals*)	39
XII.	TREES 1. OLD TREES: Walter Savage Landor 2. YEW-TREES: William Wordsworth 3. A FOREST: Percy Bysshe Shelley 4. GREENWOOD TREES: Thomas Love Peacock	45
XIII.	THE VISION OF THE ANGEL GUARDS 1. FROM 2 *Kings* vi 2. FROM BERNAL DIAZ'S *Conquest of New Spain* (1519) 3. THE GREAT TWIN BRETHREN (From *The Battle of Lake Regillus*, by Lord Macaulay)	50
XIV.	ROMEO AND JULIET (From Shakespeare's *Romeo and Juliet*, ii, 2)	55
XV.	MY UNCLE TOBY'S APOLOGY: Laurence Sterne (From *Tristram Shandy*)	61
XVI.	FIVE POEMS BY HERRICK 1. CORINNA'S GOING A-MAYING 2. TO BLOSSOMS 3. TO MEDDOWES 4. TO ANTHEA, WHO MAY COMMAND HIM ANY THING 5. GRACE FOR A CHILD	63

CONTENTS

		PAGE
XVII.	MR. MANTALINI AT BREAKFAST: Charles Dickens . . . . (From *Nicholas Nickleby*)	68
XVIII.	THE UNIVERSAL CHORUS: Percy Bysshe Shelley . . . . 1. From *Prometheus Unbound* 2. From *Hellas*	72
XIX.	OWLD BOCOCK'S MARE: E. Œ. Somerville and M. Ross . . . . (From *Some Experiences of an Irish R.M.*, by courtesy of Messrs. Longmans Green)	76
XX.	A RIDE ON AN ALLIGATOR: Charles Waterton (From *Wanderings in South America*)	82
XXI.	KING HENRY AT TOWTON FIELD: Shakespeare . . . . (From *III King Henry VI*, ii, 5)	85
XXII.	MR. SKIMPOLE AND COAVINSES: Charles Dickens . . . . (From *Bleak House*)	87
XXIII.	TWO POEMS: Austin Dobson . . . 1. A GENTLEMAN OF THE OLD SCHOOL 2. A GENTLEWOMAN OF THE OLD SCHOOL (By courtesy of Mr. A. T. A. Dobson and the Oxford University Press)	92
XXIV.	ELWES THE MISER: Edward Topham . (From *Life of the Late John Elwes*, 1790)	99
XXV.	FOUR PARABLES . . . . . 1. THE PRODIGAL SON (From *Luke xv*) 2. THE LABOURERS IN THE VINEYARD (From *Matthew xx*) 3. THE GREAT SUPPER (From *Luke xiv*) 4. THE PHARISEE AND THE PUBLICAN (From *Luke xviii*)	103
XXVI.	FROM 'THE SCHOLAR-GIPSY': Matthew Arnold	106

		PAGE
XXVII.	ELIJAH AND THE RAIN . . . . 112 (From 1 *Kings xviii*)	
XXVIII.	POETRY AND PURITANS: Charles Kingsley 116 (From *Plays and Puritans*)	
XXIX.	SLEEP . . . . 120 1. From Bernal Diaz's *Conquest of New Spain* 2. By Sir Philip Sidney 3. By Thomas Sackville, Lord Buckhurst 4. From Shakespeare's *II Henry IV*, iii, 1 5. By Charles Mackay 6. From *Don Quixote*, by Cervantes	
XXX.	THE CIRCUMLOCUTION OFFICE: Charles Dickens . . . . 123 (From *Little Dorrit*)	
XXXI.	NELSON . . . . 127 1. From *The Life of Nelson*, by Robert Southey 2. From *Ecclesiasticus, xliv*	
XXXII.	SCOTT IN ADVERSITY . . . . 131 (From Sir Walter Scott's *Journals*, 1825–6)	
XXXIII.	FOUR POEMS BY GEORGE HERBERT . 135 1. LIFE 2. THE QUIP 3. THE PULLEY 4. MAN	
XXXIV.	NORSE TALES: Sir G. W. Dasent . . . 139 1. WHY THE SEA IS SALT 2. THE LAD AND THE DEIL	
XXXV.	THE DEFENCE OF LUCKNOW: Alfred, Lord Tennyson . . . . 144 (By courtesy of Messrs. Macmillan)	
XXXVI.	CHARLES LAMB TO A FRIEND IN CHINA 150	
XXXVII.	1. NAVAL BALLADS . . . . . 153 1. WE CONQUER TO SAVE 2. THE ISLAND 3. BLACK-EYED SUSAN 2. THE ENGLISHMAN'S IDOLATRY: George Savile, Marquess of Halifax	

CONTENTS

		PAGE
XXXVIII.	FROM DR. JOHNSON	158
	1. JOHNSON'S DICTIONARY (From the Preface)	
	2. JOHNSON ON PATIENCE (From *The Rambler*, No. 32)	
	3. EPITAPH ON ROBERT LEVETT	
XXXIX.	GERARD, DENYS AND THE BEAR: Charles Reade	162
	(From *The Cloister and the Hearth*)	
XL.	THREE POEMS BY MARVELL . . .	166
	1. BERMUDAS	
	2. THE GARDEN	
	3. A DIALOGUE BETWEEN THE RESOLVED SOUL AND CREATED PLEASURE	
XLI.	STORY OF THE FALCON: Boccaccio . .	172
XLII.	SAVOY SONGS: Sir W. S. Gilbert . .	177
	1. THE MIKADO'S SONG (From *The Mikado*)	
	2. KING GOODHEART (From *The Gondoliers*)	
	3. THE MAJOR-GENERAL'S SONG (From *The Pirates of Penzance*)	
	4. 'IS LIFE A BOON?' (From *The Yeomen of the Guard*)	
	5. TITWILLOW (From *The Mikado*) (By courtesy of Lady Gilbert and Messrs. Macmillan)	
XLIII.	THE MIGHTY WORKS OF GOD . .	183
	1. From *Job xxxviii–xxxix* 2. By Joseph Addison	
XLIV.	THE TRIAL OF FAITHFUL: John Bunyan .	188
	(From *The Pilgrim's Progress*)	
XLV.	FROM SIR WALTER RALEIGH . .	192
	1. THE END OF ALL THINGS (From *History of the World*, 1614)	
	2. 'EVEN SUCH IS TIME' (Written the night before his death)	

		PAGE
XLVI.	THE JUST MAN . . . . 1. SOCRATES TO HIS JUDGES (From Jowett's translation of Plato's *Apology*) 2. By W. S. LANDOR	194
XLVII.	THE PUNISHMENT OF KHIPIL: George Meredith . . . . (From *The Shaving of Shagpat*, by courtesy of Mr. W. M. Meredith and Messrs. Constable)	198
XLVIII.	INSPIRED MOMENTS: William Wordsworth . (From *The Prelude*)	204
XLIX.	AT A WESTERN HOTEL: E. Œ. Somerville and M. Ross . . . . (From *In Mr. Knox's Country*, by courtesy of Messrs. Longmans Green)	207
L.	TAM O' SHANTER: Robert Burns . .	212
LI.	THE MARRIED STATE . . . . (From *The Tatler*, Nov. 16, 1709)	218
LII.	THE TEMPTATION OF CYMOCHLES: Edmund Spenser . . . . . . (From *The Faery Queen*)	223
LIII.	DIE VERNON: Sir Walter Scott . . . (From *Rob Roy*)	227
LIV.	THE WONDERS OF THE WORLD . . 1. From the Book of John Mandeville (1359) 2. From Dickens's *Great Expectations*	231
LV.	1. ST. PAUL'S VOYAGE AND SHIPWRECK (From *Acts xxvii*) 2. 'THEY THAT GO DOWN TO THE SEA' (From *Psalms cvii*)	236
LVI.	AN IDEAL OF EMPIRE: Edmund Burke . (From the *Speech on Conciliation with America*, 1775)	239
LVII.	1. THE HAPPY WARRIOR: William Wordsworth . . . . 2. THE VIRTUOUS MAN: Katherine Philips (1631–1664)	241

CONTENTS

		PAGE
LVIII.	THE FUSILIER BRIGADE AT ALBUERA: Sir William Napier (From *The History of the War in the Peninsula*)	245
LIX.	A TRIANGULAR DUEL: Captain F. Marryat (From *Mr. Midshipman Easy*)	249
LX.	1. THE ISLE OF WIGHT: Sir A. Geikie (From *Landscape in History*, by courtesy of Messrs. Macmillan) 2. 'GREEN FIELDS OF ENGLAND.' Arthur Hugh Clough	254
LXI.	THE DRAMA AND THE CRUMMLES COMPANY: Charles Dickens (From *Nicholas Nickleby*)	258
LXII.	A SAVAGE PEOPLE: Charles Darwin (From *The Voyage of the Beagle*)	263
LXIII.	THE DONCASTER ST. LEGER: Sir F. H. Doyle	268
LXIV.	SOME EARLY NATURAL HISTORY: Pliny (From the Translation by Philemon Holland, 1601)	275
LXV.	1. THE GOLDEN IMAGE (From *Daniel iii*) 2. 'AGAINST THE THREATS OF MALICE' (From Milton's *Comus*)	279
LXVI.	HOW TO MANAGE A SEA-FIGHT: Captain John Smith (From *Sea Grammar*, 1627)	282
LXVII.	SOME IRISH POEMS 1. DARK ROSALEEN: James Clarence Mangan 2. A RETORT: Emily Lawless 3. CORRYMEELA: Moira O'Neill (From *Songs of the Glens of Antrim*, by courtesy of the Author and Messrs. Blackwood)	287
LXVIII.	A RIDE ON A BUFFALO: Captain Mayne Reid (From *The Scalp-Hunters*)	292
LXIX.	SCROOGE'S VISITORS: Charles Dickens (From *A Christmas Carol*)	296

INTRODUCTION

THE anthology contained in this volume, as in the first *Book of Broadsheets* published last year, differs from others of the kind in having a definite historical interest. It is a reproduction—not indeed complete, but sufficiently representative—of the pocket literature provided by *The Times* for the men in the trenches during the early days of the War. The selection therefore is neither a new one, as in most anthologies of the kind, nor the work of any one individual. Every item in it was printed during the autumn of the year 1915 in the form of a 'Broadsheet'—a single page of thin paper suitable for inclusion in a letter—and distributed in hundreds of thousands to the forces in the field or at sea. Moreover, though *The Times* may claim some credit for the organization and production of the scheme, it had its origin elsewhere and was kept alive by innumerable volunteers. Very few complete bound collections of the original Broadsheets are known to be still in existence, though a good deal of evidence has been forthcoming since the first anthology was published that many people preserved isolated sheets; and their reproduction now, at the end of the first decade of peace, affords a welcome opportunity to pay tribute to some of those who invented and furthered the project, assisted it with their suggestions, and in certain cases waived valuable copyrights in so good a cause.

The idea, like many others, sprang from the fertile imagination of Mr. Lionel Curtis, who recalls that he first conceived it when some young soldiers, home on leave from the trenches in the early days of August, 1915, were discussing in his house their favourite passages in English literature. Some of these passages were read aloud by Sir William Marris, who was also of the party. 'As he read,' writes Mr. Curtis, 'we all felt as though a great wind was sweeping away the clouds and the sunlight was breaking through.' One of the officers present exclaimed that 'it was a thousand pities that such stuff could not be read in the trenches,' and from that moment the Broadsheets had their beginning. The practical possibilities were discussed at once. A letter from Mr. Curtis two or three days later inquired whether *The Times* would undertake the necessary organization. Mr. Bruce Richmond, then as now in charge of *The Times Literary Supplement*, was promptly and willingly brought into the scheme and bore much of the burden of it for many months afterwards. Sir Walter Raleigh, Professor of English Literature at Oxford, was suggested as an ideal colleague in the choice of extracts, and responded to the invitation with enthusiasm. To these two, more than to any others, the present volume owes its range and its variety.

Variety indeed was Raleigh's chief preoccupation from the beginning. 'I covet infinite variety,' he was telling a friend on August 17 in one of the letters published after his death.

'I wish you would send references of anything that occurs to you, from bits of the Book of Job to accounts of a prize-fight. No standard except "good of its kind". There is room for every one's pets, except elephants. So, for a time at least, I've got a job.'

By the end of the month the scheme was ready for announcement, and Raleigh was invited to explain it in a letter to *The Times*.

'What is wanted,' he wrote, 'and what you have generously undertaken to supply, is a numerous and various selection of the best passages, grave and gay, from English verse and prose, to be printed on flyleaves or broadsheets, and sold in mixed sets at a very low price. One of these broadsheets can be enclosed in a letter, without adding to the cost of postage. Whole assortments of them can be sent to officers and distributed according to taste among the men of their command.'

And he added a passage which might well stand alone for the introduction to the present collection.

'I confess I like the idea of this library. Apart from its main use, it seems to me to symbolize the cause for which we are fighting. The Germans are right when they call us frivolous, if it may be permitted in the name of politeness to assume that by frivolous they mean playful. They are right; we have playful minds, and they have not, so that we are often embarrassed in our converse with them. They are full of a simple unquestioning faith in Germany, in things German, in the great deeds they have done and the great deeds they are about to do, in all that is large, heavy, solid and persistent. They think of these things, if their own account is just, relentlessly and eternally, without mitigation or fatigue. They do not want Heine in their trenches; there is a danger that he might not be serious. We could not think of ourselves as they do, magnificently, for years together; some one would be sure to laugh. We are not very good at hating, and we do not believe in hate. We continue to believe in life, and in the variety and surprise of life. If we submit ourselves to rigid discipline, as we are quite willing to do, it is not that we wish to be like them, but that we hope to save life from being crushed under their machine. We believe in freedom, and we mean to keep it. We will fight as long as we can stand, so that the world may still be a place where spontaneous and playful persons, especially women and children, may lead a life free from fear. There is no better expression of freedom, in all its senses, than English literature.'

The first series of broadsheets, thirty-six in number, was published on August 30. They were divided into sets of six, each set being sold in an envelope for a penny, with special rates for large quantities, such as were purchased and distributed by the Camps Library and other organizations of the kind. The price can hardly have covered the cost of production, but it was announced from the outset that, if there should be any small profit it would be devoted to the Red Cross Fund which *The Times* maintained throughout the war.

As for the choice of extracts, Raleigh's first selection set the standard, and from the moment of their publication a flood of suggestions for future packets began to pour into Printing House Square. Within a week the game of choosing subjects for broadsheets, which Raleigh had described as 'better fun than I knew', was being played wherever *The Times* was read.

Neither space nor memory would suffice to tell the names of all those whose ideas were adopted in the thirty sets eventually produced in the autumn of 1915. Some of the most interesting came from the trenches—among them a demand for certain extracts from Hardy and for 'passages on scientific subjects'. Men of letters, publishers, prelates, correspondents of every sort and kind made their contribution to the common stock. But it is permissible, perhaps, now that both are gone from us, to record that two of those to whom *The Times* owed much help and encouragement in those days were Dean Ryle of Westminster, and Professor W. P. Ker of All Souls; while for another reason special acknowledgment must be made to Mr. E. V. Lucas, who not only took his share in the work of selection at the time but is the originator as well as the publisher of the present volume and its predecessor.

The work of distribution, though largely and intentionally left to individual correspondents, was also carried out in bulk by a number of agencies concerned with the welfare of the troops in the field, afloat, and in hospital. Among these—in addition to the Camps Library, already mentioned —were such bodies as the Y.M.C.A., the War Library, the Overseas Club, and the Church of England Temperance Association, and to them also recognition is due. It was thanks largely to their co-operation that by September 8 (just a week after the scheme was launched) *The Times* was able to announce that the sale of the first series of broadsheets had reached the round figure of one million. A little later Lord Derby was arranging a consignment for those Lancashire battalions in which he was interested—an example which was followed in other instances—while the National Institute for the Blind, headed by Mr. Arthur Pearson, was busily engaged in reproducing the broadsheets in Braille type for the use of blinded soldiers. Meanwhile the work of production went forward fast. Within the first six weeks twenty-four sets, or 144 broadsheets, were selected, printed, and published. By December these figures had grown to thirty sets of 180 broadsheets, and the series was crowned with a special Christmas set which is represented in the earlier anthology by its two final extracts—the story of

INTRODUCTION

Scott's last Christmas in the Antarctic and the Mellstock Carols.

There was never any question of the popularity of the broadsheets among those for whom they were originally put together. In the archives of *The Times* are many treasured letters of gratitude—one, for example, which describes a 'prosaic sergeant, painfully recapturing' a familiar poem of his youth, and 'annoying those around him by intoning the stanzas as he moved up and down the trench'; another complaining that the writer had been compelled to read aloud Mr. Micawber twice over to the men in his dug-out and the Game of Cribbage three times; another inspired to compare the broadsheets to 'a cool spring rippling through an arid sand-waste'; another moved, more practically, to 'take the Izaak Walton one to the 86th on the Tigris'. 'The beggars are so keen on fishing', he explained, 'that they make rods of the centre rib of the date palm.'

Nor were contemporary authors any less grateful for the compliment which included extracts from their writings in the series; and, since this *Second Book of Broadsheets* contains a notable passage from *Mr. Knox's Country*, it is of interest to recall Miss Somerville's testimony (from 'Irish Memories') to the satisfaction which its original appearance gave to her friend and collaborator Martin Ross.

'Nothing' she wrote, 'ever gave Martin more pleasure than that passages from the "Irish R.M." should have been included among the Broad Sheets that *The Times* sent out to the soldiers. It was in the last summer of her life, little as we thought it, that this honour was paid to our stories, and had she been told how brief her time was to be, and been asked to choose the boon that she would like best, I believe that to be numbered among that elect company of consolers was what she would most gladly have chosen.'

Was it equally worth while, after ten years of peace, to preserve the collection for other readers under wholly different conditions? To that question also the answer is preserved in a contemporary letter, written in December 1915, from 'A Hospital, Somewhere in France'.

'It would be interesting,' it runs, 'to have all these broadsheets, and whatever are to follow, bound in one volume, as an example of English literature's beguilement, comfort and sustainment for the warrior. Such a volume, I suppose, cannot be published, but if ever I get back and am able to preserve them (and yet how can I, when every decent motive dictates that I must pass them on to others?) I shall see that mine are stitched into a cover. Another reason for binding the Broadsheets is that, as it happens, the collection would not be very different had the desire been to amuse and hearten not men of war but men of peace.'

These two *Books of Broadsheets* are an attempt to fulfil that ambition—and to let others share in its fulfilment

GEOFFREY DAWSON

September, 1929

A SECOND BOOK OF BROADSHEETS

I

FOUR POEMS ON THE WAR

'FOR ALL WE HAVE AND ARE'

FOR all we have and are,
    For all our children's fate,
    Stand up and meet the war.
The Hun is at the gate!
Our world has passed away
In wantonness o'erthrown.
There is nothing left to-day
But steel and fire and stone.

    Though all we knew depart,
    The old commandments stand:
    'In courage keep your heart,
    In strength lift up your hand.'

Once more we hear the word
That sickened earth of old:
'No law except the sword
Unsheathed and uncontrolled.'
Once more it knits mankind,
Once more the nations go
To meet and break and bind
A crazed and driven foe.

Comfort, content, delight—
The ages' slow-bought gain
They shrivelled in a night;
Only ourselves remain
To face the naked days
In silent fortitude
Through perils and dismays
Renewed and re-renewed.

Though all we made depart,
The old commandments stand:
'In patience keep your heart,
In strength lift up your hand.'

No easy hopes or lies
Shall bring us to our goal,
But iron sacrifice
Of body, will, and soul.
There is but one task for all—
For each one life to give.
Who stands if freedom fall?
Who dies if England live?

INTO BATTLE

The naked earth is warm with Spring,
    And with green grass and bursting trees
Leans to the sun's gaze glorying,
    And quivers in the sunny breeze;

And Life is Colour and Warmth and Light,
    And a striving evermore for these;
And he is dead who will not fight;
    And who dies fighting has increase.

The fighting man shall from the sun
  Take warmth, and life from the glowing earth;
Speed with the light-foot winds to run,
  And with the trees to newer birth;
And find, when fighting shall be done,
  Great rest, and fullness after dearth.

All the bright company of Heaven
  Hold him in their high comradeship,
The Dog-Star and the Sisters Seven,
  Orion's Belt and sworded hip.

The woodland trees that stand together,
  They stand to him each one a friend;
They gently speak in the windy weather;
  They guide to valley and ridges' end.

The kestrel hovering by day,
  And the little owls that call by night,
Bid him be swift and keen as they,
  As keen of ear, as swift of sight.

The blackbird sings to him, 'Brother, brother,
  'If this be the last song you shall sing
'Sing well, for you may not sing another;
  'Brother, sing.'

In dreary doubtful waiting hours,
  Before the brazen frenzy starts,
The horses show him nobler powers;
  O patient eyes, courageous hearts!

And when the burning moment breaks,
  And all things else are out of mind,
And only Joy-of-Battle takes
  Him by the throat, and makes him blind,

Through joy and blindness he shall know,
  Not caring much to know, that still
Nor lead nor steel shall reach him, so
  That it be not the Destined Will.

The thundering line of battle stands,
  And in the air Death moans and sings;
But Day shall clasp him with strong hands,
  And Night shall fold him in soft wings.

TO WOMEN

Your hearts are lifted up, your hearts
That have foreknown the utter price,
Your hearts burn upward as a flame
Of splendour and of sacrifice.

For you, you too to battle go,
Not with the marching drums and cheers,
But in the watch of solitude
And through the boundless night of fears,

Swift, swifter than those hawks of war,
Those threatening wings that pulse the air,
Far as the vanward ranks are set,
You are gone before them, you are there!

And not a shot comes blind with death,
And not a stab of steel is pressed
Home, but invisibly it tore
And entered first a woman's breast.

Amid the thunder of the guns,
The lightning of the lance and sword,
Your hope, your dread, your throbbing pride,
Your infinite passion is outpoured

From hearts that are as one high heart
Withholding naught from doom and bale,
Burningly offered up—to bleed,
To bear, to break, but not to fail.

THE WIFE OF FLANDERS

Low and brown barns thatched and repatched and tattered,
  Where I had seven sons until to-day,
A little hill of hay your spur has scattered . . .
  This is not Paris. You have lost the way.

You, staring at your sword to find it brittle,
  Surprised at the surprise that was your plan,
Who shaking and breaking barriers not a little
  Find never more the death-door of Sedan.

Must I for more than carnage call you claimant,
  Paying you a penny for each son you slay?
Man, the whole globe in gold were no repayment
  For what *you* have lost. And how shall I repay?

What is the price of that red spark that caught me
  From a kind farm that never had a name?
What is the price of that dead man they brought me?
  For other dead men do not look the same.

How should I pay for one poor graven steeple
  Whereon you shattered what you shall not know;
How should I pay you, miserable people?
  How should I pay you everything you owe?

Unhappy, can I give you back your honour?
  Though I forgave would any man forget?
While all the great green land has trampled on her
  The treason and terror of the night we met.

Not any more in vengeance or in pardon
  An old wife bargains for a bean that's hers.
You have no word to break: no heart to harden.
  Ride on and prosper. You have lost your spurs.

II

THREE ESSAYS BY FRANCIS BACON

OF DEATH

MEN fear death, as children fear to go in to the dark; and as that natural fear in children is increased with tales, so is the other. Certainly the contemplation of death, as the wages of sin, and passage to another world, is holy and religious; but the fear of it, as a tribute due unto nature, is weak. Yet in religious meditations, there is sometimes mixture of vanity and of superstition. You shall read in some of the friars books of mortification, that a man should think with himself, what the pain is, if he have but his finger's end pressed or tortured; and thereby imagine what the pains of death are, when the whole body is corrupted and dissolved; when many times death passeth with less pain than the torture of a limb: for the most vital parts are not the quickest of sense. And by him that spake only as a philosopher, and natural man, it was well said, 'Pompa mortis magis terret, quam mors ipsa.' Groans and convulsions, and a discoloured face, and friends weeping, and blacks and obsequies, and the like, shew death terrible. It is worthy the observing, that there is no passion in the mind of man so weak, but it mates and masters the fear of death; and therefore death is no such terrible enemy when a man hath so many attendants about him that can win the combat of him. Revenge triumphs over death; love slights it; honour aspireth to it; grief flieth to it; fear pre-occupateth it: nay, we read, after Otho the emperor had slain himself, pity (which is the tenderest of affections) provoked many to die out of mere compassion to their sovereign, and as the truest sort of followers. Nay, Seneca adds, niceness and satiety: 'Cogita quamdiu eadem feceris; mori velle, non tantum fortis, aut miser, sed etiam fastidiosus potest.' A man would die, though he were neither valiant nor miserable, only upon a weariness to do the same thing so oft over and over. It is no less worthy to observe, how little alteration in good spirits the approaches of death make: for they appear to be the same men till the last instant. Augustus Cæsar died in a compliment: 'Livia, conjugii nostri memor, vive et vale.' Tiberius in dissimulation, as Tacitus saith of him, 'Jam Tiberium vires et corpus, non dissimulatio, deserebant': Vespasian in a jest, sitting upon the stool, 'Ut puto Deus fio': Galba with a sentence, 'Feri, si ex re sit populi Romani,' holding forth his neck: Septimius Severus in dispatch, 'Adeste, si quid mihi restat agendum,' and the like. Certainly the Stoics bestowed too much cost upon death, and by their great preparations made it appear more fearful. Better, saith he, 'qui finem vitæ extremum inter munera ponat naturæ.' It is as natural to die as to be born; and to a little infant, perhaps, the one is as painful as the other. He that dies in an earnest pursuit, is like one that is wounded in hot blood; who, for the time, scarce feels the hurt; and therefore a mind fixed and bent upon somewhat that is good, doth avert the dolours of death; but, above all, believe it, the sweetest canticle is, 'Nunc dimittis' when a man hath obtained worthy ends and expectations. Death hath this also, that it openeth the gate to good fame, and extinguisheth envy: 'Extinctus amabitur idem.'

OF REVENGE

Revenge is a kind of wild justice, which the more man's nature runs to, the more ought law to weed it out: for as for the first wrong, it doth but offend the law, but the revenge of that wrong putteth the law out of office. Certainly, in taking revenge, a man is but even with his enemy; but in passing it over, he is superior; for it is a prince's part to pardon: and Solomon, I am sure, saith, 'It is the glory of a man to pass by an offence.' That which is past is gone and irrecoverable, and wise men have enough to do with things present and to come; therefore they do but trifle with themselves, that labour in past matters. There is no man doth a wrong for the wrong's sake, but thereby to purchase himself profit, or pleasure, or honour, or the like; therefore why should I be angry with a man for loving himself better than me? And if any man should do wrong, merely out of illnature, why, yet it is but like the thorn or brier, which prick and scratch, because they can do no other. The most tolerable sort of revenge is for those wrongs which there is no law to remedy; but then, let a man take heed the revenge be such as there is no law to punish, else a man's enemy is still before hand, and it is two for one. Some, when they take revenge, are desirous the party should know whence it cometh: this is the more generous; for the delight seemeth to be not so much in doing the hurt as in making the party repent: but base and crafty cowards are like the arrow that flieth in the dark. Cosmus, duke of Florence, had a desperate saying against perfidious or neglecting friends, as if those wrongs were unpardonable. 'You shall read,' saith he, 'that we are commanded to forgive our enemies, but you never read that we are commanded to forgive our friends.' But yet the spirit of Job was in a better tune: 'Shall we,' saith he, 'take good at God's hands, and not be content to take evil also?' and so of friends in a proportion. This is certain, that a man that studieth revenge, keeps his own wounds green, which otherwise would heal and do well. Public revenges are for the most part fortunate; as that for the death of Cæsar; for the death of Pertinax; for the death of Henry the Third of France; and many more. But in private revenges it is not so; nay, rather vindictive persons live the life of witches; who, as they are mischievous, so end they unfortunate.

OF ADVERSITY

It was a high speech of Seneca (after the manner of the Stoics), that the good things which belong to prosperity are to be wished, but the good things that belong to adversity are to be admired: 'Bona rerum secundarum optabilia, adversarum mirabilia.' Certainly, if miracles be the command over nature, they appear most in adversity. It is yet a higher speech of his than the other (much too high for a heathen), 'It is true greatness to have in one the frailty of a man, and the security of a God':—'Vere magnum habere fragilitatem hominis, securitatem Dei.' This would have done better in poesy, where transcendencies are more allowed; and the poets, indeed, have been busy with it; for it is in effect the thing which is figured in that strange fiction of the ancient poets, which seemeth not to be without mystery; nay, and to have some approach to the state of a Christian, 'that Hercules, when he went to unbind Prometheus (by whom human nature is represented), sailed the length of the great ocean in an earthen pot or pitcher, lively describing Christian resolution, that saileth in the frail bark of the flesh through the waves of the world.' But to speak in a mean, the virtue of prosperity is temperance, the virtue of adversity is fortitude, which in morals is the more heroical virtue. Prosperity is the blessing of the Old Testament, adversity is the blessing of the New, which carrieth the greater benediction, and the clearer revelation of God's favour. Yet even in the Old Testament, if you listen to David's harp, you shall hear as many hearse-like airs as carols; and the pencil of the Holy Ghost hath laboured more in describing the afflictions of Job than the felicities of Solomon. Prosperity is not without many fears and distastes; and adversity is not without comforts and hopes. We see in needleworks and embroideries, it is more pleasing to have a lively work upon a sad and solemn ground, than to have a dark and melancholy work upon a lightsome ground: judge, therefore, of the pleasure of the heart by the pleasure of the eye. Certainly virtue is like precious odours, most fragrant when they are incensed, or crushed: for prosperity doth best discover vice, but adversity doth best discover virtue.

III

THE SONG OF DEBORAH

THEN sang Deborah and Barak the son of Abinoam
on that day, saying,
Praise ye the Lord for the avenging of Israel,
When the people willingly offered themselves.
Hear, O ye kings; give ear, O ye princes;
I, even I, will sing unto the Lord;
I will sing praise to the Lord God of Israel.
Lord, when thou wentest out of Seir,
When thou marchedst out of the field of Edom,
The earth trembled, and the heavens dropped,
The clouds also dropped water.
The mountains melted from before the Lord,
Even that Sinai from before the Lord God of Israel.
In the days of Shamgar the son of Anath,
In the days of Jael, the highways were unoccupied,
And the travellers walked through byways.
The inhabitants of the villages ceased, they ceased in Israel,
Until that I Deborah arose,
That I arose a mother in Israel.
They chose new gods;
Then was war in the gates:
Was there a shield or spear seen
Among forty thousand in Israel?
My heart is toward the governors of Israel,
That offered themselves willingly among the people.
Bless ye the Lord.
Speak, ye that ride on white asses,
Ye that sit in judgment,
And walk by the way.
They that are delivered from the noise of archers in the
places of drawing water,
There shall they rehearse the righteous acts of the Lord,
Even the righteous acts toward the inhabitants of his villages
in Israel:

THE SONG OF DEBORAH

Then shall the people of the Lord go down to the gates.
Awake, awake, Deborah;
Awake, awake; utter a song:
Arise, Barak, and lead thy captivity captive, thou son of Abinoam.
Then he made him that remaineth have dominion over the nobles among the people:
The Lord made me have dominion over the mighty.
Out of Ephraim was there a root of them against Amalek;
After thee, Benjamin, among thy people:
Out of Machir came down governors,
And out of Zebulun they that handle the pen of the writer.
And the princes of Issachar were with Deborah;
Even Issachar, and also Barak;
He was sent on foot into the valley.
For the divisions of Reuben there were great thoughts of heart.
Why abodest thou among the sheep-folds,
To hear the bleatings of the flocks?
For the divisions of Reuben there were great searchings of heart.
Gilead abode beyond Jordan:
And why did Dan remain in ships?
Asher continued on the sea shore,
And abode in his breaches.
Zebulun and Naphtali were a people that jeoparded their lives unto the death in the high places of the field.
The kings came and fought,
Then fought the kings of Canaan
In Taanach by the waters of Megiddo;
They took no gain of money.
They fought from heaven;
The stars in their courses fought against Sisera,
The river of Kishon swept them away,
That ancient river, the river Kishon.
O my soul, thou hast trodden down strength.
Then were the horse-hoofs broken by the means of the prancings,

The prancings of their mighty ones.
Curse ye Meroz, said the angel of the Lord,
Curse ye bitterly the inhabitants thereof;
Because they came not to the help of the Lord,
To the help of the Lord against the mighty.
Blessed above women shall Jael the wife of Heber the Kenite be;
Blessed shall she be above women in the tent.
He asked water, and she gave him milk;
She brought forth butter in a lordly dish.
She put her hand to the nail,
And her right hand to the workman's hammer;
And with the hammer she smote Sisera,
She smote off his head,
When she had pierced and stricken through his temples.
At her feet he bowed, he fell, he lay down:
At her feet he bowed, he fell:
Where he bowed, there he fell down dead.
The mother of Sisera looked out at a window,
And cried through the lattice,
Why is his chariot so long in coming?
Why tarry the wheels of his chariots?
Her wise ladies answered her,
Yea, she returned answer to herself,
Have they not sped? have they not divided the prey;
To every man a damsel or two; to Sisera a prey of divers colours,
A prey of divers colours of needlework,
Of divers colours of needlework on both sides,
Meet for the necks of them that take the spoil?
So let all thine enemies perish, O Lord:
But let them that love him be as the sun when he goeth forth in his might.

IV

THE PASHA

THE Pasha received us with the smooth, kind, gentle manner that belongs to well-bred Osmanlees; then he lightly clapped his hands, and instantly the sound filled all the lower end of the room with slaves; a syllable dropped from his lips which bowed all heads, and conjured away the attendants like ghosts (their coming and their going was thus swift and quiet, because their feet were bare, and they passed through no door, but only by the yielding folds of a purder). Soon the coffee-bearers appeared, every man carrying separately his tiny cup in a small metal stand; and presently to each of us there came a pipe-bearer, who first rested the bowl of the *tchibouque* at a measured distance on the floor, and then, on this axis, wheeled round the long cherry stick, and gracefully presented it on half-bended knee; already the well-kindled fire was glowing secure in the bowl, and so, when I pressed the amber up to mine, there was no coyness to conquer; the willing fume came up, and answered my slightest sigh, and followed softly every breath inspired, till it touched me with some faint sense and understanding of Asiatic contentment. . . . I think I should mislead you if I were to attempt to give the substance of any particular conversation with Orientals. A traveller may write and say that "the Pasha of So-and-so was particularly interested in the vast progress which has been made in the application of steam, and appeared to understand the structure of our machinery—that he remarked upon the gigantic results of our manufacturing industry—showed that he possessed considerable knowledge of our Indian affairs, and of the constitution of the Company, and expressed a lively admiration of the many sterling qualities for which the people of England are distinguished.' But the heap of commonplaces thus quietly attributed to the Pasha will have been founded perhaps on some such talking as this:—

Pasha.—The Englishman is welcome; most blessed among hours is this, the hour of his coming.

Dragoman (to the traveller).—The Pasha pays you his compliments.

Traveller.—Give him my best compliments in return and say I'm delighted to have the honour of seeing him.

Dragoman (to the Pasha).—His lordship, this Englishman, Lord of London, Scorner of Ireland, Suppressor of France, has quitted his governments, and left his enemies to breathe for a moment, and has crossed the broad waters in strict disguise, with a small but eternally faithful retinue of followers, in order that he might look upon the bright countenance of the Pasha among Pashas—the Pasha of the everlasting Pashalik of Karagholookoldour.

Traveller (to his dragoman).—What on earth have you been saying about London? The Pasha will be taking me for a mere cockney. Have not I told you *always* to say that I am from a branch of the family of Mudcombe Park, and that I am to be a magistrate for the county of Bedfordshire, only I've not qualified, and that I should have been a deputy-lieutenant if it had not been for the extraordinary conduct of Lord Mountpromise, and that I was a candidate for Goldborough at the last election, and that I should have won easy if my committee had not been bought. I wish to Heaven that if you *do* say anything about me, you'd tell the simple truth.

Dragoman [is silent].

Pasha.—What says the friendly Lord of London? is there aught that I can grant him within the Pashalik of Karagholookoldour?

Dragoman (growing sulky and literal).—This friendly Englishman—this branch of Mudcombe—this head-purveyor of Goldborough—this possible policeman of Bedfordshire, is recounting his achievements, and the number of his titles.

Pasha.—The end of his honours is more distant than the ends of the earth, and the catalogue of his glorious deeds is brighter than the firmament of heaven!

Dragoman (to the traveller).—The Pasha congratulates your Excellency.

Traveller.—About Goldborough? The deuce he does!—but I want to get at his views in relation to the present state of the Ottoman Empire. Tell him the Houses of Parliament have met, and that there has been a speech from the throne, pledging England to preserve the integrity of the Sultan's dominions.

Dragoman (to the Pasha).—This branch of Mudcombe, this possible policeman of Bedfordshire, informs your Highness that in England the talking houses have met, and that the integrity of the Sultan's dominions has been assured for ever and ever by a speech from the velvet chair.

Pasha.—Wonderful chair! Wonderful houses!—whirr! whirr! all by wheels!—whiz! whiz! all by steam!—wonderful chair! wonderful houses! wonderful people!—whirr! whirr! all by wheels!—whiz! whiz! all by steam!

Traveller (to the dragoman).—What does the Pasha mean by that whizzing? he does not mean to say, does he, that our Government will ever abandon their pledges to the Sultan?

Dragoman.—No, your Excellency; but he says the English talk by wheels, and by steam.

Traveller.—That's an exaggeration; but say that the English really have carried machinery to great perfection; tell the Pasha (he'll be struck with that) that whenever we have any disturbances to put down, even at two or three hundred miles from London, we can send troops by the thousand to the scene of action in a few hours.

Dragoman (recovering his temper and freedom of speech).—His Excellency, this Lord of Mudcombe, observes to your Highness, that whenever the Irish, or the French, or the Indians rebel against the English, whole armies of soldiers, and brigades of artillery, are dropped into a mighty chasm called Euston Square, and in the biting of a cartridge they arise up again in Manchester, or Dublin, or Paris, or Delhi, and utterly exterminate the enemies of England from the face of the earth.

Pasha.—I know it—I know all—the particulars have been faithfully related to me, and my mind comprehends locomotives. The armies of the English ride upon the vapours of boiling caldrons, and their horses are flaming coals! —whirr! whirr! all by wheels!—whiz! whiz! all by steam!

Traveller (to his dragoman).—I wish to have the opinion of an unprejudiced Ottoman gentleman as to the prospects of our English commerce and manufactures; just ask the Pasha to give me his views on the subject.

Pasha (after having received the communication of the dragoman).—The ships of the English swarm like flies; their printed calicoes cover the whole earth; and by the side of their swords the blades of Damascus are blades of grass. All India is but an item in the ledger-books of the merchants, whose lumber-rooms are filled with ancient thrones!—whirr! whirr! all by wheels!—whiz! whiz! all by steam.

Dragoman.—The Pasha compliments the cutlery of England, and also the East India Company.

Traveller.—The Pasha's right about the cutlery (I tried my scimitar with the common officers' swords belonging to our fellows at Malta, and they cut it like the leaf of a novel). Well (to the dragoman), tell the Pasha I am exceedingly gratified to find that he entertains such a high opinion of our manufacturing energy, but I should like him to know, though, that we have got something in England besides that. These foreigners are always fancying that we have nothing but ships, and railways, and East India Companies; do just tell the Pasha that our rural districts deserve his attention, and that even within the last two hundred years there has been an evident improvement in the culture of the turnip, and if he does not take any interest about that, at all events you can explain that we have our virtues in the country— that we are a truth-telling people, and, like the Osmanlees, are faithful in the performance of our promises. Oh! and, by-the-bye, whilst you are about it, you may as well just say at the end that the British yeoman is still, thank God! the British yeoman.

Pasha (after hearing the dragoman).—It is true, it is true: —through all Feringhstan the English are foremost and best; for the Russians are drilled swine, and the Germans are sleeping babes, and the Italians are the servants of songs, and the French are the sons of newspapers, and the Greeks they are weavers of lies, but the English and the Osmanlees are brothers together in righteousness; for the Osmanlees believe in one only God, and cleave to the Koran, and destroy idols, so do the English worship one God, and abominate graven images, and tell the truth, and believe in a book, and though they drink the juice of the grape, yet to say that they worship their prophet as God, or to say that they are eaters of pork, these are lies—lies born of Greeks, and nursed by Jews!

Dragoman.—The Pasha compliments the English.

Traveller (rising).—Well, I've had enough of this. Tell the Pasha I am greatly obliged to him for his hospitality, and still more for his kindness in furnishing me with horses, and say that now I must be off.

Pasha (after hearing the dragoman, and standing up on his divan).—Proud are the sires, and blessed are the dams of the horses that shall carry his Excellency to the end of his prosperous journey. May the saddle beneath him glide down to the gates of the happy city, like a boat swimming on the third river of Paradise. May he sleep the sleep of a child, when his friends are around him; and the while that his enemies are abroad, may his eyes flame red through the darkness—more red than the eyes of ten tigers! Farewell!

Dragoman.—The Pasha wishes your Excellency a pleasant journey.

So ends the visit.

V

INTIMATIONS OF IMMORTALITY

OUR birth is but a sleep and a forgetting:
    The Soul that rises with us, our life's Star,
    Hath had elsewhere its setting,
  And cometh from afar:
Not in entire forgetfulness,
And not in utter nakedness,

But trailing clouds of glory do we come
        From God, who is our home;
Heaven lies about us in our infancy!
Shades of the prison-house begin to close
        Upon the growing Boy,
But He beholds the light, and whence it flows
        He sees it in his joy;
The Youth, who daily farther from the east
        Must travel, still is Nature's Priest,
        And by the vision splendid
        Is on his way attended;
At length the Man perceives it die away,
And fade into the light of common day. . . .

        O joy! that in our embers
        Is something that doth live,
        That nature yet remembers
        What was so fugitive!
The thought of our past years in me doth breed
Perpetual benediction: not indeed
For that which is most worthy to be blest;
Delight and liberty, the simple creed
Of childhood, whether busy or at rest,
With new-fledged hope still fluttering in his breast:—
        Not for these I raise
        The song of thanks and praise;
        But for those obstinate questionings
        Of sense and outward things,
        Fallings from us, vanishings;
        Blank misgivings of a Creature
Moving about in worlds not realized,
High instincts before which our mortal Nature
Did tremble like a guilty Thing surprised:
        But for those first affections,
        Those shadowy recollections,
        Which, be they what they may,
Are yet the fountain light of all our day,

Are yet a master light of all our seeing;
  Uphold us, cherish, and have power to make
Our noisy years seem moments in the being
Of the eternal Silence: truths that wake,
    To perish never;
Which neither listlessness, nor mad endeavour,
    Nor Man nor Boy,
Nor all that is at enmity with joy,
Can utterly abolish or destroy!
      Hence in a season of calm weather,
      Though inland far we be,
Our Souls have sight of that immortal sea
    Which brought us hither,
    Can in a moment travel thither,
And see the Children sport upon the shore,
And hear the mighty waters rolling evermore.

VI

A WORTHY COMMANDER

A WORTHY commander is one that accounts learning the nourishment of military virtue, and lays that as his first foundation. He never bloudies his sword but in heat of battle; and had rather save one of his own soldiers than kill ten of his enemies. He accounts it an idle, vain-glorious, and suspected bounty to be full of good words; his rewarding, therefore, of the deserver arrives so timely, that his liberality can never be said to be gouty-handed. He holds it next his creed, that no coward can be an honest man, and dare die in it. He doth not think his body yields a more spreading shadow after a victory than before; and when he looks upon his enemy's dead body, 'tis with a kind of noble heaviness, not insultation; he is so honourably merciful to women in surprisal, that only makes him an excellent courtier. He knows the hazard of battles, not the pomp of ceremonies, are soldiers' best theatres; and strives to gain reputation, not by the multitude, but by the greatness of his actions. He is the first in giving the charge, and the last in retiring his foot. Equal toil he endures with the common soldier: from his example they all take fire, as one torch lights many. He understands in war there is no mean to err twice; the first, and least fault being sufficient to ruin an army: faults, therefore, he pardons none; they that are presidents of disorder, or mutiny, repair it by being examples of his justice. Besiege him never so strictly, so long as the air is not cut from him, his heart faints not. He hath learned so well to make use of a victory, as to get it, and in pursuing his enemy like a whirlwind carries all afore him; being assured, if ever a man would benefit himself upon his foe, then is the time, when they have lost force, wisdom, courage, and reputation. The goodness of his cause is the special motive to his valour; never is he known to slight the weakest enemy that comes armed against him in the hand of justice. Hasty and overmuch heat he accounts the stepdame to all great actions, that will not suffer them to thrive: if he cannot overcome his enemy by force, he does it by time. If ever he shake hands with war, he can die more calmly than most courtiers, for his continual dangers have been, as it were, so many meditations of death; he thinks not out of his own calling when he accounts life a continual warfare, and his prayers then best become him when armed *cap-à-pie*. He utters them like the great Hebrew general, on horseback. He casts a smiling contempt upon calumny, it meets him as if glass should encounter adamant. He thinks war is never to be given o'er, but on one of these three conditions: an assured peace, absolute victory, or an honest death. Lastly, when peace folds him up, his silver head should lean near the golden sceptre, and die in his prince's bosom.

VII

THE SECRET OF HAPPINESS

HONOUR and shame from no condition rise;
   Act well your part: there all the honour lies.
   Fortune in men has some small diff'rence made;
One flaunts in rags, one flutters in brocade,
The cobbler apron'd, and the parson gown'd;
The friar hooded, and the monarch crown'd.
'What differ more,' you cry, 'than crown and cowl?'
I'll tell you, friend! a wise man and a fool.
You'll find, if once the monarch acts the monk
Or, cobbler-like, the parson will be drunk,
Worth makes the man, and want of it the fellow,
The rest is all but leather or prunella.

  Stuck o'er with titles, and hung round with strings,
That thou mayst be by kings, or whores of kings,
Boast the pure blood of an illustrious race,
In quiet flow from Lucrece to Lucrece:
But by your fathers' worth if yours you rate,
Count me those only who were good and great.
Go! if your ancient but ignoble blood
Has crept thro' scoundrels ever since the flood,
Go! and pretend your family is young,
Nor own your fathers have been fools so long.
What can ennoble sots, or slaves, or cowards?
Alas! not all the blood of all the *Howards*.

  Look next on Greatness: say where Greatness lies.
'Where but among the heroes and the wise?'
Heroes are much the same, the point's agreed,
From Macedonia's madman to the Swede;
The whole strange purpose of their lives to find,
Or make, an enemy of all mankind!

Not one looks backward, onward still he goes,
Yet ne'er looks forward further than his nose.
No less alike the politic and wise;
All sly slow things with circumspective eyes:
Men in their loose unguarded hours they take,
Not that themselves are wise, but others weak.
But grant that those can conquer, these can cheat:
'T is phrase absurd to call a villain great.
Who wickedly is wise, or madly brave,
Is but the more a fool, the more a knave.
Who noble ends by noble means obtains,
Or failing, smiles in exile or in chains,
Like good Aurelius let him reign, or bleed
Like Socrates:—that man is great indeed!

What's fame? a fancied life in others' breath;
A thing beyond us, ev'n before our death.
Just what you hear you have; and what's unknown
The same, my lord, if Tully's or your own.
All that we feel of it begins and ends
In the small circle of our foes or friends;
To all beside as much an empty shade,
An Eugene living as a Cæsar dead;
Alike or when or where, they shone or shine,
Or on the Rubicon or on the Rhine.
A Wit's a feather, and a Chief a rod;
An Honest Man's the noblest work of God.
Fame but from death a villain's name can save,
As Justice tears his body from the grave;
When what t' oblivion better were resign'd
Is hung on high, to poison half mankind.
All fame is foreign but of true desert,
Plays round the head, but comes not to the heart:
One self-approving hour whole years outweighs
Of stupid starers and of loud huzzas:
And more true joy Marcellus exiled feels
Than Cæsar with a senate at his heels.

THE SECRET OF HAPPINESS

In Parts superior what advantage lies?
Tell (for you can) what is it to be wise?
'T is but to know how little can be known,
To see all others' faults, and feel our own,
Condemn'd in bus'ness or in arts to drudge,
Without a second, or without a judge.
Truths would you teach, or save a sinking land?
All fear, none aid you, and few understand.
Painful pre-eminence! yourself to view
Above life's weakness, and its comforts too.

Bring then these blessings to a strict account;
Make fair deductions; see to what they mount;
How much of other each is sure to cost;
How each for other oft is wholly lost;
How inconsistent greater goods with these;
How sometimes life is risk'd, and always ease.
Think, and if still the things thy envy call,
Say, wouldst thou be the man to whom they fall?
To sigh for ribands if thou art so silly,
Mark how they grace Lord Umbra or Sir Billy.
Is yellow dirt the passion of thy life?
Look but on Gripus or on Gripus' wife.
If parts allure thee, think how Bacon shined,
The wisest, brightest, meanest of mankind!
Or, ravish'd with the whistling of a name,
See Cromwell damn'd to everlasting fame!
If all united thy ambition call,
From ancient story learn to scorn them all:
There in the rich, the honour'd, famed, and great,
See the false scale of Happiness complete!
In hearts of Kings, in arms of Queens who lay,
How happy! those to ruin, these betray.
Mark by what wretched steps their glory grows;
From dirt and sea-weed, as proud Venice rose,
In each how guilt and greatness equal ran,
And all that rais'd the Hero sunk the Man:
Now Europe's laurels on their brows behold.

But stain'd with blood, or ill-exchanged for gold;
Then see them broke with toils, or sunk in ease,
Or infamous for plunder'd provinces.
O wealth ill-fated! which no act of fame
E'er taught to shine, or sanctified from shame!
What greater bliss attends their close of life?
Some greedy minion, or imperious wife,
The trophied arches, storied halls invade,
And haunt their slumbers in the pompous shade.
Alas! not dazzled with their noontide ray,
Compute the morn and ev'ning to the day;
The whole amount of that enormous fame,
A tale that blends their glory with their shame!
Know then this truth (enough for man to know),
'Virtue alone is happiness below';
The only point where human bliss stands still,
And tastes the good without the fall to ill;
Where only merit constant pay receives,
Is bless'd in what it takes and what it gives;
The joy unequall'd if its end it gain,
And, if it lose, attended with no pain;
Without satiety, tho' e'er so bless'd,
And but more relish'd as the more distress'd:
The broadest mirth unfeeling Folly wears,
Less pleasing far than Virtue's very tears:
Good from each object, from each place acquired,
For ever exercised, yet never tired;
Never elated while one man's oppress'd;
Never dejected while another's bless'd:
And where no wants, no wishes can remain,
Since but to wish more virtue is to gain.
  See the sole bliss Heav'n could on all bestow!
Which who but feels can taste, but thinks can know;
Yet poor with fortune, and with learning blind,
The bad must miss, the good untaught will find:
Slave to no sect, who takes no private road,
But looks thro' Nature up to Nature's God;
Pursues that chain which links th' immense design,

Joins Heav'n and earth, and mortal and divine;
Sees that no being any bliss can know,
But touches some above and some below;
Learns from this union of the rising whole
The first, last purpose of the human soul;
And knows where faith, law, morals, all began,
All end, in love of God and love of Man.

VIII

D'ARTAGNAN'S APPRENTICESHIP

'NOW that we are all here together, gentlemen,' said D'Artagnan, 'allow me to make my apologies.'

At the word apologies the brow of Athos darkened, a scornful smile played on Porthos' lips, and Aramis shook his head contemptuously.

'Do not misunderstand me, gentlemen,' said the Gascon, facing them proudly, while at the same moment the sun's rays happened to light up his striking features, 'do not misunderstand me. I only ask you to accept my apologies in case I should be prevented from fulfilling my engagements with you all; for M. Athos has the right to kill me first, which leaves M. Porthos a very poor chance of distinguishing himself, and practically puts you out of court altogether, M. Aramis. It is for this reason only I tender my apologies. So now, M. Athos, stand on your guard.'

As he uttered the last word the Gascon with a knightly air drew his sword from the scabbard. He was now eager for the fray, and would have faced the entire company of Musketeers, let alone three.

It was just after midday; the sun was almost at its zenith, and the barren spot chosen for the encounter was insufferably warm.

'It's devilish hot,' said Athos, as he drew his sword, 'but I cannot take off my doublet because my wound has started bleeding again, and I don't want to annoy you by the sight of blood which you have not drawn.'

'That's very thoughtful of you,' said D'Artagnan, 'and whether shed by myself or another, I regret that the blood of so brave a gentleman should be shed at all. Under the circumstances, I will keep on my doublet too.'

'Come, come, have done with compliments,' cried Porthos; 'please remember that we are both waiting for our turns.'

'Speak for yourself,' said Aramis, 'for I do not at all echo your sentiments; for my part, I think these gentlemen show a proper spirit which does them credit.'

'Are you ready?' said Athos, putting himself on guard.

'I was only waiting for the word from you,' replied D'Artagnan, and they crossed swords. But no sooner had the rapiers clashed than a company of the Cardinal's guards, headed by Jussac, came round the corner.

'The Cardinal's guards! The Cardinal's guards!' cried the two seconds in the same breath. 'Sheathe swords, gentlemen, sheathe your swords!'

But the warning came too late; the attitude of the combatants told its own tale.

'Halloa!' cried Jussac, advancing towards them, and bidding his men follow. 'Musketeers fighting again! How about the edicts? Are they made only to be broken?'

'This is hardly fair, gentlemen of the guards,' said Athos, rather bitterly; for Jussac had been one of the aggressors on the previous evening. 'I know that if we were to catch you fighting we should never dream of interfering. Let us proceed with this affair and you will have some amusement gratis.'

'Gentlemen,' said Jussac, 'it is quite out of the question; orders must be obeyed. Up swords, instantly, and fall in. You must come with us.'

'Sir,' said Aramis, mimicking Jussac's manner, 'it would give us great pleasure to accept your very kind invitation; but, unfortunately, it is quite impossible. M. de Tréville has given strict orders on the subject, and his orders must be obeyed. So pass on, gentlemen; there is nothing else for you to do.'

This flippant tone exasperated Jussac.

'If you disobey, I shall bid my men enforce my orders.'

'There are five of them,' said Athos, half to himself, 'while we are only three, so we shall get the worst of it again, and in that case I, for one, shall not leave the field alive, for I do not intend to appear before the Captain a second time as a vanquished man.'

Athos, Porthos, and Aramis instantly closed in shoulder to shoulder and Jussac formed up his men for the attack. This just gave the young Gascon time to make up his mind what part he should take in the coming conflict. It was one of those critical moments which decide a man's future. He had to choose between the King and the Cardinal, and the choice once made, there was no turning back. Of course, to fight was to break the law, to risk his life, to make an enemy of a statesman more powerful, perhaps, than the King himself. All this passed through his mind, and yet—to his honour, be it said—he did not hesitate long. Turning to the Musketeers, he cried, 'Gentlemen, I think there is some mistake. M. Athos said we were but three, but I make it four.'

'But you don't count as one of us,' said Porthos.

'It is true I do not wear the uniform of a Musketeer, but I am one at heart, and so I throw in my chances with you.'

'Young man,' cried Jussac, 'you are at liberty to retire; and if you wish to save your skin, you had better be gone quickly.'

But D'Artagnan made no move to go.

'You are the right sort,' said Athos, pressing the young man's hand.

'Come, look sharp, make up your mind one way or the other,' cried Jussac.

'Something must be decided, and that quickly,' said Porthos to Aramis.

The youth and inexperience of our young hero made them hesitate to accept his generous offer.

'Even then it would be only three and a boy,' said Athos, 'and one of the three wounded already into the bargain.'

'Still, we cannot give in,' said Porthos.

'Hardly,' replied Athos.

D'Artagnan, seeing them hesitate, cried, 'Give me a chance, gentlemen. I pledge my word that I will not leave the field unless we get the best of it.'

'Your name, my gallant fellow?' said Athos.

'D'Artagnan, sir.'

'Good, then we four stand together.'

'Come, gentlemen, have you made up your minds?' cried Jussac, for the third time.

'We have,' said Athos.

'Then what do you mean to do?'

'We are going to fight,' replied Aramis, drawing his sword.

'What! you resist! Then, guards, forward!' and the two parties furiously attacked each other. All being expert swordsmen, there was no little skill exhibited on both sides. Athos engaged Cahusac, who was a favourite of the Cardinal's, Porthos attacked Bicarat, and Aramis had to deal with two others.

In the meantime D'Artagnan had rushed at Jussac himself. He felt no fear, but his heart beat fast as he flung himself on his formidable adversary. He fought with the agility of a tiger, springing at his antagonist from every side, and changing his ground and his guard twenty times a minute. Jussac was an expert swordsman, but it took all his skill and vigilance to defend himself against such a desperate and unconventional mode of attack, while at the same time his own thrusts were parried with consummate adroitness.

Jussac's patience was at last exhausted. Incensed at being thus bearded by a mere boy, he began to strike wildly. The Gascon saw his chance, and in the next onslaught brought all his cunning to bear, and attacked him with renewed vigour. Jussac, thinking the time had come when he could put an end to this, made a furious lunge at his antagonist; but D'Artagnan was on the look out for this and, parrying the blow, glided like a snake under his opponent's sword-arm, and before Jussac could recover himself, ran him through the body. The Captain fell like a dead man.

D'Artagnan now had time to recover breath, and looked round to see how his comrades were faring.

Aramis had killed one of his assailants, but was still hotly engaged with the other.

Porthos had received a thrust in his arm, and had wounded his opponent in the thigh. But neither wound was serious, and they only fought on the more fiercely.

Athos had been wounded by Cahusac, but though he looked pale, he was holding his own. He had, however, shifted his sword to the left hand.

By the then laws of duelling, D'Artagnan could go to the help of any comrade as he thought best. He had not quite made up his mind, when a glance from Athos decided him. That appealing look spoke volumes, though probably nothing on earth would have induced him to call out for help.

With one bound D'Artagnan sprang at Cahusac, shouting, 'Stand on your guard, sir, or I will run you through.'

'Don't kill him, for heaven's sake!' cried Athos, who had sunk breathless on his knees. 'I have an old affair to settle with him as soon as I am fit to fight again. So if you could only disarm him—Bravo! that's splendid!' he continued, seeing Cahusac's sword fly through the air and fall twenty paces from him. Cahusac sprang forward to recover it, but the Gascon was too active for him, and had his foot on the blade before he could get there. Cahusac then pounced on the sword of the guardsman who had been killed by Aramis, and again rushed to attack D'Artagnan. But as he turned he encountered Athos, who had recovered his breath in the interval and was most anxious to finish his fight with Cahusac. D'Artagnan saw at once that Athos preferred to do without his assistance, and in a few minutes Cahusac fell with an ugly wound in his throat.

Almost at the same moment Aramis had got his other antagonist on the ground, and had compelled him to cry for mercy. There were now only Porthos and Bicarat left fighting. Porthos made all kind of jests at the expense of his opponent, but he could not get him off his guard or reach him anyway, for Bicarat was one of those men with nerves of steel who never give in.

But there was no time to be lost. The patrol might come up at any moment and arrest them all, King's Musketeers and Cardinal's guard. So Athos, Aramis, and D'Artagnan surrounded Bicarat and called on him to surrender. But though all alone and wounded in the thigh, Bicarat was loth to yield. Then Jussac, who lay wounded, raised himself on his elbow and urged him to surrender. But Bicarat was a Gascon too, and paid no attention to Jussac, but, pointing to a spot of ground with his sword, cried with the utmost nonchalance, 'On this spot will Bicarat die, the only one left of his company.'

'But it's four against one,' cried Jussac. 'As your Captain, I order you to surrender.'

'If you order me, that's another matter,' said Bicarat. 'As my commander you must, of course, be obeyed.'

But not wishing to give up his sword, he broke it across his knee, threw the pieces over the monastery wall, crossed his arms, and began to whistle an air which was a favourite among the Cardinal's guards.

Courage always wins respect, even in an enemy. The Musketeers gave Bicarat a military salute and returned their swords to the scabbards. D'Artagnan did the same. Then with Bicarat's help, he carried Cahusac and the guard that Aramis had wounded to the porch of the monastery. The fourth, as we know, was dead. Then they rang the cloister bell, and taking with them the four swords which they had captured, directed their steps towards the residence of M. de Tréville, half-mad with exultation.

Arm in arm they strode along, taking up almost the whole width of the street, and telling the glad news to every Musketeer they met, who then, as a matter of course, joined the triumphal procession. D'Artagnan was in the seventh heaven of delight as he marched down the street between Athos and Porthos.

'Although I am not yet enrolled in the ranks of the Musketeers,' said he to his new friends as they entered the courtyard, 'at any rate, I have had my first fight for them.'

IX

ELEGY WRITTEN IN A COUNTRY CHURCHYARD

THE Curfew tolls the knell of parting day,
    The lowing herd winds slowly o'er the lea,
    The plowman homeward plods his weary way,
And leaves the world to darkness and to me.

Now fades the glimmering landscape on the sight,
    And all the air a solemn stillness holds,
Save where the beetle wheels his droning flight,
    And drowsy tinklings lull the distant folds:

Save that from yonder ivy-mantled tow'r
    The moping owl does to the moon complain
Of such as, wand'ring near her secret bow'r,
    Molest her ancient solitary reign.

Beneath those rugged elms, that yew-tree's shade,
    Where heaves the turf in many a mould'ring heap,
Each in his narrow cell for ever laid,
    The rude Forefathers of the hamlet sleep.

The breezy call of incense-breathing Morn,
    The swallow twitt'ring from the straw-built shed,
The cock's shrill clarion, or the echoing horn,
    No more shall rouse them from their lowly bed.

For them no more the blazing hearth shall burn,
    Or busy housewife ply her evening care:
No children run to lisp their sire's return,
    Or climb his knee the envied kiss to share.

Oft did the harvest to their sickle yield,
   Their furrow oft the stubborn glebe has broke:
How jocund did they drive their team afield!
   How bow'd the woods beneath their sturdy stroke!

Let not Ambition mock their useful toil,
   Their homely joys, and destiny obscure;
Nor Grandeur hear with a disdainful smile
   The short and simple annals of the poor.

The boast of heraldry, the pomp of pow'r,
   And all that beauty, all that wealth e'er gave,
Awaits alike th' inevitable hour.
   The paths of glory lead but to the grave.

Nor you, ye Proud, impute to These the fault,
   If Mem'ry o'er their Tomb no Trophies raise,
Where through the long-drawn isle and fretted vault
   The pealing anthem swells the note of praise.

Can storied urn or animated bust
   Back to its mansion call the fleeting breath?
Can Honour's voice provoke the silent dust,
   Or Flatt'ry soothe the dull cold ear of death?

Perhaps in this neglected spot is laid
   Some heart once pregnant with celestial fire;
Hands, that the rod of empire might have sway'd,
   Or wak'd to ecstasy the living lyre.

But Knowledge to their eyes her ample page
   Rich with the spoils of time did ne'er unroll;
Chill Penury repress'd their noble rage,
   And froze the genial current of the soul.

Full many a gem of purest ray serene,
   The dark unfathom'd caves of ocean bear:
Full many a flower is born to blush unseen,
   And waste its sweetness on the desert air.

Some village-Hampden, that with dauntless breast
  The little Tyrant of his fields withstood,
Some mute inglorious Milton here may rest,
  Some Cromwell guiltless of his country's blood.

Th' applause of list'ning senates to command,
  The threats of pain and ruin to despise,
To scatter plenty o'er a smiling land,
  And read their hist'ry in a nation's eyes,

Their lot forbad: nor circumscrib'd alone
  Their growing virtues, but their crimes confin'd;
Forbad to wade through slaughter to a throne,
  And shut the gates of mercy on mankind,

The struggling pangs of conscious truth to hide,
  To quench the blushes of ingenuous shame,
Or heap the shrine of Luxury and Pride
  With incense kindled at the Muse's flame.

Far from the madding crowd's ignoble strife,
  Their sober wishes never learn'd to stray;
Along the cool sequester'd vale of life
  They kept the noiseless tenor of their way.

Yet ev'n these bones from insult to protect
  Some frail memorial still erected nigh,
With uncouth rhymes and shapeless sculpture deck'd,
  Implores the passing tribute of a sigh.

Their name, their years, spelt by th' unletter'd muse,
  The place of fame and elegy supply:
And many a holy text around she strews,
  That teach the rustic moralist to die.

For who to dumb Forgetfulness a prey,
  This pleasing anxious being e'er resign'd,
Left the warm precincts of the cheerful day,
  Nor cast one longing ling'ring look behind?

On some fond breast the parting soul relies,
  Some pious drops the closing eye requires;
E'en from the tomb the voice of Nature cries,
  E'en in our Ashes live their wonted Fires.

For thee, who, mindful of th' unhonour'd Dead,
  Dost in these lines their artless tale relate;
If chance, by lonely contemplation led,
  Some kindred spirit shall inquire thy fate,—

Haply some hoary-headed Swain may say,
  'Oft have we seen him at the peep of dawn
Brushing with hasty steps the dews away
  To meet the sun upon the upland lawn.

'Him have we seen the Green-wood Side along,
  While o'er the Heath we hied, our Labours done,
Oft as the Woodlark piped her farewell Song,
  With wistful eyes pursue the setting Sun.

'There at the foot of yonder nodding beech,
  That wreathes its old fantastic roots so high,
His listless length at noontide would he stretch,
  And pore upon the brook that babbles by.

'Hard by yon wood, now smiling as in scorn,
  Mutt'ring his wayward fancies he would rove,
Now drooping, woeful-wan, like one forlorn,
  Or craz'd with care, or cross'd in hopeless love.

'One morn I miss'd him on the custom'd hill,
  Along the heath, and near his fav'rite tree;
Another came; nor yet beside the rill,
  Nor up the lawn, nor at the wood was he:

'The next, with dirges due in sad array
  Slow thro' the church-way path we saw him borne,—
Approach and read (for thou can'st read) the lay,
  Grav'd on the stone beneath yon aged thorn.'

THE EPITAPH

Here rests his head upon the lap of Earth
  A Youth, to Fortune and to Fame unknown,
Fair Science frown'd not on his humble birth,
  And Melancholy mark'd him for her own.

Large was his bounty, and his soul sincere,
  Heav'n did a recompence as largely send:
He gave to Mis'ry (all he had) a tear,
  He gain'd from Heav'n ('twas all he wish'd) a friend.

No farther seek his merits to disclose,
  Or draw his frailties from their dread abode,
(There they alike in trembling hope repose,)
  The bosom of his Father and his God.

X

THE CITY AT NIGHT

THE POET: WORDSWORTH

EARTH has not any thing to show more fair:
  Dull would he be of soul who could pass by
  A sight so touching in its majesty:
This City now doth, like a garment, wear
The beauty of the morning; silent, bare,
Ships, towers, domes, theatres, and temples lie
Open unto the fields, and to the sky,
All bright and glittering in the smokeless air.
Never did sun more beautifully steep
In his first splendour, valley, rock, or hill;
Ne'er saw I, never felt, a calm so deep!
The river glideth at his own sweet will:
Dear God! the very houses seem asleep;
And all that mighty heart is lying still!

THE PHILOSOPHER: CARLYLE

'*Ach, mein Lieber!*' said he once, at midnight, when we had returned from the Coffee-house in rather earnest talk, 'it is a true sublimity to dwell here. These fringes of lamplight, struggling up through smoke and thousandfold exhalation, some fathoms into the ancient reign of Night, what thinks Boötes of them, as he leads his Hunting-Dogs over the Zenith in their leash of sidereal fire? That stifled hum of Midnight, when Traffic has lain down to rest; and the chariot-wheels of Vanity, still rolling here and there through distant streets, are bearing her to Halls roofed-in, and lighted to the due pitch for her; and only Vice and Misery to prowl or to moan like nightbirds, are abroad: that hum, I say, like the stertorous, unquiet slumber of sick Life, is heard in Heaven! Oh, under that hideous coverlet of vapours, and putrefactions, and unimaginable gases, what a Fermenting-vat lies simmering and hid! The joyful and the sorrowful are there; men are dying there, men are being born; men are praying,—on the other side of a brick partition, men are cursing; and around them all is the vast, void Night. The proud Grandee still lingers in his perfumed saloons, or reposes within damask curtains; Wretchedness cowers into truckle-beds, or shivers hunger-stricken into its lair of straw: in obscure cellars, *Rouge-et-Noir* languidly emits its voice-of-destiny to haggard hungry Villains; while Councillors of State sit plotting, and playing their high chess-game, whereof the pawns are Men. The Lover whispers his mistress that the coach is ready; and she, full of hope and fear, glides down, to fly with him over the borders: the Thief, still more silently, sets-to his picklocks and crowbars, or lurks in wait till the watchmen first snore in their boxes. Gay mansions, with supper-rooms and dancing-rooms, are full of light and music and high-swelling hearts; but, in the Condemned Cells, the pulse of life beats tremulous and faint, and bloodshot eyes look out through the darkness, which is around and within, for the light of a stern last morning. Six men are to be hanged on the morrow: comes no hammering from the

Rabenstein?—their gallows must even now be o' building. Upwards of five-hundred-thousand two-legged animals without feathers lie round us, in horizontal positions; their heads all in nightcaps, and full of the foolishest dreams. Riot cries aloud, and staggers and swaggers in his rank dens of shame; and the Mother, with streaming hair, kneels over her pallid dying infant, whose cracked lips only her tears now moisten.—All these heaped and huddled together, with nothing but a little carpentry and masonry between them;—crammed in, like salted fish in their barrel;—or weltering, shall I say, like an Egyptian pitcher of tamed vipers, each struggling to get its *head above* the others: *such* work goes on under that smoke-counterpane!—But I, *mein Werther*, sit above it all; I am alone with the Stars.'

THE CONSTABLE: SHAKESPEARE

Enter DOGBERRY *and* VERGES *with the Watch.*

Dog. Are you good men and true?

Verg. Yea, or else it were pity but they should suffer salvation, body and soul.

Dog. Nay, that were a punishment too good for them, if they should have any allegiance in them, being chosen for the prince's watch.

Verg. Well, give them their charge, neighbour Dogberry.

Dog. First, who think you the most desartless man to be constable?

First Watch. Hugh Otecake, sir, or George Seacole; for they can write and read.

Dog. Come hither, neighbour Seacole. God hath blessed you with a good name: to be a well-favoured man is the gift of fortune; but to write and read comes by nature.

Sec. Watch. Both which, master constable,—

Dog. You have: I knew it would be your answer. Well, for your favour, sir, why, give God thanks, and make no boast of it; and for your writing and reading, let that appear when there is no need of such vanity. You are thought here to be the most senseless and fit man for the constable of the watch; therefore bear you the lantern. This is your charge: you shall comprehend all vagrom men; you are to bid any man stand, in the prince's name.

Sec. Watch. How if a' will not stand?

Dog. Why, then, take no note of him, but let him go; and presently call the rest of the watch together, and thank God you are rid of a knave.

Verg. If he will not stand when he is bidden, he is none of the prince's subjects.

Dog. True, and they are to meddle with none but the prince's subjects. You shall also make no noise in the streets; for, for the watch to babble and to talk is most tolerable and not to be endured.

Watch. We will rather sleep than talk: we know what belongs to a watch.

Dog. Why, you speak like an ancient and most quiet watchman; for I cannot see how sleeping could offend: only, have a care that your bills be not stolen. Well, you are to call at all the ale-houses, and bid those that are drunk get them to bed.

Watch. How if they will not?

Dog. Why, then, let them alone till they are sober: if they make you not then the better answer, you may say they are not the men you took them for.

Watch. Well, sir.

Dog. If you meet a thief, you may suspect him, by virtue of your office, to be no true man; and, for such kind of men, the less you meddle or make with them, why, the more is for your honesty.

Watch. If we know him to be a thief, shall we not lay hands on him?

Dog. Truly, by your office, you may; but I think they that touch pitch will be defiled: the most peaceable way for you, if you do take a thief, is to let him show himself what he is, and steal out of your company.

Verg. You have been always called a merciful man, partner.

Dog. Truly, I would not hang a dog by my will, much more a man who hath any honesty in him.

Verg. If you hear a child cry in the night, you must call to the nurse and bid her still it.

Watch. How if the nurse be asleep and will not hear us?

Dog. Why, then, depart in peace, and let the child wake her with crying; for the ewe that will not hear her lamb when it baes will never answer a calf when he bleats.

Verg. 'Tis very true.

Dog. This is the end of the charge:—you, constable, are to present the prince's own person: if you meet the prince in the night, you may stay him.

Verg. Nay, by'r lady, that I think a' cannot.

Dog. Five shillings to one on't, with any man that knows the statues, he may stay him; marry, not without the prince be willing; for, indeed, the watch ought to offend no man; and it is an offence to stay a man against his will.

Verg. By'r lady, I think it be so.

Dog. Ha, ah, ha! Well, masters, good night: an there be any matter of weight chances, call up me: keep your fellows' counsels and your own; and good night. Come, neighbour.

Watch. Well, masters, we hear our charge: let us go sit here upon the church-bench till two, and then all to bed.

Dog. One word more, honest neighbours. I pray you, watch about Signior Leonato's door; for the wedding being there to-morrow, there is a great coil to-night. Adieu: be vigilant, I beseech you.

XI

BOB ACRES' DUEL

SIR LUCIUS O'TRIGGER. Pray, my friend, what has brought you so suddenly to Bath?

Acres. Faith! I have followed Cupid's Jack-a-lantern, and find myself in a quagmire at last.—In short, I have been very ill-used, Sir Lucius.—I don't choose to mention names, but look on me as on a very ill-used gentleman. . . . Mark me, Sir Lucius, I fall as deep as need be in love with a young lady—her friends take my part—I follow her to Bath—send word of my arrival; and receive answer, that the lady is to be otherwise disposed of.—This, Sir Lucius, I call being ill-used.

Sir L. Very ill, upon my conscience.—Pray, can you divine the cause of it?

Acres. Why, there's the matter; she has another lover, one Beverley, who, I am told, is now in Bath.—Odds slanders and lies! he must be at the bottom of it.

Sir L. A rival in the case, is there?—and you think he has supplanted you unfairly?

Acres. Unfairly! to be sure he has. He never could have done it fairly.

Sir L. Then sure you know what is to be done!

Acres. Not I, upon my soul!

Sir L. We wear no swords here, but you understand me.

Acres. What! fight him.

Sir L. Ay, to be sure: what can I mean else?

Acres. But he has given me no provocation.

Sir L. Now, I think he has given you the greatest provocation in the world. Can a man commit a more heinous offence against another man than to fall in love with the same woman? Oh, by my soul! it is the most unpardonable breach of friendship.

Acres. Breach of friendship! ay, ay; but I have no acquaintance with this man. I never saw him in my life.

Sir L. That's no argument at all—he has the less right then to take such a liberty.

Acres. Gad, that's true—I grow full of anger, Sir Lucius! I fire apace! Odds hilts and blades! I find a man may have a deal of valour in him, and not know it! But couldn't I contrive to have a little right on my side?

Sir L. What the devil signifies right, when your honour is concerned? Do you think Achilles, or my little Alexander the Great, ever inquired where the right lay? No, by my soul, they drew their broad-swords, and left the lazy sons of peace to settle the justice of it.

Acres. Your words are a grenadier's march to my heart! I believe courage must be catching! I certainly do feel a kind of valour rising as it were—a kind of courage, as I may say.—Odds flints, pans, and triggers! I'll challenge him directly.

Sir L. Ah, my little friend, if I had Blunderbuss Hall here, I could show you a range of ancestry, in the old O'Trigger line, that would furnish the new room; every one of whom had killed his man!—For though the mansion-house and dirty acres have slipped through my fingers, I thank heaven our honour and the family-pictures are as fresh as ever.

Acres. O, Sir Lucius! I have had ancestors too!—every man of 'em colonel or captain in the militia!—Odds balls and barrels! say no more—I'm braced for it. The thunder of your words has soured the milk of human kindness in my breast:—Zounds! as the man in the play says, *I could do such deeds!*

Sir L. Come, come, there must be no passion at all in the case—these things should always be done civilly.

Acres. I must be in a passion, Sir Lucius—I must be in a rage.—Dear Sir Lucius, let me be in a rage, if you love me. Come, here's pen and paper.—[*Sits down to write.*] I would the ink were red!

Scene III.—*King's-Mead-Fields.*

Enter O'Trigger *and* Acres, *with pistols.*

Acres. By my valour! then, Sir Lucius, forty yards is a good distance. Odds levels and aims!—I say it is a good distance.

Sir L. Is it for muskets or small field-pieces? Upon my conscience, Mr. Acres, you must leave those things to me.— Stay now—I'll show you.—[*Measures paces along the stage.*] There now, that is a very pretty distance—a pretty gentleman's distance.

Acres. Zounds! we might as well fight in a sentry box!

I tell you, Sir Lucius, the farther he is off, the cooler I shall take my aim.

Sir L. Faith! then I suppose you would aim at him best of all if he was out of sight!

Acres. No, Sir Lucius; but I should think forty or eight and thirty yards——

Sir L. Pho! pho! nonsense! three or four feet between the mouths of your pistols is as good as a mile.

Acres. Odds bullets, no!—by my valour! there is no merit in killing him so near; do, my dear Sir Lucius, let me bring him down at a long shot—a long shot, Sir Lucius, if you love me.

Sir L. Well, the gentleman's friend and I must settle that.—But tell me now, Mr. Acres, in case of an accident, is there any little will or commission I could execute for you? . . . You may think there's no being shot at without a little risk—and if an unlucky bullet should carry a quietus with it—I say it will be no time then to be bothering you about family matters.

Acres. A quietus!

Sir L. For instance, now—if that should be the case— would you choose to be pickled and sent home?—or would it be the same to you to lie here in the Abbey? I'm told there is very snug lying in the Abbey.

Acres. Pickled!—Snug lying in the Abbey!—Odds tremors! Sir Lucius, don't talk so!

Sir L. I suppose, Mr. Acres, you never were engaged in an affair of this kind before?

Acres. No, Sir Lucius, never before.

Sir L. Ah! that's a pity!—there's nothing like being used to a thing. Pray now, how would you receive the gentleman's shot?

Acres. Odds files!—I've practised that—there, Sir Lucius—there. [*Puts himself in an attitude.*] A side-front, hey? Odds! I'll make myself small enough? I'll stand edgeways.

Sir L. Now—you're quite out—for if you stand so when I take my aim——[*Levelling at him.*]

Acres. Zounds! Sir Lucius—are you sure it is not cocked?

Sir L. Never fear.

Acres. But—but—you don't know—it may go off of its own head!

Sir L. Pho! be easy.—Well, now if I hit you in the body, my bullet has a double chance—for if it misses a vital part of your right side, 'twill be hard if it don't succeed on the left!

Acres. A vital part.

Sir L. But there—fix yourself so—[*Placing him*]—let him see the broad-side of your full front—there—now a ball or two may pass clean through your body, and never do any harm.

Acres. Clean through me!—a ball or two clean through me!

Sir L. Ay—may they—and it is much the genteelest attitude into the bargain.

Acres. Look'ee! Sir Lucius—I'd just as lieve be shot in an awkward posture as a genteel one; so, by my valour! I will stand edgeways.

Sir L. [*Looking at his watch.*] Sure they don't mean to disappoint us—Hah!—no, faith—I think I see them coming.

Acres. Hey!—what!—coming!——

Sir L. Ay.—Who are those yonder getting over the stile?

Acres. There are two of them indeed!—well—let them come—hey, Sir Lucius!—we—we—we—we—won't run.

Sir L. Run!

Acres. No—I say—we won't run, by my valour!

Sir L. What the devil's the matter with you?

Acres. Nothing—nothing—my dear friend—my dear Sir Lucius—but I—I—I don't feel quite so bold, somehow, as I did.

Sir L. O fy!—consider your honour.

Acres. Ay—true—my honour. Do, Sir Lucius, edge in a word or two every now and then about my honour.

Sir L. Well, here they're coming. [*Looking.*

Acres. Sir Lucius—if I wa'n't with you, I should almost think I was afraid.—If my valour should leave me! Valour will come and go.

Sir L. Then pray keep it fast, while you have it.

Acres. Sir Lucius—I doubt it is going—yes—my valour is certainly going!—it is sneaking off!—I feel it oozing out as it were at the palms of my hands!

Sir L. Your honour—your honour.—Here they are.

Acres. O mercy!—now—that I was safe at Clod Hall! or could be shot before I was aware!

Enter FAULKLAND *and* CAPTAIN ABSOLUTE.

Sir L. Gentlemen, your most obedient.—Hah!—what Captain Absolute!

Acres. What, Jack!—my dear Jack!—my dear friend!

Abs. Hark'ee, Bob, Beverley's at hand.

Sir L. Well, Mr. Acres—I don't blame your saluting the gentleman civilly.—[*To* FAULKLAND.] So, Mr. Beverley, if you'll choose your weapons, the captain and I will measure the ground.

Faulk. My weapons, sir!

Acres. Odds life! Sir Lucius, I'm not going to fight Mr. Faulkland; these are my particular friends.

Sir L. What, sir, did you not come here to fight Mr. Acres?

Faulk. Not I, upon my word, sir.

Sir L. Well, now, that's mighty provoking! But I hope, Mr. Faulkland, as there are three of us come on purpose for the game, you won't be so cantankerous as to spoil the party by sitting out.

Abs. O pray, Faulkland, fight to oblige Sir Lucius.

Faulk. Nay, if Mr. Acres is so bent on the matter——

Acres. No, no, Mr. Faulkland;—I'll bear my disappointment like a Christian.—Look'ee, Sir Lucius, there's no occasion at all for me to fight; and if it is the same to you, I'd as lieve let it alone.

Sir L. Observe me, Mr. Acres—I must not be trifled with. You have certainly challenged somebody—and you came here to fight him. Now, if that gentleman is willing to represent him—I can't see, for my soul, why it isn't just the same thing.

Acres. Why no—Sir Lucius—I tell you, 'tis one Beverley I've challenged—a fellow, you see, that dare not show his face!—if he were here, I'd make him give up his pretensions directly!

Abs. Hold, Bob—let me set you right—there is no such man as Beverley in the case.—The person who assumed that name is before you; and as his pretensions are the same in both characters, he is ready to support them in whatever way you please.

Sir L. Well, this is lucky.—Now you have an opportunity——

Acres. What, quarrel with my dear friend, Jack Absolute?—not if he were fifty Beverleys! Zounds! Sir Lucius, you would not have me so unnatural.

Sir L. Upon my conscience, Mr. Acres, your valour has oozed away with a vengeance!

Acres. Not in the least! Odds backs and abettors! I'll be your second with all my heart—and if you should get a quietus, you may command me entirely. I'll get you snug lying in the Abbey here; or pickle you, and send you over to Blunderbuss Hall, or anything of the kind, with the greatest pleasure.

XII

TREES

OLD TREES: LANDOR

LANDOR. I am pleased, as I observed, by the palace opposite, not having seen in Italy, until now, a house of any kind with a span of turf before it. Like yours and that opposite, they generally encroach on some lane, following its windings and angles, lest a single inch of ground should be lost; and the roofs fight for the centre of the road. I am inclined to believe that the number of houses of which the fronts are uneven, is greater than of the even;

and that there are more cramped with iron than uncramped. These deformities are always left visible, though the house is plastered, that the sum expended on the iron and labour may be evident. If an Italian of condition spends a lira, he must be seen to spend it: his stables, his laundry, his domestics, his peasants, must strike the eye together: his pigsty must have witnesses like his will. Every tree is accursed, as that of which the holy cross was fabricated, and ought to be swept away. You are surely the most hospitable people in the world: even that edifice which derives its existence and its name from privacy, stands exposed and wide-open to the stranger, wherever it stands at all.

When I resided on the Lake of Como, I visited the palace of Marchese Odeschalchi. Before it swelled in majesty that sovran of inland waters; behind it was a pond surrounded with brickwork in which about twenty young goldfish jostled and gasped for room. The Larius had sapped the foundation of his palace, and the Marchese had exerted all his genius to avenge himself: he composed this bitter parody. I inquired of his cousin Don Pepino who conducted me, when the roof would be put on: he looked at me, doubting if he understood me, and answered in a gentle tone, 'It was finished last summer.' My error originated from observing red pantiles, kept in their places by heavy stones, loose, and laid upon them irregularly.

'What a beautiful swell, Don Pepino, is this upon the right,' exclaimed I: 'the little hill seems sensible of pleasure as he dips his foot into the Larius.'

'There will be the offices.'

'What! and hide Grumello? Let me enjoy the sight while I can. He appears instinct with life, nodding the network of vines upon his head, and beckoning and inviting us, while the fig-trees and mulberries and chestnuts and walnuts, and those lofty and eternal cypresses, stand motionless around. His joyous mates, all different in form and features, push forward; and, if there is not something in the air, or something in my eyesight, illusory, they are running a race along the borders. Stop a moment: how shall we climb over these two enormous pines? Ah, Don Pepino! old trees in their living state are the only things that money cannot command. Rivers leave their beds, run into cities, and traverse mountains for it; obelisks and arches, palaces and temples, amphitheatres and pyramids, rise up like exhalations at its bidding; even the free spirit of Man, the only thing great on earth, crouches and cowers in its presence. It passes away and vanishes before venerable trees. What a sweet odour is here! whence comes it? sweeter it appears to me and stronger than of the pine itself.'

'I imagine,' said he, 'from the linden; yes, certainly.'

'Is that a linden? It is the largest, and I should imagine, the oldest upon earth, if I could perceive that it had lost any of its branches.'

'Pity that it hides half the row of yon houses from the palace! It will be carried off with the two pines in the autumn.'

'O Don Pepino!' cried I; 'the French, who abhor whatever is old and whatever is great, have sparèd it; the Austrians, who sell their fortresses and their armies, nay, sometimes their daughters, have not sold it: must it fall! Shall the cypress of Soma be without a rival? I hope to have left Lombardy before it happens; for, events which you will tell me ought never to interest me at all, not only do interest me, but make me (I confess it) sorrowful.'

Who in the world could ever cut down a linden, or dare in his senses to break a twig from off one? To a linden was fastened the son of William Tell, when the apple was cloven on his head. Years afterward, often did the father look higher and lower, and search laboriously, to descry if any mark were remaining of the cord upon its bark! often must he have inhaled this very odour! what a refreshment was it to a father's breast! The flowers of the linden should be the only incense offered up in the churches to God. Happy the man whose aspirations are pure enough to mingle with it!

How many fond and how many lively thoughts have been nurtured under this tree! how many kind hearts have beaten here! Its branches are not so numerous as the couples they have invited to sit beside it, nor its blossoms and leaves as the expressions of tenderness it has witnessed. What appeals to the pure all-seeing heavens! what similitudes to the everlasting mountains! what protestations of eternal truth and constancy! from those who now are earth; they, and their shrouds, and their coffins! The caper and fig-tree have split the monument. Emblems of past loves and future hopes, severed names which the holiest rites united, broken letters of brief happiness, bestrew the road, and speak to the passer-by in vain.

YEW-TREES: WORDSWORTH

There is a Yew-tree, pride of Lorton Vale,
Which to this day stands single, in the midst
Of its own darkness, as it stood of yore:
Not loth to furnish weapons for the bands
Of Umfraville or Percy ere they marched
To Scotland's heaths; or those that crossed the sea
And drew their sounding bows at Azincour,
Perhaps at earlier Crecy, or Poictiers.
Of vast circumference and gloom profound
This solitary Tree! a living thing
Produced too slowly ever to decay;
Of form and aspect too magnificent
To be destroyed. But worthier still of note
Are those fraternal Four of Borrowdale,
Joined in one solemn and capacious grove;
Huge trunks! and each particular trunk a growth
Of intertwisted fibres serpentine
Up-coiling, and inveterately convolved;
Nor uninformed with Phantasy, and looks
That threaten the profane; a pillared shade,
Upon whose grassless floor of red-brown hue,
By sheddings from the pining umbrage tinged
Perennially—beneath whose sable roof
Of boughs, as if for festal purpose decked
With unrejoicing berries—ghostly Shapes
May meet at noontide; Fear and trembling Hope,
Silence and Foresight; Death the Skeleton

And Time the Shadow;—there to celebrate,
As in a natural temple scattered o'er
With altars undisturbed of mossy stone,
United worship; or in mute repose
To lie, and listen to the mountain flood
Murmuring from Glaramara's inmost caves.

A FOREST: SHELLEY

The path through which that lovely twain
  Have passed, by cedar, pine, and yew,
  And each dark tree that ever grew,
  Is curtained out from heaven's wide blue.
Nor sun nor moon nor wind nor rain
Can pierce its interwoven bowers;
  Nor aught save where some cloud of dew,
Drifted along the earth-creeping breeze
Between the trunks of the hoar trees,
  Hangs each a pearl in the pale flowers
    Of the green laurel blown anew,
  And bends,—and then fades silently—
  One frail and fair anemone.
  Or when some star, of many a one
    That climbs and wanders through steep night,
  Has found the cleft through which alone
  Beams fall from high those depths upon,—
  Ere it is borne away—away,
  By the swift heavens that cannot stay,—
  It scatters drops of golden light,
  Like lines of rain that ne'er unite;
And the gloom divine is all around,
And underneath is the mossy ground.

GREENWOOD TREES: PEACOCK

Had either been less sylvan, the other might have been more saintly; but they will now never hear matins but those of the lark, nor reverence vaulted aisle but that of the greenwood canopy. They are twin plants of the forest, and are identified with its growth.

For the slender beech and the sapling oak,
    That grow by the shadowy rill,
You may cut down both at a single stroke,
    You may cut down which you will.

But this you must know, that as long as they grow,
    Whatever change may be,
You never can teach either oak or beech
    To be aught but a greenwood tree.

XIII

THE VISION OF THE ANGEL GUARDS

ELISHA

THEN the king of Syria warred against Israel, and took counsel with his servants, saying, In such and such a place shall be my camp. And the man of God sent unto the king of Israel, saying, Beware that thou pass not such a place; for thither the Syrians are come down. And the king of Israel sent to the place which the man of God told him and warned him of, and saved himself there, not once nor twice. Therefore the heart of the king of Syria was sore troubled for this thing; and he called his servants, and said unto them, Will ye not shew me which of us is for the king of Israel? And one of his servants said, None, my lord, O king: but Elisha, the prophet that is in Israel, telleth the king of Israel the words that thou speakest in thy bedchamber. And he said, Go and spy where he is, that I may send and fetch him. And it was told him, saying, Behold, he is in Dothan. Therefore sent he thither horses, and chariots, and a great host: and they came by night, and compassed the city about.

And when the servant of the man of God was risen early, and gone forth, behold, an host compassed the city both with horses and chariots. And his servant said unto him, Alas, my master! how shall we do? And he answered, Fear not: for they that be with us are more than they that be with them. And Elisha prayed, and said, Lord, I pray thee, open his eyes, that he may see. And the Lord opened the eyes of the young man: and he saw: and, behold, the mountain was full of horses and chariots of fire round about Elisha.

BERNAL DIAZ

It is on this occasion that Francisco López de Gomara says that Francisco de Morla set out on a dapple gray horse before Cortés and the other horsemen arrived, and that the sainted apostles Señor Santiago and Señor San Pedro appeared. I say that all our doings and our victories are at the hands of our Lord Jesus Christ, and that in this battle there were so many Indians to every one of us that they could have blinded us with the dust they raised but for the pity of God who always helped us. It may be that as Gomara says the Glorious Apostles Señor Santiago and Señor San Pedro came to our aid and that I, being a sinner, was not worthy to behold them. What I saw was Francisco de Morla, on a chestnut horse, who came up at the same time as Cortés; and it seems to me that now as I write I can see again with these sinful eyes all that battle in the very way that it took place, and although I am a poor sinner and not worthy to see either of those glorious apostles, there were there in our company over four hundred soldiers and Cortés himself and many other gentlemen, and it would have been talked about, and evidence would have been taken, and a church would have been built when the town was founded, and the town would have been named Santiago de la Victoria, or San Pedro de la Victoria instead of Santa Maria de la Victoria. If it was as Gomara says we must have all been very bad Christians, when our Lord God sent his holy Apostle to us, not to recognize the great favour that he was showing to us, and not daily to have venerated that church. I wish to God it were as the historian Gomara says, but, until I read his history, one never heard about it among the conquistadores who were there at the time.

THE GREAT TWIN BRETHREN

SO spake he; and was buckling
    Tighter black Auster's band,
    When he was aware of a princely pair
That rode at his right hand.
So like they were, no mortal
    Might one from other know:
White as snow their armour was;
    Their steeds were white as snow.
Never on earthly anvil
    Did such rare armour gleam;
And never did such gallant steeds
    Drink of an earthly stream.

And all who saw them trembled,
    And pale grew every cheek;
And Aulus the Dictator
    Scarce gathered voice to speak.
'Say by what name men call you?
    What city is your home?
And wherefore ride ye in such guise
    Before the ranks of Rome?'

'By many names men call us;
    In many lands we dwell:
Well Samothracia knows us;
    Cyrene knows us well.
Our house in gay Tarentum
    Is hung each morn with flowers:
High o'er the masts of Syracuse
    Our marble portal towers;
But by the proud Eurotas
    Is our dear native home;
And for the right we come to fight
    Before the ranks of Rome.'

So answered those strange horsemen,
  And each couched low his spear;
And forthwith all the ranks of Rome
  Were bold, and of good cheer:
And on the thirty armies
  Came wonder and affright,
And Ardea wavered on the left,
  And Cora on the right.
'Rome to the charge!' cried Aulus;
  'The foe begins to yield!
Charge for the hearth of Vesta!
  Charge for the Golden Shield!
Let no man stop to plunder,
  But slay, and slay, and slay;
The Gods who live for ever
  Are on our side to-day.'

. . . . .

Sempronius Atratinus
  Sate in the Eastern Gate,
Beside him were three Fathers,
  Each in his chair of state;
Fabius, whose nine stout grandsons
  That day were in the field,
And Manlius, eldest of the Twelve
  Who keep the Golden Shield;
And Sergius, the High Pontiff,
  For wisdom far renowned;
In all Etruria's colleges
  Was no such Pontiff found.
And all around the portal,
  And high above the wall,
Stood a great throng of people,
  But sad and silent all;
Young lads and stooping elders
  That might not bear the mail,
Matrons with lips that quivered,
  And maids with faces pale.

Since the first gleam of daylight,
    Sempronius had not ceased
To listen for the rushing
    Of horse-hoofs from the east.
The mist of eve was rising,
    The sun was hastening down,
When he was aware of a princely pair
    Fast pricking towards the town.
So like they were, man never
    Saw twins so like before;
Red with gore their armour was,
    Their steeds were red with gore.

'Hail to the great Asylum!
    Hail to the hill-tops seven!
Hail to the fire that burns for aye,
    And the shield that fell from heaven!
This day, by Lake Regillus,
    Under the Porcian height,
All in the lands of Tusculum
    Was fought a glorious fight.
To-morrow your Dictator
    Shall bring in triumph home
The spoils of thirty cities
    To deck the shrines of Rome!'

Then burst from that great concourse
    A shout that shook the towers,
And some ran north, and some ran south,
    Crying, 'The day is ours!'
But on rode these strange horsemen,
    With slow and lordly pace;
And none who saw their bearing
    Durst ask their name or race.
On rode they to the Forum,
    While laurel-boughs and flowers,
From house-tops and from windows,
    Fell on their crests in showers.

When they drew nigh to Vesta,
  They vaulted down amain,
And washed their horses in the well
  That springs by Vesta's fane.
And straight again they mounted,
  And rode to Vesta's door;
Then, like a blast, away they passed,
  And no man saw them more.

XIV

ROMEO AND JULIET

Enter ROMEO

Rom. He jests at scars that never felt a wound.
          [*Juliet appears above at a window*
But, soft! what light through yonder window breaks?
It is the east, and Juliet is the sun!
Arise, fair sun, and kill the envious moon,
Who is already sick and pale with grief,
That thou her maid art far more fair than she:
Be not her maid, since she is envious;
Her vestal livery is but sick and green,
And none but fools do wear it; cast it off.
It is my lady; O, it is my love!
O, that she knew she were!
She speaks, yet she says nothing: what of that?
Her eye discourses, I will answer it.
I am too bold, 'tis not to me she speaks:
Two of the fairest stars in all the heaven,
Having some business, do intreat her eyes
To twinkle in their spheres till they return.
What if her eyes were there, they in her head?
The brightness of her cheek would shame those stars,
As daylight doth a lamp; her eyes in heaven
Would through the airy region stream so bright
That birds would sing and think it were not night.

See, how she leans her cheek upon her hand!
O, that I were a glove upon that hand,
That I might touch that cheek!
    Jul.   Ay me!
    Rom.   She speaks!
O, speak again, bright angel! for thou art
As glorious to this night, being o'er my head,
As is a winged messenger of heaven
Unto the white-upturned wondering eyes
Of mortals that fall back to gaze on him,
When he bestrides the lazy-pacing clouds
And sails upon the bosom of the air.
    Jul. O Romeo, Romeo! wherefore art thou Romeo?
Deny thy father and refuse thy name!
Or if thou wilt not, be but sworn my love,
And I'll no longer be a Capulet.
    Rom. [*Aside*] Shall I hear more, or shall I speak at this?
    Jul. 'Tis but thy name that is my enemy;
Thou art thyself, though not a Montague.
What's Montague? it is nor hand, nor foot,
Nor arm, nor face, nor any other part
Belonging to a man. O, be some other name!
What's in a name? that which we call a rose
By any other name would smell as sweet;
So Romeo would, were he not Romeo call'd,
Retain that dear perfection which he owes
Without that title. Romeo, doff thy name,
And for thy name, which is no part of thee,
Take all myself.
    Rom.   I take thee at thy word:
Call me but love, and I'll be new baptized;
Henceforth I never will be Romeo.
    Jul. What man art thou, that, thus bescreen'd in night,
So stumblest on my counsel?
    Rom.   By a name
I know not how to tell thee who I am:
My name, dear saint, is hateful to myself,
Because it is an enemy to thee;

Had I it written, I would tear the word.

Jul. My ears have yet not drunk a hundred words
Of thy tongue's uttering, yet I know the sound:
Art thou not Romeo, and a Montague?

Rom. Neither, fair maid, if either thee dislike.

Jul. How camest thou hither, tell me, and wherefore?
The orchard walls are high and hard to climb,
And the place death, considering who thou art,
If any of my kinsmen find thee here.

Rom. With love's light wings did I o'er-perch these walls,
For stony limits cannot hold love out:
And what love can do, that dares love attempt;
Therefore thy kinsmen are no let to me.

Jul. If they do see thee, they will murder thee.

Rom. Alack, there lies more peril in thine eye
Than twenty of their swords: look thou but sweet,
And I am proof against their enmity.

Jul. I would not for the world they saw thee here.

Rom. I have night's cloak to hide me from their eyes;
And but thou love me, let them find me here:
My life were better ended by their hate,
Than death prorogued, wanting of thy love.

Jul. By whose direction found'st thou out this place?

Rom. By love, that first did prompt me to inquire;
He lent me counsel, and I lent him eyes.
I am no pilot; yet, wert thou as far
As that vast shore wash'd with the farthest sea,
I would adventure for such merchandise.

Jul. Thou know'st the mask of night is on my face,
Else would a maiden blush bepaint my cheek
For that which thou hast heard me speak to-night.
Fain would I dwell on form, fain, fain deny
What I have spoke: but farewell compliment!
Dost thou love me? I know thou wilt say 'Ay,'
And I will take thy word: yet, if thou swear'st,
Thou mayst prove false: at lovers' perjuries,
They say, Jove laughs. O gentle Romeo!

If thou dost love, pronounce it faithfully:
Or if thou think'st I am too quickly won,
I'll frown and be perverse and say thee nay,
So thou wilt woo; but else, not for the world.
In truth, fair Montague, I am too fond;
And therefore thou mayst think my 'haviour light:
But trust me, gentleman, I'll prove more true
Than those that have more cunning to be strange.
I should have been more strange, I must confess,
But that thou overheard'st, ere I was ware,
My true love's passion: therefore pardon me,
And not impute this yielding to light love,
Which the dark night hath so discovered.

Rom. Lady, by yonder blessed moon I swear,
That tips with silver all these fruit-tree tops,—

Jul. O, swear not by the moon, th' inconstant moon,
That monthly changes in her circled orb,
Lest that thy love prove likewise variable.

Rom. What shall I swear by?

Jul. Do not swear at all;
Or, if thou wilt, swear by thy gracious self,
Which is the god of my idolatry,
And I'll believe thee.

Rom. If my heart's dear love—

Jul. Well, do not swear: although I joy in thee,
I have no joy of this contract to-night:
It is too rash, too unadvised, too sudden,
Too like the lightning, which doth cease to be
Ere one can say 'It lightens.' Sweet, good night!
This bud of love, by summer's ripening breath,
May prove a beauteous flower when next we meet.
Good night, good night! as sweet repose and rest
Come to thy heart as that within my breast!

Rom. O, wilt thou leave me so unsatisfied?

Jul. What satisfaction canst thou have to-night?

Rom. The exchange of thy love's faithful vow for mine.

Jul. I gave thee mine before thou didst request it:
And yet I would it were to give again.

Rom. Wouldst thou withdraw it? for what purpose, love?

Jul. But to be frank, and give it thee again.
And yet I wish but for the thing I have:
My bounty is as boundless as the sea,
My love as deep; the more I give to thee,
The more I have, for both are infinite.
I hear some noise within; dear love, adieu!

[*Nurse calls within.*

Anon, good nurse! Sweet Montague, be true.
Stay but a little, I will come again. [*Exit*

Rom. O blessed, blessed night! I am afeard,
Being in night, all this is but a dream,
Too flattering-sweet to be substantial.

Re-enter JULIET, *above.*

Jul. Three words, dear Romeo; and good night indeed.
If that thy bent of love be honourable,
Thy purpose marriage, send me word to-morrow,
By one that I'll procure to come to thee,
Where and what time thou wilt perform the rite,
And all my fortunes at thy foot I'll lay,
And follow thee my lord throughout the world.

Nurse. [*Within*] Madam!

Jul. I come, anon.—But if thou mean'st not well,
I do beseech thee—

Nurse. [*Within*] Madam!

Jul. By and by, I come:—
To cease thy suit, and leave me to my grief:
To-morrow will I send.

Rom. So thrive my soul,—

Jul. A thousand times good night! [*Exit.*

Rom. A thousand times the worse, to want thy light.
Love goes toward love, as schoolboys from their books,
But love from love, toward school with heavy looks.

[*Retiring slowly.*

Re-enter JULIET, *above.*

Jul. Hist! Romeo, hist!—O, for a falconer's voice,
To lure this tassel-gentle back again!
Bondage is hoarse, and may not speak aloud;
Else would I tear the cave where Echo lies,
And make her airy tongue more hoarse than mine,
With repetition of my Romeo's name.
Romeo!

Rom. It is my soul that calls upon my name:
How silver-sweet sound lovers' tongues by night,
Like softest music to attending ears!

Jul. Romeo!

Rom. My dear?

Jul. At what o'clock to-morrow
Shall I send to thee?

Rom. At the hour of nine.

Jul. I will not fail: 'tis twenty years till then.
I have forgot why I did call thee back.

Rom. Let me stand here till thou remember it.

Jul. I shall forget, to have thee still stand there,
Remembering how I love thy company.

Rom. And I'll still stay, to have thee still forget,
Forgetting any other home but this.

Jul. 'Tis almost morning; I would have thee gone:
And yet no farther than a wanton's bird,
Who lets it hop a little from her hand,
Like a poor prisoner in his twisted gyves,
And with a silk thread plucks it back again,
So loving-jealous of his liberty.

Rom. I would I were thy bird.

Jul. Sweet, so would I:
Yet I should kill thee with much cherishing.
Good night, good night! parting is such sweet sorrow
That I shall say good night till it be morrow. [*Exit.*

Rom. Sleep dwell upon thine eyes, peace in thy breast!
Would I were sleep and peace, so sweet to rest!

XV

MY UNCLE TOBY'S APOLOGY
FOR WISHING TO CONTINUE THE WAR

I AM not insensible, brother Shandy, that when a man whose profession is arms, wishes, as I have done, for war —it has an ill aspect to the world:—and that, how just and right soever his motives and intentions may be,—he stands in an uneasy posture in vindicating himself from private views in doing it.

For this cause, if a soldier is a prudent man, which he may be without being a jot the less brave, he will be sure not to utter his wish in the hearing of an enemy; for, say what he will, an enemy will not believe him.—He will be cautious of doing it even to a friend,—lest he may suffer in his esteem;— but if his heart is overcharged, and a secret sigh for arms must have its vent, he will reserve it for the ear of a brother, who knows his character to the bottom, and what his true notions, dispositions, and principles of honour are. What, I hope, I have been in all these, brother Shandy, would be unbecoming in me to say:—much worse, I know, have I been than I ought,—and something worse, perhaps, than I think: but such as I am, you, my dear brother Shandy, who have sucked the same breasts with me,—and with whom I have been brought up from the cradle, and from whose knowledge, from the first hours of our boyish pastimes, down to this, I have concealed no one action of my life, and scarce a thought in it;—such as I am, brother, you must by this time know me, with all my vices, and with all my weaknesses too, whether of my age, my temper, my passions, or my understanding.

Tell me then, my dear brother Shandy, upon which of them it is that, when I condemned the peace of Utrecht, and grieved the war was not carried on with vigour a little longer, you should think your brother did it upon unworthy views; or that, in wishing for war, he should be bad enough to wish more of his fellow-creatures slain,—more slaves made,—and more families driven from their peaceful habitations, merely for his own pleasure.—Tell me, brother Shandy, upon what one deed of mine do you ground it?—[*The devil a deed do I know of, dear Toby, but one for a hundred pounds, which I lent thee to carry on these cursed sieges.*]

If, when I was a schoolboy, I could not hear a drum beat, but my heart beat with it,—was it my fault?—Did I plant the propensity there?—Did I sound the alarm within—or Nature?

When *Guy, Earl of Warwick*, and *Parismus*, and *Parismenus*, and *Valentine* and *Orson*, and the *Seven Champions of England*, were handed around the school,—were they not all purchased with my own pocket-money?—Was that selfish, brother Shandy?—When we read over the siege of Troy, which lasted ten years and eight months;—though, with such a train of artillery as we had at Namur, the town might have been carried in a week,—was I not as much concerned for the destruction of the Greeks and Trojans as any boy of the whole school?—Did any one of you shed more tears for Hector?—And when King Priam came to the camp to beg his body, and returned weeping back to Troy without it,—you know, brother, I could not eat my dinner.

Did that bespeak me cruel?—Or, because, brother Shandy, my blood flew out into the camp, and my heart panted for war,—was it a proof it could not ache for the distresses of war too?

O brother! 'tis one thing for a soldier to gather laurels,—and 'tis another to scatter cypress.—[*Who told thee, my dear Toby, that cypress was used by the ancients on mournful occasions?*—] 'Tis one thing, brother Shandy, for a soldier to hazard his own life,—to leap first down into the trench, where he is sure to be cut in pieces;—'Tis one thing, from public spirit and a thirst for glory, to enter the breach the first man,—to stand in the foremost rank, and march bravely on with drums and trumpets, and colours flying about his ears:—'Tis one thing, I say, brother Shandy, to do this;—and 'tis another thing to reflect on the miseries of war:—to view the desolations of whole countries and consider the intolerable fatigues and hardships which the soldier himself, the instrument who works them, is forced (for sixpence a day, if he can get it) to undergo.

Need I be told, dear Yorick, as I was by you, in Le Fevre's funeral sermon, *That so soft and gentle a creature, born to love, to mercy, and kindness, as man is, was not shaped for this?*—But why did you not add, Yorick,—If not by *Nature*, that he is so by *necessity?*—For what is war? what is it, Yorick, when fought, as ours has been, upon principles of *liberty*, and upon principles of *honour*—what is it, but the getting together of quiet and harmless people, with their swords in their hands, to keep the ambitious and the turbulent within bounds?—And Heaven is my witness, brother Shandy, that the pleasure I have taken in these things,—and that infinite delight, in particular, which has attended my sieges in my bowling-green, has arose within me, and, I hope, in the Corporal too, from the consciousness we both had that, in carrying them on, we were answering the great end of our creation.

XVI

FIVE POEMS BY HERRICK

CORINNA'S GOING A-MAYING

GET up, get up for shame, the Blooming Morne
    Upon her wings presents the god unshorne.
    See how Aurora throwes her faire
Fresh-quilted colours through the aire:
Get up, sweet Slug-a-bed, and see
The Dew-bespangling Herbe and Tree.

Each Flower has wept, and bow'd toward the East,
Above an houre since; yet you not drest,
   Nay! not so much as out of bed?
   When all the Birds have Mattens seyd,
   And sung their thankful Hymnes: 'tis sin,
   Nay, profanation to keep in,
Whenas a thousand Virgins on this day,
Spring, sooner than the Lark, to fetch in May.

Rise; and put on your Foliage, and be seene
To come forth, like the Spring-time, fresh and greene;
   And sweet as Flora. Take no care
   For Jewels for your Gowne, or Haire:
   Feare not; the leaves will strew
   Gemms in abundance upon you:
Besides, the childhood of the Day has kept,
Against you come, some Orient Pearls unwept:
   Come, and receive them while the light
   Hangs on the Dew-locks of the night:
   And Titan on the Eastern hill
   Retires himselfe, or else stands still
Till you come forth. Wash, dresse, be briefe in praying:
Few Beads are best, when once we goe a Maying.

Come, my Corinna, come; and comming, marke
How each field turns a street; each street a Parke
   Made green, and trimm'd with trees: see how
   Devotion gives each House a Bough,
   Or Branch: Each Porch, each doore, ere this,
   An Arke a Tabernacle is
Made up of white-thorn neatly enterwove;
As if here were those cooler shades of love.
   Can such delights be in the street,
   And open fields, and we not see't?
   Come, we'll abroad; and let's obay
   The Proclamation made for May:
And sin no more, as we have done, by staying:
But my Corinna, come, let's goe a Maying.

There's not a budding Boy, or Girle, this day,
But is got up, and gone to bring in May.
   A deale of Youth, ere this, is come
   Back, and with White-thorn laden home.
   Some have dispatcht their Cakes and Creame,
   Before that we have left to dreame:
And some have wept, and woo'd, and plighted Troth,
And chose their Priest, ere we can cast off sloth.
   Many a green-gown has been given;
   Many a kisse, both odde and even:
   Many a glance too has been sent
   From out the eye, Love's Firmament:
Many a jest told of the Keyes betraying
This night, and Locks pickt, yet w'are not a Maying.

Come, let us goe, while we are in our prime;
And take the harmlesse follie of the time.
   We shall grow old apace, and die
   Before we know our liberty.
   Our life is short; and our dayes run
   As fast away as do's the Sunne:
And as a vapour, or a drop of raine
Once lost, can ne'er be found againe:
   So when or you or I are made
   A fable, song, or fleeting shade;
   All love, all liking, all delight
   Lies drown'd with us in endlesse night.
Then while time serves, and we are but decaying,
Come, my Corinna, come, let's goe a Maying.

TO BLOSSOMS

   Faire pledges of a fruitful Tree,
      Why do yee fall so fast?
      Your date is not so past,
But you may stay yet here a while,
      To blush and gently smile,
         And go at last.

What, were yee borne to be
    An houre or half's delight,
    And so to bid goodnight?
'Twas pitie Nature brought yee forth
    Merely to shew your worth,
      And lose you quite.

But you are lovely Leaves, where we
    May read how soon things have
    Their end, though ne'er so brave:
And after they have shown their pride,
    Like you a while they glide
      Into the Grave.

TO MEDDOWES

Ye have been fresh and green,
    Ye have been fill'd with flowers:
And ye the Walks have been
    Where Maids have spent their houres.

You have beheld how they
    With Wicker Arks did come
To kisse, and beare away
    The richer Couslips home.

Y'ave heard them sweetly sing,
    And seen them in a Round:
Each Virgin, like a Spring,
    With Hony-succles crown'd.

But now we see none here,
    Whose silv'rie feet did tread,
And with dishevell'd Haire
    Adorn'd this smoother Mead.

Like Unthrifts, having spent
    Your stock, and needy grown,
Y'are left here to lament
    Your poore estates, alone.

TO ANTHEA, WHO MAY COMMAND HIM ANY THING

Bid me to live, and I will live
  Thy Protestant to be:
Or bid me love, and I will give
  A loving heart to thee.

A heart as soft, a heart as kind,
  A heart as sound and free,
As in the whole world thou canst find,
  That heart I'll give to thee.

Bid that heart stay, and it will stay,
  To honour thy Decree:
Or bid it languish quite away,
  And 't shall doe so for thee.

Bid me to weep, and I will weep,
  While I have eyes to see;
And having none, yet I will keep
  A heart to weep for thee.

Bid me despaire, and I'll despaire,
  Under that Cypresse tree:
Or bid me die, and I will dare
  E'en Death, to die for thee.

Thou art my life, my love, my heart,
  The very eyes of me:
And hast command of every part,
  To live and die for thee.

GRACE FOR A CHILD

Here a little child I stand,
Heaving up my either hand;
Cold as Paddocks [1] though they be,
Here I lift them up to Thee,
For a Benizon to fall
On our meat, and on us all. *Amen.*

[1] Frogs.

XVII

MR. MANTALINI AT BREAKFAST

IT was with a heavy heart, and many sad forebodings which no effort could banish, that Kate Nickleby, on the morning appointed for the commencement of her engagement with Madame Mantalini, left the city when its clocks yet wanted a quarter of an hour of eight, and threaded her way alone, amid the noise and bustle of the streets, towards the west end of London.

At this early hour many sickly girls, whose business, like that of the poor worm, is to produce, with patient toil, the finery that bedecks the thoughtless and luxurious, traverse our streets, making towards the scene of their daily labour, and catching, as if by stealth, in their hurried walk, the only gasp of wholesome air and glimpse of sunlight which cheers their monotonous existence during the long train of hours that make a working day. As she drew nigh to the more fashionable quarter of the town, Kate marked many of this class as they passed by, hurrying like herself to their painful occupation, and saw, in their unhealthy looks and feeble gait, but too clear an evidence that her misgivings were not wholly groundless.

She arrived at Madame Mantalini's some minutes before the appointed hour, and after walking a few times up and down, in the hope that some other female might arrive and spare her the embarrassment of stating her business to the servant, knocked timidly at the door: which, after some delay, was opened by the footman, who had been putting on his striped jacket as he came upstairs, and was now intent on fastening his apron.

'Is Madame Mantalini in?' faltered Kate.

'Not often out at this time, Miss,' replied the man in a tone which rendered 'Miss' something more offensive than 'My dear.'

'Can I see her?' asked Kate.

'Eh?' replied the man, holding the door in his hand, and

honouring the inquirer with a stare and a broad grin, 'Lord, no.'

'I came by her own appointment,' said Kate; 'I am—I am —to be employed here.'

'Oh! you should have rung the workers' bell,' said the footman, touching the handle of one in the door-post. 'Let me see, though, I forgot—Miss Nickleby, is it?'

'Yes,' replied Kate.

'You're to walk upstairs then, please,' said the man. 'Madame Mantalini wants to see you—this way—take care of these things on the floor.'

Cautioning her, in these terms, not to trip over a heterogeneous litter of pastrycook's trays, lamps, waiters full of glasses, and piles of rout seats which were strewn about the hall, plainly bespeaking a late party on the previous night, the man led the way to the second story, and ushered Kate into a back room, communicating by folding-doors with the apartment in which she had first seen the mistress of the establishment.

'If you'll wait here a minute,' said the man, 'I'll tell her presently.' Having made this promise with much affability, he retired and left Kate alone.

There was not much to amuse in the room; of which the most attractive feature was a half-length portrait in oil of Mr. Mantalini, whom the artist had depicted scratching his head in an easy manner, and thus displaying to advantage a diamond ring, the gift of Madame Mantalini before her marriage. There was, however, the sound of voices in conversation in the next room; and as the conversation was loud and the partition thin, Kate could not help discovering that they belonged to Mr. and Mrs. Mantalini.

'If you will be odiously, demnebly outr*ige*ously jealous, my soul,' said Mr. Mantalini, 'you will be very miserable— horrid miserable—demnition miserable.' And then, there was a sound as though Mr. Mantalini were sipping his coffee.

'I *am* miserable,' returned Madame Mantalini, evidently pouting.

'Then you are an ungrateful, unworthy, demd unthankful little fairy,' said Mr. Mantalini.

'I am not,' returned Madame, with a sob.

'Do not put itself out of humour,' said Mr. Mantalini, breaking an egg. 'It is a pretty, bewitching little demd countenance, and it should not be out of humour, for it spoils its loveliness, and makes it cross and gloomy like a frightful, naughty, demd hobgoblin.'

'I am not to be brought round in that way, always,' rejoined Madame, sulkily.

'It shall be brought round in any way it likes best, and not brought round at all if it likes that better,' retorted Mr. Mantalini, with his egg-spoon in his mouth.

'It's very easy to talk,' said Mrs. Mantalini.

'Not so easy when one is eating a demnition egg,' replied Mr. Mantalini; 'for the yolk runs down the waistcoat, and yolk of egg does not match any waistcoat but a yellow waistcoat, demmit.'

'You were flirting with her during the whole night,' said Madame Mantalini, apparently desirous to lead the conversation back to the point from which it had strayed.'

'No, no, my life.'

'You were,' said Madame; 'I had my eye upon you all the time.'

'Bless the little winking twinking eye; was it on me all the time!' cried Mantalini, in a sort of lazy rapture. 'Oh, demmit!'

'And I say once more,' resumed Madame, 'that you ought not to waltz with anybody but your own wife; and I will not bear it, Mantalini, if I take poison first.'

'She will not take poison and have horrid pains, will she?' said Mantalini, who, by the altered sound of his voice, seemed to have moved his chair, and taken up his position nearer to his wife. 'She will not take poison, because she has a demd fine husband who might have married two countesses and a dowager——'

'Two countesses,' interposed Madame. 'You told me one before!'

'Two!' cried Mantalini. 'Two demd fine women, real countesses and splendid fortunes, demmit.'

'And why didn't you?' asked Madame, playfully.

'Why didn't I!' replied her husband. 'Had I not seen, at a morning concert, the demdest little fascinator in all the world, and while that little fascinator is my wife, may not all the countesses and dowagers in England be——'

Mr. Mantalini did not finish the sentence, but he gave Madame Mantalini a very loud kiss, which Madame Mantalini returned; after which, there seemed to be some more kissing mixed up with the progress of the breakfast.

'And what about the cash, my existence's jewel?' said Mantalini, when these endearments ceased. 'How much have we in hand?'

'Very little indeed,' replied Madame.

'We must have some more,' said Mantalini; 'we must have some discount out of old Nickleby to carry on the war with, demmit.'

'You can't want any more just now,' said Madame coaxingly.

'My life and soul,' returned her husband, 'there is a horse for sale at Scrubbs's, which it would be a sin and a crime to lose—going, my senses' joy, for nothing.'

'For nothing,' cried Madame, 'I am glad of that.'

'For actually nothing,' replied Mantalini. 'A hundred guineas down will buy him; mane, and crest, and legs, and tail, all of the demdest beauty. I will ride him in the park before the very chariots of the rejected countesses. The demd old dowager will faint with grief and rage; the other two will say "He is married, he has made away with himself, it is a demd thing, it is all up!" They will hate each other demnebly, and wish you dead and buried. Ha! ha! Demmit.'

Madame Mantalini's prudence, if she had any, was not proof against these triumphal pictures; after a little jingling of keys, she observed that she would see what her desk contained, and rising for that purpose, opened the folding-door, and walked into the room where Kate was seated.

'Dear me, child!' exclaimed Madame Mantalini, recoiling in surprise. 'How came you here?'

'Child!' cried Mantalini, hurrying in. 'How came—eh! —oh—demmit, how d'ye do?'

'I have been waiting here some time, ma'am,' said Kate, addressing Madame Mantalini. 'The servant must have forgotten to let you know that I was here, I think.'

'You really must see to that man,' said Madame, turning to her husband. 'He forgets everything.'

'I will twist his demd nose off his countenance for leaving such a very pretty creature all alone by herself,' said her husband.

'Mantalini,' cried Madame, 'you forget yourself.'

'I don't forget *you*, my soul, and never shall, and never can,' said Mantalini, kissing his wife's hand, and grimacing aside to Miss Nickleby, who turned away.

Appeased by this compliment, the lady of the business took some papers from her desk which she handed over to Mr. Mantalini, who received them with great delight. She then requested Kate to follow her, and after several feints on the part of Mr. Mantalini to attract the young lady's attention, they went away: leaving that gentleman extended at full length on the sofa, with his heels in the air and a newspaper in his hand.

XVIII

THE UNIVERSAL CHORUS
FROM 'PROMETHEUS UNBOUND'

Ione. There is a sense of words upon mine ear.
Panthea. An universal sound like words: Oh, list!

Demogorgon.

Thou, Earth, calm empire of a happy soul,
  Sphere of divinest shapes and harmonies,
Beautiful orb! gathering as thou dost roll
  The love which paves thy path along the skies:

The Earth.

I hear: I am as a drop of dew that dies.

Demogorgon.

Thou, Moon, which gazest on the nightly Earth
  With wonder, as it gazes upon thee;
Whilst each to men, and beasts, and the swift birth
  Of birds, is beauty, love, calm, harmony:

The Moon.

I hear: I am a leaf shaken by thee!

Demogorgon.

Ye Kings of suns and stars, Dæmons and Gods,
  Aetherial Dominations, who possess
Elysian, windless, fortunate abodes
  Beyond Heaven's constellated wilderness:

A Voice from above.

Our great Republic hears, we are blest, and bless.

Demogorgon.

Ye happy Dead, whom beams of brightest verse
  Are clouds to hide, not colours to portray,
Whether your nature is that universe
  Which once ye saw and suffered—

A Voice from beneath.

              Or as they
Whom we have left, we change and pass away.

Demogorgon.

Ye elemental Genii, who have homes
  From man's high mind even to the central stone
Of sullen lead; from heaven's star-fretted domes
  To the dull weed some sea-worm battens on.

A confused Voice.

We hear: thy words waken Oblivion.

Demogorgon.

Spirits, whose homes are flesh: ye beasts and birds,
  Ye worms, and fish; ye living leaves and buds;
Lightning and wind; and ye untameable herds,
  Meteors and mists, which throng air's solitudes:—

A Voice.

Thy voice to us is wind among still woods.

Demogorgon.

Man, who wert once a despot and a slave;
  A dupe and a deceiver; a decay;
A traveller from the cradle to the grave
  Through the dim night of this immortal day:

All.

Speak: thy strong words may never pass away.

Demogorgon.

This is the day, which down the void abysm
At the Earth-born's spell yawns for Heaven's despotism,
  And Conquest is dragged captive through the deep:
Love, from its awful throne of patient power
In the wise heart, from the last giddy hour
  Of dread endurance, from the slippery, steep,
And narrow verge of crag-like agony, springs
And folds over the world its healing wings.

Gentleness, Virtue, Wisdom, and Endurance,
These are the seals of that most firm assurance
  Which bars the pit over Destruction's strength;
And if, with infirm hand, Eternity,
Mother of many acts and hours, should free
  The serpent that would clasp her with his length;
These are the spells by which to reassume
An empire o'er the disentangled doom.

To suffer woes which Hope thinks infinite;
To forgive wrongs darker than death or night;
  To defy Power, which seems omnipotent;
To love, and bear; to hope till Hope creates
From its own wreck the thing it contemplates;
  Neither to change, nor falter, nor repent;
This, like thy glory, Titan, is to be
Good, great and joyous, beautiful and free;
This is alone Life, Joy, Empire, and Victory.

FROM 'HELLAS'

The world's great age begins anew,
  The golden years return,
The earth doth like a snake renew
  Her winter weeds outworn;
Heaven smiles, and faiths and empires gleam,
Like wrecks of a dissolving dream.

A brighter Hellas rears its mountains
  From waves serener far;
A new Peneus rolls his fountains
  Against the morning star.
Where fairer Tempes bloom, there sleep
Young Cyclads on a sunnier deep.

A loftier Argo cleaves the main,
  Fraught with a later prize;
Another Orpheus sings again,
  And loves, and weeps, and dies.
A new Ulysses leaves once more
Calypso for his native shore.

Oh, write no more the tale of Troy,
  If earth Death's scroll must be!
Nor mix with Laian rage the joy
  Which dawns upon the free:
Although a subtler Sphinx renew
Riddles of death Thebes never knew.

Another Athens shall arise,
    And to remoter time
Bequeath, like sunset to the skies,
    The splendour of its prime;
And leave, if nought so bright may live,
All earth can take or Heaven can give.

Saturn and Love their long repose
    Shall burst, more bright and good,
Than all who fell, than One who rose,
    Than many unsubdued:
Not gold, not blood, their altar dowers,
But votive tears and symbol flowers.

Oh, cease! must hate and death return?
    Cease! must men kill and die?
Cease! drain not to its dregs the urn
    Of bitter prophecy.
The world is weary of the past,
Oh, might it die or rest at last!

XIX

OWLD BOCOCK'S MARE

WE gained the inner room at last, a cheerless apartment, adorned with sacred pictures, a sewing-machine, and an array of supplementary tumblers and wineglasses; but, at all events, we had it so far to ourselves. At intervals during the next half-hour Mary Kate burst in with cups and plates, cast them on the table and disappeared, but of food there was no sign. After a further period of starvation and of listening to the noise in the shop, Flurry made a sortie, and, after lengthy and unknown adventures, reappeared carrying a huge brown teapot, and driving before him Mary Kate with the remainder of the repast. The bread tasted of mice, the butter of turf-smoke, the tea of brown paper, but we had got past the critical stage. I had entered upon my third round of bread and butter when the door was flung open, and my valued acquaintance, Slipper, slightly advanced in liquor, presented himself to our gaze. His bandy legs sprawled consequentially, his nose was redder than a coal of fire, his prominent eyes rolled crookedly upon us, and his left hand swept behind him the attempt of Mary Kate to frustrate his entrance.

'Good-evening to my vinerable friend, Mr. Flurry Knox!' he began, in the voice of a town crier, 'and to the Honourable Major Yeates, and the English gintleman!'

This impressive opening immediately attracted an audience from the shop, and the doorway filled with grinning faces as Slipper advanced farther into the room.

'Why weren't ye at the races, Mr. Flurry?' he went on, his roving eye taking a grip of us all at the same time; 'sure the Miss Bennetts and all the ladies was asking where were ye.'

'It'd take some time to tell them that,' said Flurry, with his mouth full; 'but what about the races, Slipper? Had you good sport?'

'Sport is it? Divil so pleasant an afternoon ever you seen,' replied Slipper. He leaned against a side table, and all the glasses on it jingled. 'Does your honour know O'Driscoll?' he went on irrelevantly. 'Sure you do. He was in your honour's stable. It's what we were all sayin'; it was a great pity your honour was not there, for the likin' you had to Driscoll.'

'That's thrue,' said a voice at the door.

'There wasn't one in the Barony but was gethered in it, through and fro,' continued Slipper, with a quelling glance at the interrupter; 'and there was tints for sellin' porther, and whisky as pliable as new milk, and boys goin' round the tints outside, feeling for heads with the big ends of their blackthorns, and all kinds of recreations, and the Sons of Liberty's piffler and dhrum band from Skebawn; though faith! there was more of thim runnin' to look at the races than what was playin' in it; not to mintion different occasions that the bandmasther was atin' his lunch within in the whisky tint.'

'But what about Driscoll?' said Flurry.

'Sure it's about him I'm tellin' ye,' replied Slipper, with the practised orator's watchful eye on his growing audience. ''Twas within in the same whisky tint meself was, with the bandmasther and a few of the lads, an' we buyin' a ha'porth o' crackers, when I see me brave Driscoll landin' into the tint, and a pair o' thim long boots on him; him that hadn't a shoe nor a stocking to his foot when your honour had him picking grass out o' the stones behind in your yard. "Well," says I to meself, "we'll knock some spoort out of Driscoll!"

'"Come here to me, acushla!" says I to him; "I suppose it's some way wake in the legs y'are," says I, "an' the docthor put them on ye the way the people wouldn't thrample ye!"

'"May the divil choke ye!" says he, pleasant enough, but I knew by the blush he had he was vexed.

'"Then I suppose 'tis a left-tenant colonel y'are," says I; "yer mother must be proud out o' ye!" says I, "an' maybe ye'll lend her a loan o' thim waders when she's rinsin' yer bauneen in the river!" says I.

'"There'll be work out o' this!" says he, lookin' at me both sour and bitther.

'"Well indeed, I was thinkin' you were blue moulded for want of a batin'," says I. He was for fightin' us then, but afther we had him pacificated with about a quarther of a naggin o' sperrits, he told us he was goin' ridin' in a race.

'"An' what'll ye ride?" says I.

'"Owld Bocock's mare," says he.

'"Knipes!" says I, sayin' a great curse; "is it that little staggeen from the mountains; sure she's somethin' about the one age with meself," says I. "Many's the time Jamesy Geoghegan and meself used to be dhrivin' her to Macroom with pigs an' all soorts," says I; "an' is it leppin' stone walls ye want her to go now?"

'"Faith, there's walls and every vari'ty of obstackle in it," says he.

'"It'll be the best o' your play, so," says I, "to leg it away home out o' this."

'"An' who'll ride her, so?" says he.

'"Let the divil ride her," says I.'

Leigh Kelway, who had been leaning back seemingly half asleep, obeyed the hypnotism of Slipper's gaze, and opened his eyes.

'That was now all the conversation that passed between himself and meself,' resumed Slipper, 'and there was no great delay afther that till they said there was a race startin' and the dickens a one at all was goin' to ride only two, Driscoll, and one Clancy. With that then I seen Mr. Kinahane, the Petty Sessions clerk, goin' round clearin' the coorse, an' I gethered a few o' the neighbours, an' we walked the fields hither and over till we seen the most of th' obstacles.

'"Stand aisy now by the plantation," says I; "if they get to come as far as this, believe me ye'll see spoort," says I, "an' 'twill be a convanient spot to encourage the mare if she's anyway wake in herself," says I, cuttin' somethin' about five foot of an ash sapling out o' the plantation.

'"That's yer sort!" says owld Bocock, that was thravellin' the racecoorse, peggin' a bit o' paper down with a thorn in front of every lep, the way Driscoll 'd know the handiest place to face her at it.

'Well, I hadn't barely thrimmed the ash plant . . . when I heard the people screechin', an' I seen Driscoll an' Clancy comin' on, leppin' all before them, an' owld Bocock's mare bellusin' an' powdherin' along, an' bedad! whatever obstackle wouldn't throw *her* down, faith, she'd throw *it* down, an' there's the thraffic they had in it.

'"I declare to me sowl," says I, "if they continue on this way there's a great chance some one o' thim 'll win," says I.

'"Ye lie!" says the bandmasther, bein' a thrifle fulsome after his luncheon.

'"I do not," says I, "in regard of seein' how soople them two boys is. Ye might observe," says I, "that if they have no convanient way to sit on the saddle, they'll ride the neck o' the horse till such time as they gets an occasion to lave it," says I.

'"Arrah, shut yer mouth!" says the bandmasther; "they're puckin' out this way now, an' may the divil admire me!" says he, "but Clancy has the other bet out, and the divil such leatherin' and beltin' of owld Bocock's mare ever you seen as what's in it!" says he.

'Well, when I seen them comin' to me, and Driscoll about the length of the plantation behind Clancy, I let a couple of bawls.

'"Skelp her, ye big brute!" says I. "What good's in ye that ye aren't able to skelp her?"'

The yell and the histrionic flourish of his stick with which Slipper delivered this incident brought down the house. . . .

'Well, Mr. Flurry, and gintlemen,' recommenced Slipper. 'I declare to ye when owld Bocock's mare heard thim roars she shtretched out her neck like a gandher, and when she passed me out she give a couple of grunts, and looked at me as ugly as a Christian.

'"Hah!" says I, givin' her a couple o' dhraws o' th' ash plant across the butt o' the tail, the way I wouldn't blind her; "I'll make ye grunt!" says I, "I'll nourish ye!"

'I knew well she was very frightful of th' ash plant since the winter Tommeen Sullivan had her under a sidecar. But now, in place of havin' any obligations to me, ye'd be surprised if ye heard the blaspheemious expressions of that young boy that was ridin' her; and whether it was overanxious he was, turnin' around the way I'd hear him cursin', or whether it was some slither or slide came to owld Bocock's mare, I dunno, but she was bet up agin the last obstackle but two, and before ye could say "Schnipes," she was standin' on her two ears beyond in th' other field! I declare to ye, on the vartue of me oath, she stood that way till she reconnoithered what side would Driscoll fall, an' she turned about then and rolled on him as cosy as if he was meadow grass!'

Slipper stopped short; the people in the doorway groaned appreciatively; Mary Kate murmured 'The Lord save us!'

'The blood was dhruv out through his nose and ears,' continued Slipper, with a voice that indicated the cream of the narration, 'and you'd hear his bones crackin' on the ground! You'd have pitied the poor boy.'

'Good heavens!' said Leigh Kelway, sitting up very straight in his chair.

'Was he hurt, Slipper?' asked Flurry casually.

'Hurt is it?' echoed Slipper in high scorn; 'killed on the spot!' He paused to relish the effect of the *dénouement* on Leigh Kelway. 'Oh, divil so pleasant an afthernoon ever you seen; and indeed, Mr. Flurry, it's what we were all sayin', it was a great pity your honour was not there for the likin' you had for Driscoll.'

As he spoke the last word there was an outburst of singing and cheering from a car-load of people who had just pulled up at the door. Flurry listened, leaned back in his chair, and began to laugh.

'It scarcely strikes one as a comic incident,' said Leigh Kelway, very coldly to me; 'in fact, it seems to me that the police ought——'

'Show me Slipper!' bawled a voice in the shop; 'show me that dirty little undherlooper till I have his blood! Hadn't I the race won only for he souring the mare on me! What's that you say? I tell ye he did! He left seven slaps on her with the handle of a hay-rake——'

There was in the room in which we were sitting a second door, leading to the back yard, a door consecrated to the unobtrusive visits of so-called 'Sunday travellers.' Through it Slipper faded away like a dream, and, simultaneously, a tall young man, with a face like a red-hot potato tied up in a bandage, squeezed his way from the shop into the room.

'Well, Driscoll,' said Flurry, 'since it wasn't the teeth of the rake he left on the mare, you needn't be talking!'

Leigh Kelway looked from one to the other with a wilder expression in his eye than I had thought it capable of. I read in it a resolve to abandon Ireland to her fate.

XX

A RIDE ON AN ALLIGATOR

WE found a cayman, ten feet and a half long, fast to the end of the rope. Nothing now remained to do, but to get him out of the water without injuring his scales, *hoc opus, hic labor*. We mustered strong: there were three Indians from the creek, there was my own Indian, Yan; Daddy Quashi, the negro from Mrs. Peterson's; James, Mr. R. Edmonstone's man, whom I was instructing to preserve birds; and, lastly, myself.

I informed the Indians that it was my intention to draw him quietly out of the water, and then secure him. They looked and stared at each other, and said I might do it myself, but they would have no hand in it; the cayman would worry some of us. On saying this, *consedere duces*, they squatted on their hams with the most perfect indifference.

The Indians of these wilds have never been subject to the least restraint; and I knew enough of them to be aware, that if I tried to force them against their will, they would take off, and leave me and my presents unheeded, and never return.

Daddy Quashi was for applying to our guns, as usual, considering them our best and safest friends. I immediately offered to knock him down for his cowardice, and he shrank back, begging that I would be cautious, and not get myself worried; and apologizing for his own want of resolution. My Indian was now in conversation with the others, and they asked me if I would allow them to shoot a dozen arrows into him, and thus disable him. This would have ruined all. I had come above three hundred miles on purpose to get a cayman uninjured, and not to carry back a mutilated specimen. I rejected their proposition with firmness, and darted a disdainful eye upon the Indians.

Daddy Quashi was again beginning to remonstrate, and I chased him on the sandbank for a quarter of a mile. He told me afterwards, he thought he should have dropped down dead with fright, for he was firmly persuaded, if I had caught him, I should have bundled him into the cayman's jaws. Here then we stood, in silence, like a calm before a thunderstorm. *Hoc res summa loco. Scinditur in contraria vulgus.* They wanted to kill him, and I wanted to take him alive.

I now walked up and down the sand, revolving a dozen projects in my head. The canoe was at a considerable distance, and I ordered the people to bring it round to the place where we were. The mast was eight feet long, and not much thicker than my wrist. I took it out of the canoe, and wrapped the sail round the end of it. Now it appeared clear to me, that if I went down upon one knee, and held the mast in the same position as the soldier holds his bayonet when rushing to the charge, I could force it down the cayman's throat, should he come open-mouthed at me. When this was told to the Indians they brightened up, and said they would help me to pull him out of the river.

'Brave squad!' said I to myself, '*Audax omnia perpeti*, now that you have got me betwixt yourselves and danger.' I then mustered all hands for the last time before the battle. We were, four South American savages, two negroes from Africa, a creole from Trinidad, and myself, a white man from Yorkshire. In fact, a little Tower of Babel group, in dress, no dress, address, and language.

Daddy Quashi hung in the rear; I showed him a large Spanish knife, which I always carried in the waistband of my trousers: it spoke volumes to him, and he shrugged up his shoulders in absolute despair. The sun was just peeping over the high forests on the eastern hills, as if coming to look on, and bid us act with becoming fortitude. I placed all the people at the end of the rope, and ordered them to pull till the cayman appeared on the surface of the water; and then, should he plunge, to slacken the rope and let him go again into the deep.

I now took the mast of the canoe in my hand (the sail being tied round the end of the mast) and sank down upon one knee, about four yards from the water's edge, determining to thrust it down his throat, in case he gave me an opportunity. I certainly felt somewhat uncomfortable in this situation, and I thought of Cerberus on the other side of the Styx ferry. The people pulled the cayman to the surface; he plunged furiously as soon as he arrived in these upper regions, and immediately went below again: on their slackening the rope I saw enough not to fall in love at first sight. I now told them we would run all risks, and have him on land immediately. They pulled again, and out he came—*monstrum horrendum, informe.* This was an interesting moment. I kept my position firmly, with my eye fixed steadfast on him.

By the time the cayman was within two yards of me, I saw he was in a state of fear and perturbation: I instantly dropped the mast, sprang up, and jumped on his back, turning half round as I vaulted, so that I gained my seat with my face in a right position. I immediately seized his fore-legs, and by main force twisted them on his back; thus they served me for a bridle.

He now seemed to have recovered from his surprise, and probably fancying himself in hostile company, he began to plunge furiously, and lashed the sand with his long and powerful tail. I was out of reach of the strokes of it, by being near his head. He continued to plunge and strike, and made my seat very uncomfortable. It must have been a fine sight for an unoccupied spectator.

The people roared out in triumph, and were so vociferous, that it was some time before they heard me tell them to pull me and my beast of burthen farther inland. I was apprehensive the rope might break, and then there would have been every chance of going down to the regions under water with the cayman. That would have been more perilous than Arion's marine morning ride:—

'*Delphini insidens vada cærula sulcat Arion.*'

The people now dragged us about forty yards on the sand; it was the first and last time I was ever on a cayman's back. Should it be asked how I managed to keep my seat, I would answer—I hunted some years with Lord Darlington's foxhounds.

After repeated attempts to regain his liberty the cayman gave in, and became tranquil through exhaustion. I now managed to tie up his jaws, and firmly secured his fore-feet in the position I had held them. We had now another severe struggle for superiority, but he was soon overcome, and again remained quiet. While some of the people were pressing upon his head and shoulders, I threw myself on his tail, and by keeping it down to the sand, prevented him from kicking up another dust. He was finally conveyed to the canoe, and then to the place where we had suspended our hammocks. There I cut his throat; and after breakfast was over, commenced the dissection.

XXI

KING HENRY AT TOWTON FIELD

King. This battle fares like to the morning's war,
When dying clouds contend with growing light,
What time the shepherd, blowing of his nails,
Can neither call it perfect day nor night.
Now sways it this way, like a mighty sea
Forced by the tide to combat with the wind;
Now sways it that way, like the selfsame sea
Forced to retire by fury of the wind:
Sometime the flood prevails, and then the wind;
Now one the better, then another best;
Both tugging to be victors, breast to breast,
Yet neither conqueror nor conquered:
So is the equal poise of this fell war.
Here on this molehill will I sit me down.
To whom God will, there be the victory!
For Margaret my queen, and Clifford too,
Have chid me from the battle; swearing both
They prosper best of all when I am thence.
Would I were dead! if God's good will were so;
For what is in this world but grief and woe?

O God! methinks it were a happy life,
To be no better than a homely swain;
To sit upon a hill, as I do now,
To carve out dials quaintly, point by point,
Thereby to see the minutes how they run,
How many make the hour full complete;
How many hours bring about the day;
How many days will finish up the year;
How many years a mortal man may live.
When this is known, then to divide the times:
So many hours must I tend my flock;
So many hours must I take my rest;
So many hours must I contemplate;
So many hours must I sport myself;
So many days my ewes have been with young;
So many weeks ere the poor fools will ean;
So many years ere I shall shear the fleece:
So minutes, hours, days, months, and years,
Pass'd over to the end they were created,
Would bring white hairs unto a quiet grave.
Ah, what life were this! how sweet! how lovely!
Gives not the hawthorn-bush a sweeter shade
To shepherds looking on their silly sheep,
Than doth a rich embroider'd canopy
To kings that fear their subjects' treachery?
O, yes, it doth; a thousand-fold it doth.
And to conclude, the shepherd's homely curds,
His cold thin drink out of his leather bottle,
His wonted sleep under a fresh tree's shade,
All which secure and sweetly he enjoys,
Is far beyond a prince's delicates,
His viands sparkling in a golden cup,
His body couched in a curious bed,
When care, mistrust, and treason waits on him.

XXII

MR. SKIMPOLE AND COAVINSES

MR. SKIMPOLE could play on the piano, and the violoncello; and he was a composer—had composed half an opera once, but got tired of it—and played what he composed with taste. After tea we had quite a little concert, in which Richard—who was enthralled by Ada's singing, and told me that she seemed to know all the songs that ever were written—and Mr. Jarndyce, and I, were the audience. After a little while I missed, first Mr. Skimpole, and afterwards Richard; and while I was thinking how could Richard stay away so long, and lose so much, the maid who had given me the keys looked in at the door, saying, 'If you please, miss, could you spare a minute?'

When I was shut out with her in the hall, she said, holding up her hands, 'Oh if you please, miss, Mr. Carstone says would you come up-stairs to Mr. Skimpole's room. He has been took, miss!'

'Took?' said I.

'Took, miss. Sudden,' said the maid.

I was apprehensive that his illness might be of a dangerous kind; but of course, I begged her to be quiet and not disturb anyone; and collected myself, as I followed her quickly up-stairs, sufficiently to consider what were the best remedies to be applied if it should prove to be a fit. She threw open a door, and I went into a chamber; where, to my unspeakable surprise, instead of finding Mr. Skimpole stretched upon the bed, or prostrate on the floor, I found him standing before the fire smiling at Richard, while Richard, with a face of great embarrassment, looked at a person on the sofa, in a white great-coat, with smooth hair upon his head and not much of it, which he was wiping smoother, and making less of, with a pocket-handkerchief.

'Miss Summerson,' said Richard, hurriedly, 'I am glad you are come. You will be able to advise us. Our friend, Mr. Skimpole—don't be alarmed!—is arrested for debt.'

'And really, my dear Miss Summerson,' said Mr. Skimpole, with his agreeable candour, 'I never was in a situation, in which that excellent sense, and quiet habit of method and usefulness, which anybody must observe in you who has the happiness of being a quarter of an hour in your society, was more needed.'

The person on the sofa, who appeared to have a cold in his head, gave such a very loud snort, that he startled me.

'Are you arrested for much, sir?' I inquired of Mr. Skimpole.

'My dear Miss Summerson,' said he, shaking his head pleasantly, 'I don't know. Some pounds, odd shillings, and half-pence, I think were mentioned.'

'It's twenty-four pound, sixteen, and sevenpence ha'-penny,' observed the stranger. 'That's wot it is.'

'And it sounds—somehow it sounds,' said Mr. Skimpole, 'like a small sum?'

The strange man said nothing, but made another snort. It was such a powerful one, that it seemed quite to lift him out of his seat.

'Mr. Skimpole,' said Richard to me, 'has a delicacy in applying to my cousin Jarndyce, because he has lately— I think, sir, I understood you that you had lately——'

'Oh, yes!' returned Mr. Skimpole, smiling. 'Though I forgot how much it was, and when it was. Jarndyce would readily do it again; but I have the epicure-like feeling that I would prefer a novelty in help; that I would rather,' and he looked at Richard and me, 'develop generosity in a new soil, and in a new form of flower.'

'What do you think will be best, Miss Summerson?' said Richard, aside.

I ventured to inquire, generally, before replying, what would happen if the money were not produced.

'Jail,' said the strange man, coolly putting his handkerchief into his hat, which was on the floor at his feet. 'Or Coavinses.'

'May I ask, sir, what is——'

'Coavinses?' said the strange man. 'A 'ouse.'

Richard and I looked at one another again. It was a most singular thing that the arrest was our embarrassment, and not Mr. Skimpole's. He observed us with a genial interest; but there seemed, if I may venture on such a contradiction, nothing selfish in it. He had entirely washed his hands of the difficulty, and it had become ours.

'I thought,' he suggested, as if good-naturedly to help us out, 'that being parties in a Chancery suit concerning (as people say) a large amount of property, Mr. Richard or his beautiful cousin, or both, could sign something, or make over something, or give some sort of undertaking, or pledge, or bond? I don't know what the business name of it may be, but I suppose there is some instrument within their power that would settle this?'

'Not a bit on it,' said the strange man.

'Really?' returned Mr. Skimpole. 'That seems odd, now, to one who is no judge of these things!'

'Odd or even,' said the stranger, gruffly, 'I tell you, not a bit on it!'

'Keep your temper, my good fellow, keep your temper!' Mr. Skimpole gently reasoned with him, as he made a little drawing of his head on the fly-leaf of a book. 'Don't be ruffled by your occupation. We can separate you from your office; we can separate the individual from the pursuit. We are not so prejudiced as to suppose that in private life you are otherwise than a very estimable man, with a great deal of poetry in your nature, of which you may not be conscious.'

The stranger only answered with another violent snort; whether in acceptance of the poetry-tribute, or in disdainful rejection of it, he did not express to me.

'Now, my dear Miss Summerson, and my dear Mr. Richard,' said Mr. Skimpole, gaily, innocently, and confidingly, as he looked at his drawing with his head on one side: 'here you see me utterly incapable of helping myself, and entirely in your hands! I only ask to be free. The butterflies are free. Mankind will surely not deny to Harold Skimpole what it concedes to the butterflies!'

'My dear Miss Summerson,' said Richard, in a whisper, 'I have ten pounds that I received from Mr. Kenge. I must try what that will do.'

I possessed fifteen pounds, odd shillings, which I had saved from my quarterly allowance during several years. I had always thought that some accident might happen which would throw me, suddenly, without any relation, or any property, on the world; and had always tried to keep some little money by me, that I might not be quite penniless. I told Richard of my having this little store, and having no present need of it; and I asked him delicately to inform Mr. Skimpole, while I should be gone to fetch it, that we would have the pleasure of paying his debt.

When I came back, Mr. Skimpole kissed my hand, and seemed quite touched. Not on his own account (I was again aware of that perplexing and extraordinary contradiction), but on ours; as if personal considerations were impossible with him, and the contemplation of our happiness alone affected him. Richard, begging me, for the greater grace of the transaction, as he said, to settle with Coavinses (as Mr. Skimpole now jocularly called him), I counted out the money and received the necessary acknowledgment. This, too, delighted Mr. Skimpole.

His compliments were so delicately administered, that I blushed less than I might have done; and settled with the stranger in the white coat, without making any mistakes. He put the money in his pocket, and shortly said, 'Well, then, I'll wish you a good evening, miss.'

'My friend,' said Mr. Skimpole, standing with his back to the fire, after giving up the sketch when it was half finished, 'I should like to ask you something, without offence.'

I think the reply was, 'Cut away, then!'

'Did you know this morning, now, that you were coming out on this errand?' said Mr. Skimpole.

'Know'd it yes'day aft'noon at tea-time,' said Coavinses.

'It didn't affect your appetite? Didn't make you at all uneasy?'

'Not a bit,' said Coavinses. 'I know'd if you wos missed to-day, you wouldn't be missed to-morrow. A day makes no such odds.'

'But when you came down here,' proceeded Mr. Skimpole, 'it was a fine day. The sun was shining, the wind was blowing, the lights and shadows were passing across the fields, the birds were singing.'

'Nobody said they warn't, in *my* hearing,' returned Coavinses.

'No,' observed Mr. Skimpole. 'But what did you think upon the road?'

'Wot do you mean?' growled Coavinses, with an appearance of strong resentment. 'Think! I've got enough to do, and little enough to get for it, without thinking. Thinking!' (with profound contempt).

'Then you didn't think, at all events,' proceeded Mr. Skimpole, 'to this effect. "Harold Skimpole loves to see the sun shine; loves to hear the wind blow; loves to watch the changing lights and shadows; loves to hear the birds, those choristers in Nature's great cathedral. And does it seem to me that I am about to deprive Harold Skimpole of his share in such possessions, which are his only birthright!" You thought nothing to that effect?'

'I—certainly—did—NOT,' said Coavinses, whose doggedness in utterly renouncing the idea was of that intense kind, that he could only give adequate expression to it by putting a long interval between each word, and accompanying the last with a jerk that might have dislocated his neck.

'Very odd and very curious, the mental process is, in you men of business!' said Mr. Skimpole, thoughtfully. 'Thank you, my friend. Good night.'

XXIII

TWO POEMS BY AUSTIN DOBSON

A GENTLEMAN OF THE OLD SCHOOL

HE lived in that past Georgian day,
    When men were less inclined to say
    That 'Time is Gold,' and overlay
        With toil their pleasure;
He held some land, and dwelt thereon,—
Where, I forget,—the house is gone;
His Christian name, I think, was John,—
        His surname, Leisure.

Reynolds has painted him,—a face
Filled with a fine, old-fashioned grace,
Fresh coloured, frank, with ne'er a trace
        Of trouble shaded;
The eyes are blue, the hair is drest
In plainest way,—one hand is prest
Deep in a flapped canary vest,
        With buds brocaded.

He wears a brown old Brunswick coat,
With silver buttons,—round his throat,
A soft cravat;—in all you note
        An elder fashion,—
A strangeness, which, to us who shine
In shapely hats,—whose coats combine
All harmonies of hue and line,—
        Inspires compassion.

He lived so long ago, you see!
Men were untravelled then, but we,
Like Ariel post o'er land and sea
        With careless parting;

He found it quite enough for him
To smoke his pipe in 'garden trim,'
And watch, about the fish-tank's brim,
    The swallows darting.

He liked the well-wheel's creaking tongue,—
He liked the thrush that fed her young,—
He liked the drone of flies among
    His netted peaches;
He liked to watch the sunlight fall
Athwart his ivied orchard wall;
Or pause to catch the cuckoo's call
    Beyond the beeches.

His were the times of Paint and Patch,
And yet no Ranelagh could match
The sober doves that round his thatch
    Spread tails and sidled;
He liked their ruffling, puffed content,—
For him their drowsy wheelings meant
More than a Mall of Beaux that bent,
    Or Belles that bridled.

Not that, in truth, when life began,
He shunned the flutter of the fan;
He too had maybe 'pinked his man'
    In Beauty's quarrel;
But now his 'fervent youth' had flown
Where lost things go; and he was grown
As staid and slow-paced as his own
    Old hunter, Sorrel.

Yet still he loved the chase, and held
That no composer's score excelled
The merry horn, when Sweetlip swelled
    Its jovial riot;

But most his measured words of praise
Caressed the angler's easy ways,—
His idly meditative days,—
>> His rustic diet.

Not that his 'meditating' rose
Beyond a sunny summer doze;
He never troubled his repose
>> With fruitless prying;
But held, as law for high and low,
What God withholds no man can know,
And smiled away inquiry so,
>> Without replying.

We read—alas, how much we read!
The jumbled strifes of creed and creed
With endless controversies feed
>> Our groaning tables;
His books—and they sufficed him—were
Cotton's 'Montaigne,' 'The Grave' of Blair,
A 'Walton'—much the worse for wear—
>> And 'Æsop's Fables.'

One more,—'The Bible.' Not that he
Had searched its page as deep as we;
No sophistries could make him see
>> Its slender credit;
It may be that he could not count
The sires and sons to Jesse's fount,—
He liked the 'Sermon on the Mount,'—
>> And more, he read it.

Once he had loved, but failed to wed,
A red-cheeked lass who long was dead;
His ways were far too slow, he said,
>> To quite forget her;

And still when time had turned him gray
The earliest hawthorn buds in May
Would find his lingering feet astray,
          Where first he met her.

'*In Coelo Quies*' heads the stone
On Leisure's grave,—now little known,
A tangle of wild-rose has grown
          So thick across it;
The 'Benefactions' still declare
He left the clerk an elbow-chair,
And '12 Pence Yearly to Prepare
          A Christmas Posset.'

Lie softly, Leisure! Doubtless you
With too serene a conscience drew
Your easy breath, and slumbered through
          The gravest issue;
But we, to whom our age allows
Scarce space to wipe our weary brows,
Look down upon your narrow house,
          Old friend, and miss you!

A GENTLEWOMAN OF THE OLD SCHOOL

She lived in Georgian era too.
Most women then, if bards be true,
Succumbed to Routs and Cards, or grew
          Devout and acid.
But hers was neither fate. She came
Of good west-country folk, whose fame
Has faded now. For us her name
          Is 'Madam Placid'.

Patience or Prudence,—what you will,
Some prefix faintly fragrant still
As those old musky scents that fill
          Our grandams' pillows;

And for her youthful portrait take
Some long-waist child of Hudson's make,
Stiffly at ease beside a lake
        With swans and willows.

I keep her later semblance placed
Beside my desk,—'tis lawned and laced,
In shadowy sanguine stipple traced
        By Bartolozzi;
A placid face, in which surprise
Is seldom seen, but yet there lies
Some vestige of the laughing eyes
        Of arch Piozzi.

For her e'en Time grew debonair.
He, finding cheeks unclaimed of care,
With late-delayed faint roses there,
        And lingering dimples,
Had spared to touch the fair old face,
And only kissed with Vauxhall grace
The soft white hand that stroked her lace,
        Or smoothed her wimples.

So left her beautiful. Her age
Was comely as her youth was sage,
And yet she once had been the rage;—
        It hath been hinted,
Indeed, affirmed by one or two,
Some spark at Bath (as sparks will do)
Inscribed a song to 'Lovely Prue,'
        Which Urban printed.

I know she thought; I know she felt;
Perchance could sum, I doubt she spelt;
She knew as little of the Celt
        As of the Saxon;

I know she played and sang, for yet
We keep the tumble-down spinet
To which she quavered ballads set
      By Arne or Jackson.

Her tastes were not refined as ours;
She liked plain food and homely flowers,
Refused to paint, kept early hours,
      Went clad demurely;
Her art was sampler work design,
Fireworks for her were 'vastly fine,'
Her luxury was elder-wine,—
      She loved that 'purely.'

She was renowned, traditions say,
For June conserves, for curds and whey,
For finest tea (she called it 'tay'),
      And ratafia;
She knew, for sprains, what bands to choose,
Could tell the sovereign wash to use
For freckles, and was learned in brews
      As erst Medea.

Yet studied little. She would read,
On Sundays, 'Pearson on the Creed,'
Though, as I think, she could not heed
      His text profoundly;
Seeing she chose for her retreat
The warm west-looking window-seat,
Where, if you chanced to raise your feet,
      You slumbered soundly.

This, 'twixt ourselves. The dear old dame,
In truth, was not so much to blame;
The excellent divine I name
      Is scarcely stirring;

Her plain-song piety preferred
Pure life to precept. If she erred,
She knew her faults. Her softest word
           Was for the erring.

If she had loved, or if she kept
Some ancient memory green, or wept
Over the shoulder-knot that slept
           Within her cuff-box,
I know not. Only this I know,
At sixty-five she'd still her beau,
A lean French exile, lame and slow,
           With monstrous snuff-box.

Younger than she, well-born and bred.
She'd found him in St. Giles', half dead
Of teaching French for nightly bed
           And daily dinners;
Starving, in fact, 'twixt want and pride;
And so, henceforth, you always spied
His rusty 'pigeon-wings' beside
           Her Mechlin pinners.

He worshipped her, you may suppose.
She gained him pupils, gave him clothes,
Delighted in his dry bons mots
           And cackling laughter;
And when, at last, the long duet
Of conversation and picquet
Ceased with her death, of sheer regret
           He died soon after.

Dear Madam Placid! Others knew
Your worth as well as he, and threw
Their flowers upon your coffin too,
           I take for granted.
Their loves are lost; but still we see
Your kind and gracious memory
Bloom yearly with the almond tree
           The Frenchman planted.

XXIV

ELWES THE MISER

IT has been remarked that Mr. Elwes was one of the best gentlemen riders in the kingdom. Sir Sydney Meadows, who is *the law* upon this subject, always allowed it. His knowledge in horses was in no way inferior; and, therefore, while he rode before the whole county of Suffolk, the horses he rode were the admiration of everybody. As no bad proof of this, he had offered him for one of his hunters the sum of three hundred guineas, and for another two hundred and fifty; a sum in those days almost incredible, when a very good horse might be bought for fifteen pounds.

To modern sportsmen, accustomed to warm cloathing and hot stables, his manner of treating them may appear singular. As soon as they were perfectly dry after hunting, if the weather was clear, he always turned them out for two or three hours, let the cold be ever so intense. Thus they walked off the stiffness occasioned by fatigue, and preserved their feet—and to this he attributed their being able to carry him when one of them was twenty-two years old.

To Mr. Elwes, an inn upon the road, and an apothecary's bill, were equal subjects of aversion. The words '*give*' and '*pay*' were not found in his vocabulary; and therefore when he once received a very dangerous kick from one of his horses, who fell in going over a leap, nothing could persuade him to have any assistance. He rode the chace through, with his leg cut to the bone; and it was only some days afterwards, when it was feared an amputation would be necessary, that he consented to go up to London, and, hard day! part with some money for advice.

No hounds were more killing ones than those of Mr. Elwes. The *wits* of the country used to say, 'it must be so, or they would get nothing to eat.' In truth, it may be credited they lived but sparingly; though scarcely will it be believed by the Meynells, the Cokes, and Pantons of the present day, that the whole fox-hunting establishment of Mr.

Elwes, huntsman, dogs, and horses, did not cost him three hundred pounds a year!

In the summer, they always passed their lives with the different tenants, where they had 'more meat and less work'; and were collected together a few days before the season began.

During this time, while he kept hounds, and which consumed a period of nearly fourteen years, Mr. Elwes almost totally resided at Stoke, in Suffolk. From thence he made frequent excursions to Newmarket—but he never engaged on the turf.

A kindness, however, which he performed there, should not pass away without remembrance.

Lord Abingdon, who was slightly known to Mr. Elwes in Berkshire, had made a match for seven thousand pounds, which it was supposed he would be obliged to forfeit, from an inability to produce the sum, though the odds were greatly in his favour. Unasked, unsolicited, Mr. Elwes made him an offer of the money, which he accepted, and won his engagement. The generosity of this act no one will deny; but it was the fate of Mr. Elwes to combine some great actions with a meanness so extraordinary, that he no longer appeared one and the same person.

The anecdote which accompanied it, I had not long ago from a clergyman, on whose authority I can place the most perfect reliance.

On the day when this match was to be run, he had agreed to accompany Mr. Elwes to see the fate of it. They were to go, as was the custom of Mr. Elwes, on horseback, and were to set out at seven in the morning. Imagining they were to breakfast at Newmarket, the gentleman took no refreshment, and away they went. They reached Newmarket about eleven, and Mr. Elwes began to busy himself, in enquiries and conversation, till twelve, when the match was decided in favour of Lord Abingdon. He then thought they should move off to the town, to take some breakfast; but old Elwes still continued riding about, till three, and then four arrived. At which time the gentleman grew so impatient, that he mentioned something of the *keen air of*

Newmarket Heath, and the comforts of a good dinner—'*Very true*,' said old Elwes, '*very true—so here, do as I do*!'—offering him at the same time, from his great-coat pocket, a piece of an *old crushed pancake*, which, he said, he had brought from his house at Marcham, two months before—but '*that it was as good as new.*'

The sequel of the story was, that they did not reach home till nine in the evening, when the gentleman was so tired, that he gave up all refreshment but rest! and old Elwes, having hazarded *seven thousand pounds* in the morning, went happily to bed with the reflection—he had saved *three shillings*! Such were the extraordinary contradictions of this *extraordinary man*! But not amongst strangers alone, was money with him the dearest object of his life. He had brought with him his two sons out of Berkshire, and certainly if he liked anything, it was these boys. But no money would he lavish on their education; for he declared that 'putting things into people's heads was the sure way to take money out of their pockets.'

When Mr. Elwes was at Marcham, two very ancient maiden ladies, in his neighbourhood, had, for some neglect, incurred the displeasure of the spiritual court, and were threatened with immediate '*excommunication.*'—The whole import of the word they did not perfectly understand, but they had heard something about standing in a church and a penance, and their ideas immediately ran upon a *white sheet*. They concluded, if they once got into that, it was all over with them; and as the excommunication was to take place the next day, away they hurried to Mr. Elwes, to know how they could make submission, and how the sentence might be prevented. No time was to be lost. Mr. Elwes did that which, fairly speaking, not one man in five thousand would have done; he had his horse saddled, and putting, according to usual custom, a couple of hard eggs in his pocket, he set out for London that evening, and reached it early enough the next morning to notify the submission of the culprit damsels. Riding 60 miles in the night, to confer a favour on two antiquated virgins, to whom he had no particular obligation, was really, what not one man in five thousand would have done: but where personal fatigue could serve, Mr. Elwes never spared it.

The ladies were so overjoyed—so thankful: So much trouble and expence!—What returns could they make? To ease their consciences on this head, an old Irish gentleman, their neighbour, who knew Mr. Elwes's mode of travelling, wrote these words—'My Dears, is it *expence* you are talking of? send him *six-pence*, and he gains *two-pence* by the journey.'

In giving his character, I have entered into the minutiæ, and all the little anecdotes of private life—for there, and there only, can the real character be seen.—Life when 'full dressed,' is always alike. It resembles the soldier on the parade, habited in one uniform, and acting with an uniformity that is equal to his habit.

The sentiment, which, doubtless, will arise in the minds of those who have perused this account, will, perhaps, thus close with me, the result of all I have said.

Mr. Elwes, as one of the commons of England, in three successive parliaments, maintained a conduct which purer times might have been glad to boast, and which later times may be proud to follow. The minister that influenced him was—*his conscience.* He obeyed no mandate, but his opinion. He gave that opinion as he held it to be right.

In one word, his public conduct lives after him, pure, and without a stain!

In private life, he was chiefly an enemy to himself. To others he lent much—to himself he denied everything. But in the pursuit of his property, or the recovery of it, I have not, in my remembrance, one unkind thing that was ever done by him.

But that great object which rises highest to the view out of the prospect of his varied life—let me again enforce upon this page. That object is, the *insufficiency of wealth alone* to confer happiness. For who, after the perusal of the life of Mr. Elwes shall say—I am *rich*—and therefore I shall be happy?

Every circumstance of the memoirs here written proves the fallacy of this hope. But still has such a life had its purpose. For if it should add one circumstance consolatory to poverty—while it enforces the extreme and perfect *vanity of wealth*—then has such a life, as that of Mr. Elwes, not been in vain.

XXV

FOUR PARABLES

THE PRODIGAL SON

AND he said, A certain man had two sons: and the younger of them said to his father, Father, give me the portion of goods that falleth to me. And he divided unto them his living. And not many days after the younger son gathered all together, and took his journey into a far country, and there wasted his substance with riotous living. And when he had spent all, there arose a mighty famine in that land; and he began to be in want. And he went and joined himself to a citizen of that country; and he sent him into his fields to feed swine. And he would fain have filled his belly with the husks that the swine did eat: and no man gave unto him. And when he came to himself, he said, How many hired servants of my father's have bread enough and to spare, and I perish with hunger! I will arise and go to my father, and will say unto him, Father, I have sinned against heaven, and before thee, and am no more worthy to be called thy son: make me as one of thy hired servants.

And he arose, and came to his father. But when he was yet a great way off, his father saw him, and had compassion, and ran, and fell on his neck, and kissed him. And the son said unto him, Father, I have sinned against heaven, and in thy sight, and am no more worthy to be called thy son. But the father said to his servants, Bring forth the best robe, and put it on him; and put a ring on his hand, and shoes on his feet; and bring hither the fatted calf, and kill it; and let us eat, and be merry; for this my son was dead, and is alive again; he was lost, and is found. And they began to be merry.

Now his elder son was in the field: and as he came and drew nigh to the house, he heard music and dancing. And he called one of the servants, and asked what these things meant. And he said unto him, Thy brother is come; and thy father hath killed the fatted calf, because he hath received him safe and sound. And he was angry, and would not go in: therefore came his father out, and intreated him. And he answering said to his father, Lo, these many years do I serve thee, neither transgressed I at any time thy commandment; and yet thou never gavest me a kid, that I might make merry with my friends: but as soon as this thy son was come, which hath devoured thy living with harlots, thou hast killed for him the fatted calf. And he said unto him, Son, thou art ever with me, and all that I have is thine. It was meet that we should make merry and be glad: for this thy brother was dead, and is alive again; and was lost, and is found.

THE LABOURERS IN THE VINEYARD

For the kingdom of heaven is like unto a man that is an householder, which went out early in the morning to hire labourers into his vineyard. And when he had agreed with the labourers for a penny a day, he sent them into his vineyard. And he went out about the third hour, and saw others standing idle in the market-place, and said unto them, Go ye also into the vineyard, and whatsoever is right I will give you. And they went their way. Again he went out about the sixth and ninth hour, and did likewise. And about the eleventh hour he went out, and found others standing idle, and saith unto them, Why stand ye here all the day idle? They say unto him, Because no man hath hired us. He saith unto them, Go ye also into the vineyard; and whatsoever is right, that ye shall receive. So when even was come, the lord of the vineyard saith unto his steward, Call the labourers, and give them their hire, beginning from the last unto the first. And when they came that were hired about the eleventh hour, they received every man a penny. But when the first came, they supposed that they should have received more; and they likewise received every man a penny. And when they had received it, they murmured against the goodman of the house, saying, These last have wrought but one hour, and thou hast made them equal unto us, which have borne the burden and heat of the day. But he answered one of them, and said, Friend, I do thee no wrong: didst not thou agree with me for a penny? Take that thine is, and go thy way: I will give unto this last, even as unto thee. Is it not lawful for me to do what I will with mine own? Is thine eye evil, because I am good? So the last shall be first, and the first last: for many be called, but few chosen.

THE GREAT SUPPER

Then said he also to him that bade him, When thou makest a dinner or a supper, call not thy friends, nor thy brethren, neither thy kinsmen, nor thy rich neighbours; lest they also bid thee again, and a recompense be made thee. But when thou makest a feast, call the poor, the maimed, the lame, the blind: and thou shalt be blessed; for they cannot recompense thee: for thou shalt be recompensed at the resurrection of the just.

And when one of them that sat at meat with him heard these things, he said unto him, Blessed is he that shall eat bread in the kingdom of God. Then said he unto him, A certain man made a great supper, and bade many: and sent his servant at supper time to say to them that were bidden, Come; for all things are now ready. And they all with one consent began to make excuse. The first said unto him, I have bought a piece of ground, and I must needs go and see it: I pray thee have me excused. And another said, I have bought five yoke of oxen, and I go to prove them: I pray thee have me excused. And another said, I have married a wife, and therefore I cannot come. So that servant came, and shewed his lord these things. Then the master of the house, being angry, said to his servant, Go out quickly into the streets and lanes of the city, and bring in hither the poor, and the maimed, and the halt, and the blind. And the servant said, Lord, it is done as thou hast commanded, and yet there is room. And the lord said unto the servant, Go out into the highways and hedges, and compel them to come in, that my house may be filled. For I say unto you, That none of those men which were bidden shall taste of my supper.

THE PHARISEE AND THE PUBLICAN

And he spake this parable unto certain which trusted in themselves that they were righteous, and despised others: Two men went up into the temple to pray; the one a Pharisee, and the other a publican. The Pharisee stood and prayed thus with himself, God, I thank thee, that I am not as other men are, extortioners, unjust, adulterers, or even as this publican. I fast twice in the week, I give tithes of all that I possess. And the publican, standing afar off, would not lift up so much as his eyes unto heaven, but smote upon his breast, saying, God be merciful to me a sinner. I tell you, this man went down to his house justified rather than the other: for every one that exalteth himself shall be abased; and he that humbleth himself shall be exalted.

XXVI

FROM 'THE SCHOLAR-GIPSY'

GO, for they call you, shepherd, from the hill;
    Go, shepherd, and untie the wattled cotes!
    No longer leave thy wistful flock unfed,
Nor let thy bawling-fellows rack their throats,
  Nor the cropp'd grasses shoot another head;
    But when the fields are still,
And the tired men and dogs all gone to rest,
  And only the white sheep are sometimes seen
    Cross and recross the strips of moon-blanched green,
Come, shepherd, and again renew the quest.

FROM 'THE SCHOLAR-GIPSY'

Here, where the reaper was at work of late,
   In this high field's dark corner, where he leaves
   His coat, his basket, and his earthen cruse,
And in the sun all morning binds the sheaves,
   Then here, at noon, comes back his stores to use—
     Here will I sit and wait,
While to my ear from uplands far away
   The bleating of the folded flocks is borne,
   With distant cries of reapers in the corn—
All the live murmur of a summer's day.

Screen'd is this nook o'er the high, half-reap'd field,
   And here till sun-down, shepherd, will I be.
   Through the thick corn the scarlet poppies peep,
And round green roots and yellowing stalks I see
   Pale blue convolvulus in tendrils creep;
     And air-swept lindens yield
Their scent, and rustle down their perfumed showers
   Of bloom on the bent grass where I am laid,
   And bower me from the August sun with shade;
And the eye travels down to Oxford's towers.

And near me on the grass lies Glanvil's book—
   Come, let me read the oft-read tale again!
   The story of that Oxford scholar poor,
Of pregnant parts and quick inventive brain,
   Who, tired of knocking at preferment's door,
     One summer morn forsook
His friends, and went to learn the gipsy lore,
   And roam'd the world with that wild brotherhood,
   And came, as most men deem'd, to little good,
But came to Oxford and his friends no more.

But once, years after, in the country lanes,
   Two scholars, whom at college erst he knew,
   Met him, and of his way of life enquired;
Whereat he answer'd, that the gipsy-crew,
   His mates, had arts to rule as they desired
     The workings of men's brains:

And they can bind them to what thoughts they will;
    'And I,' he said, 'the secret of their art,
    When fully learn'd, will to the world impart;
But it needs heaven-sent moments for this skill.'

This said, he left them, and return'd no more.—
    But rumours hung about the country-side
        That the lost Scholar long was seen to stray,
    Seen by rare glimpses, pensive and tongue-tied,
        In hat of antique shape, and cloak of grey,
            The same the gipsies wore.
    Shepherds had met him on the Hurst in spring;
        At some lone alehouse in the Berkshire moors,
        On the warm ingle-bench, the smock-frock'd boors
    Had found him seated at their entering.

But, 'mid their drink and clatter, he would fly;
    And I myself seem half to know thy looks,
        And put the shepherds, wanderer, on thy trace;
    And boys who in lone wheatfields scare the rooks
        I ask if thou has pass'd their quiet place;
            Or in my boat I lie
    Moor'd to the cool bank in the summer-heats,
        'Mid wide grass meadows which the sunshine fills,
        And watch the warm, green-muffled Cumnor hills,
    And wonder if thou haunt'st their shy retreats.

For most, I know, thou lov'st retired ground!
    Thee at the ferry Oxford riders blithe,
        Returning home on summer nights, have met
    Crossing the stripling Thames at Bab-lock-hithe,
        Trailing in the cool stream thy fingers wet,
            As the punt's rope chops round;
    And leaning backward in a pensive dream,
        And fostering in thy lap a heap of flowers
        Pluck'd in shy fields and distant Wychwood bowers,
    And thine eyes resting on the moonlit stream.
                *   *   *   *

And once, in winter, on the causeway chill
  Where home through flooded fields foot-travellers go,
    Have I not pass'd thee on the wooden bridge,
  Wrapt in thy cloak and battling with the snow,
    Thy face towards Hinksey and its wintry ridge?
      And thou hast climb'd the hill,
  And gain'd the white brow of the Cumnor range;
    Turn'd once to watch, while thick the snowflakes fall,
    The line of festal light in Christ-Church hall—
  Then sought thy straw in some sequester'd grange.

But what—I dream! Two hundred years are flown
  Since first thy story ran through Oxford halls,
    And the grave Glanvil did the tale inscribe
  That thou wert wander'd from the studious walls
    To learn strange arts, and join a gipsy tribe;
      And thou from earth art gone
  Long since, and in some quiet churchyard laid—
    Some country-nook, where o'er thy unknown grave
    Tall grasses and white flowering nettles wave,
  Under a dark, red-fruited yew-tree's shade.

—No, no, thou hast not felt the lapse of hours!
  For what wears out the life of mortal men?
    'Tis that from change to change their being rolls;
  'Tis that repeated shocks, again, again,
    Exhaust the energy of strongest souls,
      And numb the elastic powers.
  Till having used our nerves with bliss and teen,
    And tired upon a thousand schemes our wit,
    To the just-pausing Genius we remit
  Our well-worn life, and are—what we have been.

Thou hast not lived, why should'st thou perish, so?
  Thou hadst *one* aim, *one* business, *one* desire;
    Else wert thou long since number'd with the dead!
  Else hadst thou spent, like other men, thy fire!
    The generations of thy peers are fled,
      And we ourselves shall go;

But thou possessest an immortal lot,
  And we imagine thee exempt from age,
  And living as thou liv'st on Glanvil's page,
Because thou hadst—what we, alas! have not.

For early didst thou leave the world, with powers
  Fresh, undiverted to the world without,
    Firm to their mark, not spent on other things:
  Free from the sick fatigue, the languid doubt,
    Which much to have tried, in much been baffled, brings.
    O life unlike to ours!
  Who fluctuate idly without term or scope,
    Of whom each strives, nor knows for what he strives,
    And each half lives a hundred different lives;
  Who wait like thee, but not, like thee, in hope.

Thou waitest for the spark from heaven! and we,
  Light half-believers of our casual creeds,
    Who never deeply felt, nor clearly will'd,
  Whose insight never has borne fruit in deeds,
    Whose vague resolves never have been fulfill'd;
      For whom each year we see
    Breeds new beginnings, disappointments new;
      Who hesitate and falter life away,
      And lose to-morrow the ground won to-day—
  Ah! do not we, wanderer, await it too?

Yes, we await it!—but it still delays,
  And then we suffer! and amongst us one,
    Who most has suffer'd, takes dejectedly
  His seat upon the intellectual throne;
    And all his store of sad experience he
      Lays bare of wretched days;
    Tells us his misery's birth and growth and signs,
      And how the dying spark of hope was fed,
      And how the breast was soothed, and how the head,
    And all his hourly varied anodynes.

This for our wisest! and we others pine,
  And wish the long unhappy dream would end,
    And waive all claim to bliss, and try to bear
  With close-lipp'd patience for our only friend,
    Sad patience, too near neighbour to despair—
      But none has hope like thine!
  Thou through the fields and through the wood dost stray,
    Roaming the country-side, a truant-boy,
    Nursing thy project in unclouded joy,
  And every doubt long blown by time away.

O born in days when wits were fresh and clear,
  And life ran gaily as the sparkling Thames;
    Before this strange disease of modern life,
  With its sick hurry, its divided aims,
    Its heads o'ertax'd, its palsied hearts, was rife—
      Fly hence, our contact fear!
  Still fly, plunge deeper in the bowering wood!
    Averse, as Dido did with gesture stern
    From her false friend's approach in Hades turn,
  Wave us away, and keep thy solitude!

Still nursing the unconquerable hope,
  Still clutching the inviolable shade,
    With a free, onward impulse brushing through,
  By night, the silver'd branches of the glade—
    Far on the forest-skirts, where none pursue,
      On some mild pastoral slope
  Emerge, and resting on the moonlit pales
    Freshen thy flowers as in former years
    With dew, or listen with enchanted ears,
  From the dark dingles, to the nightingales!

But fly our paths, our feverish contact fly!
  For strong the infection of our mental strife,
    Which, though it gives no bliss, yet spoils for rest;
  And we should win thee from thy own fair life,
    Like us distracted, and like us unblest.
      Soon, soon thy cheer would die,

Thy hopes grow timorous, and unfix'd thy powers,
  And thy clear aims be cross and shifting made;
  And then thy glad perennial youth would fade,
Fade, and grow old at last, and die like ours.

Then fly our greetings, fly our speech and smiles!
  —As some grave Tyrian trader, from the sea,
    Descried at sunrise an emerging prow
  Lifting the cool-hair'd creepers stealthily,
    The fringes of a southward-facing brow
      Among the Ægean isles;
  And saw the merry Grecian coaster come,
    Freighted with amber grapes, and Chian wine,
    Green, bursting figs, and tunnies steep'd in brine;
  And knew the intruders on his ancient home,

The young light-hearted masters of the waves;
  And snatch'd his rudder, and shook out more sail,
    And day and night held on indignantly
  O'er the blue Midland waters with the gale,
    Betwixt the Syrtes and soft Sicily,
      To where the Atlantic raves
  Outside the western straits, and unbent sails
    There where down cloudy cliffs, through sheets of foam,
    Shy traffickers, the dark Iberians come;
And on the beach undid his corded bales.

XXVII

ELIJAH AND THE RAIN

AND it came to pass, after many days, that the word of the Lord came to Elijah in the third year, saying, Go, shew thyself unto Ahab; and I will send rain upon the earth. And Elijah went to show himself unto Ahab. And there was a sore famine in Samaria. And

ELIJAH AND THE RAIN

Ahab called Obadiah, which was the governor of his house. (Now Obadiah feared the Lord greatly: for it was so, when Jezebel cut off the prophets of the Lord, that Obadiah took an hundred prophets, and hid them by fifty in a cave, and fed them with bread and water.) And Ahab said unto Obadiah, Go into the land, unto all fountains of water, and unto all brooks: peradventure we may find grass to save the horses and mules alive, that we lose not all the beasts. So they divided the land between them, to pass throughout it: Ahab went one way by himself, and Obadiah went another way by himself.

And as Obadiah was in the way, behold, Elijah met him: and he knew him, and fell on his face, and said, Art thou that my lord Elijah? And he answered him, I am: go, tell thy lord, Behold, Elijah is here. And he said, What have I sinned, that thou wouldest deliver thy servant into the hand of Ahab, to slay me? As the Lord thy God liveth, there is no nation or kingdom, whither my lord hath not sent to seek thee: and when they said, He is not there; he took an oath of the kingdom and nation, that they found thee not. And now thou sayest, Go, tell thy lord, Behold, Elijah is here. And it shall come to pass, as soon as I am gone from thee, that the Spirit of the Lord shall carry thee whither I know not; and so when I come and tell Ahab, and he cannot find thee, he shall slay me: but I thy servant fear the Lord from my youth. Was it not told my lord what I did when Jezebel slew the prophets of the Lord, how I hid an hundred men of the Lord's prophets by fifty in a cave, and fed them with bread and water? And now thou sayest, Go, tell thy Lord, Behold, Elijah is here: and he shall slay me. And Elijah said, As the Lord of hosts liveth, before whom I stand, I will surely shew myself unto him to-day. So Obadiah went to meet Ahab, and told him: and Ahab went to meet Elijah.

And it came to pass, when Ahab saw Elijah, that Ahab said unto him, Art thou he that troubleth Israel? And he answered, I have not troubled Israel; but thou and thy father's house, in that ye have forsaken the commandments of the Lord, and thou hast followed Baalim. Now therefore send, and gather to me all Israel unto mount Carmel, and the prophets of Baal four hundred and fifty, and the prophets of the groves four hundred, which eat at Jezebel's table. So Ahab sent unto all the children of Israel, and gathered the prophets together unto mount Carmel.

And Elijah came unto all the people, and said, How long halt ye between two opinions? if the Lord be God, follow him: but if Baal, then follow him. And the people answered him not a word. Then said Elijah unto the people, I, even I only, remain a prophet of the Lord; but Baal's prophets are four hundred and fifty men. Let them therefore give us two bullocks; and let them choose one bullock for themselves, and cut it in pieces, and lay it on wood, and put no fire under: and I will dress the other bullock, and lay it on wood, and put no fire under: and call ye on the name of your gods, and I will call on the name of the Lord: and the God that answereth by fire, let him be God. And all the people answered and said, It is well spoken. And Elijah said unto the prophets of Baal, Choose you one bullock for yourselves, and dress it first; for ye are many; and call on the name of your gods, but put no fire under. And they took the bullock which was given them, and they dressed it, and called on the name of Baal from morning even until noon, saying, O Baal, hear us. But there was no voice, nor any that answered. And they leaped upon the altar which was made. And it came to pass at noon, that Elijah mocked them, and said, Cry aloud: for he is a God; either he is talking, or he is pursuing, or he is in a journey, or peradventure he sleepeth, and must be awaked. And they cried aloud, and cut themselves after their manner with knives and lancets, till the blood gushed out upon them. And it came to pass, when midday was past, and they prophesied until the time of the offering of the evening sacrifice, that there was neither voice, nor any to answer, nor any that regarded. And Elijah said unto all the people, Come near unto me. And all the people came near unto him. And he repaired the altar of the Lord that was broken down. And Elijah took twelve stones, according to the number of the tribes of the sons of Jacob unto whom the word of the Lord came, saying, Israel shall be thy name: and with the stones he built an altar in the name of the Lord: and he made a trench about the altar, as great as would contain two measures of seed. And he put the wood in order, and cut the bullock in pieces, and laid him on the wood, and said, Fill four barrels with water, and pour it on the burnt sacrifice, and on the wood. And he said, Do it the second time : and they did it the second time. And he said, Do it the third time: and they did it the third time. And the water ran round about the altar; and he filled the trench also with water. And it came to pass, at the time of the offering of the evening sacrifice, that Elijah the prophet came near, and said, Lord God of Abraham, Isaac, and of Israel, let it be known this day that thou art God in Israel, and that I am thy servant, and that I have done all these things at thy word. Hear me, O Lord, hear me, that this people may know that thou art the Lord God, and that thou hast turned their heart back again. Then the fire of the Lord fell, and consumed the burnt sacrifice, and the wood, and the stones, and the dust, and licked up the water that was in the trench. And when all the people saw it, they fell on their faces: and they said, The Lord, he is the God; the Lord, he is the God. And Elijah said unto them, Take the prophets of Baal; let not one of them escape, And they took them: and Elijah brought them down to the brook Kishon, and slew them there.

And Elijah said unto Ahab, Get thee up, eat and drink; for there is a sound of abundance of rain. So Ahab went up to eat and to drink. And Elijah went up to the top of Carmel; and he cast himself down upon the earth, and put his face between his knees, and said to his servant, Go up now, look toward the sea. And he went up, and looked, and said, There is nothing. And he said, Go again seven times. And it came to pass at the seventh time, that he said, Behold, there ariseth a little cloud out of the sea, like a man's hand. And he said, Go up, say unto Ahab, prepare thy chariot, and get thee down, that the rain stop thee not. And it came to pass in the meanwhile, that the heaven was black with clouds and wind, and there was a great rain. And Ahab rode, and went to Jezreel. And the hand of the Lord was on Elijah; and he girded up his loins, and ran before Ahab to the entrance of Jezreel.

XXVIII

POETRY AND PURITANS

WAS there no poetry in these Puritans, because they wrote no poetry? We do not mean now the unwritten tragedy of the battle-psalm and the charge; but simple idyllic poetry and quiet home drama, love-poetry of the heart and the hearth, and the beauties of everyday human life? Take the most commonplace of them: was Zeal-for-Truth Thoresby, of Thoresby Rise in Deeping Fen, because his father had thought fit to give him an ugly and silly name, the less of a noble lad? Did his name prevent his being six feet high? Were his shoulders the less broad for it, his cheeks the less ruddy for it? He wore his flaxen hair of the same length that everyone now wears theirs, instead of letting it hang half-way to his waist in essenced curls; but was he therefore the less of a true Viking's son, bold-hearted as his sea-roving ancestors who won the Danelagh by Canute's side and settled there on Thoresby Rise, to grow wheat and breed horses, generation succeeding generation, in the old moated grange?

He carried a Bible in his jack-boot: but did that prevent him, as Oliver rode past him with an approving smile on Naseby field, thinking himself a very handsome fellow, with his moustache and imperial, and bright red coat, and cuirass well polished, in spite of many a dint, as he sate his father's great black horse as gracefully and firmly as any long-locked and essenced cavalier in front of him? Or did it prevent him thinking too, for a moment, with a throb of the heart, that sweet Cousin Patience, far way at home, could she but see him, might have the same opinion of him as he had of himself? Was he the worse for the thought? He was cer-

POETRY AND PURITANS

tainly not the worse for checking it the next instant, with manly shame for letting such 'carnal vanities' rise in his heart, while he was 'doing the Lord's work' in the teeth of death and hell: but was there no poetry in him then? No poetry in him, five minutes after, as the long rapier swung round his head, redder and redder at every sweep?

We are befooled by names. Call him Crusader instead of Roundhead, and he seems at once—granting him only sincerity, which he had, and that of a right awful kind—as complete a knight-errant as ever watched and prayed, ere putting on his spurs, in fantastic Gothic chapel, beneath 'storied windows richly dight.' Was there no poetry in him, either, half an hour afterwards, as he lay bleeding across the corpse of the gallant horse, waiting for his turn with the surgeon, and fumbled for the Bible in his boot and tried to hum a psalm, and thought of Cousin Patience, and his father, and his mother, and how they would hear, at least, that he had played the man in Israel that day and resisted unto blood, striving against sin and the Man of Sin?

And was there no poetry in him, too, as he came wearied along Thoresby Dyke, in the quiet autumn eve, home to the house of his forefathers, and saw afar off the knot of tall poplars rising over the broad misty flat, and the one great abele tossing its sheets of silver in the dying gusts; and knew that they stood before his father's door? Who can tell all the pretty child-memories which flitted across his brain at that sight, and made him forget that he was a wounded cripple? There is the dyke where he and his brothers snared the great pike which stole the ducklings—how many years ago?—while pretty little Patience stood by trembling, and shrieked at each snap of the brute's wide jaws; and there, down that long dark lode, ruffling with crimson in the sunset-breeze, he and his brothers skated home in triumph with Patience when his uncle died.

What a day that was! when in the clear bright winter noon, they laid the gate upon the ice and tied the beef bones under the four corners, and packed little Patience on it. How pretty she looked, though her eyes were red with weeping, as she peeped out from among the heap of blankets and horse-hides; and how merrily their long fen-runners whistled along the ice-lane, between the high banks of sighing reed, as they towed home their new treasure in triumph, at a pace like the race-horses to the dear old home among the poplar trees. And now he was going home to meet her, after a mighty victory, a deliverance from Heaven, second only in his eyes to that Red-Sea one. Was there no poetry in his heart at that thought? Did not the glowing sunset, and the reed beds which it transfigured before him into sheets of golden flame, seem tokens that the glory of God was going before him in his path? Did not the sweet clamour of the wild-fowl, gathering for one rich pæan ere they sank into rest, seem to him as God's bells chiming him home in triumph, with peals sweeter and bolder than those of Lincoln or Peterborough Steeple-house? Did not the very lapwing, as she tumbled, softly wailing, before him, as she did years ago, seem to welcome the wanderer home in the name of Heaven?

Fair Patience, too, though she was a Puritan; yet did not her cheek flush, her eye grow dim, like any other girl's, as she saw far off the red-coat, like a sliding spark of fire, coming slowly along the strait fen-bank, and flew upstairs into her chamber to pray, half that it might be, half that it might not be he? Was there no happy storm of human tears and human laughter when he entered the court-yard gate? Did not the old dog lick his Puritan hand as lovingly as if it had been a Cavalier's? Did not lads and lasses run out shouting? Did not the old yeoman father hug him, weep over him, hold him at arm's-length, and hug him again, as heartily as any other John Bull, even though the next moment he called all to kneel down and thank Him who had sent his boy home again, after bestowing on him the grace to bind kings in chains and nobles with links of iron, and contend to death for the faith delivered to the Saints? And did not Zeal-for-Truth look about as wistfully for Patience as any other man would have done, longing to see her, yet not daring even to ask for her? And when she came down at last, was she the less lovely in his eyes because she came, not flaunting with bare bosom, in tawdry finery and paint, but shrouded close in coif and pinner, hiding from all the world beauty which was there still but was meant for one alone, and that only if God willed, in God's good time? And was there no faltering of their voices, no light in their eyes, no trembling pressure of their hands, which said more, and was more, ay, and more beautiful in the sight of Him who made them, than all Herrick's Dianemes, Waller's Saccharissas, flames, darts, posies, love-knots, anagrams, and the rest of the insincere cant of the Court? What if Zeal-for-Truth had never strung two rhymes together in his life? Did not his heart go for inspiration to a loftier Helicon, when it whispered to itself 'My love, my dove, my undefilèd is but one,' than if he had filled pages with sonnets about Venuses and Cupids, love-sick shepherds and cruel nymphs?

And was there no poetry, true idyllic poetry, as of Longfellow's 'Evangeline' itself, in that trip round the old farm next morning; when Zeal-for-Truth, after looking over every heifer, and peeping into every sty, would needs canter down by his father's side to the horse-fen, with his arm in a sling; while the partridges whirred up before them, and the lurchers flashed like grey snakes after the hare, and the colts came whinnying round, with staring eyes and streaming manes; and the two chatted on in the same sober business-like English tone, alternately of 'The Lord's great dealings' by General Cromwell, the pride of all honest fen-men, and the price of troop-horses at the next Horncastle fair?

Poetry in those old Puritans? Why not? They were men of like passions with ourselves. They loved, they married, they brought up children; they feared, they sinned, they sorrowed, they fought—they conquered. There was poetry enough in them, be sure, though they acted it like men, instead of singing it like birds.

XXIX

SLEEP

BERNAL DIAZ

LET us leave him building the ships and say how we all went about in that city very much depressed, fearing that at any moment they might attack us; and our friends from Tlaxcala and Doña Marina also told the captain that an attack was probable, and Orteguilla, Montezuma's page, was always in tears. We all kept on the alert and placed a strong Guard over Montezuma, I say that we were on the alert, but there is no necessity to repeat it so often, for neither by day or night did we ever take off our arms or our gorgets or leggings, and we slept in them. Maybe some will ask when we slept and what our beds were like, —they were nothing but a little straw and a mat, and if one had a curtain, he placed it beneath him, and we slept shod and armed and with all our weapons to hand. The horses stood saddled and bridled all day long, and everything so fully prepared that on a call to arms we stood as though we had already been posted and were waiting for it. Sentinels were posted every night, and there was not a soldier who did not keep watch. There is another thing I must say, but not with the intention of boasting about it, that I grew so accustomed to go about armed, and to sleep in the way I have said, that after the conquest of New Spain I kept to the habit of sleeping in my clothes and without a bed, and I slept thus better than on a mattress.

Now when I go to the towns of my *encomienda* I do not take a bed, and if sometimes I do take one with me, it is not that I want it, but because some gentlemen may happen to go with me, and I do not wish them to think that I have not brought a bed because I do not possess a good one, but in truth I always lie on it dressed. There is another thing I must say. I am only able to sleep for a short time of a night, and have to get up and look at the heavens and the stars, and have to walk about for a time in the dew, and this I do without putting a cap or handkerchief on my head, and I am so used to it that thank God it does me no harm. I have said all this that it may be known how we the true conquistadores lived, and how accustomed we became to our arms and to keeping watch.

SIR PHILIP SIDNEY

Come, Sleep! O Sleep, the certain knot of peace,
The baiting-place of wit, the balm of woe,
The poor man's wealth, the prisoner's release,
Th' indifferent judge between the high and low;
With shield of proof shield me from out the press
Of those fierce darts Despair at me doth throw:
O make in me those civil wars to cease;
I will good tribute pay, if thou do so.
Take thou of me smooth pillows, sweetest bed,
A chamber deaf to noise and blind to light,
A rosy garland and a weary head:
And if these things, as being thine in right,
Move not thy heavy grace, thou shalt in me,
Livelier than elsewhere, Stella's image see.

THOMAS SACKVILLE

By him lay heavy Sleep, the cousin of Death,
Flat on the ground, and still as any stone,
A very corpse, save yielding forth a breath:
Small keep took he, whom Fortune frowned on,
Or whom she lifted up into the throne
Of high renown: but as a living death,
So, dead alive, of life he drew the breath.

The body's rest, the quiet of the heart,
The travail's ease, the still night's fear was he,
And of our life on earth the better part:
Reaver of sight, and yet in whom we see
Things oft that tide, and oft that never be:
Without respect, esteeming equally
King Crœsus' pomp, and Irus' poverty.

THE SLEEPLESS KING: SHAKESPEARE

How many thousand of my poorest subjects
Are at this hour asleep! O sleep, O gentle sleep,
Nature's soft nurse, how have I frighted thee,
That thou no more wilt weigh my eyelids down
And steep my senses in forgetfulness?
Why rather, sleep, liest thou in smoky cribs,
Upon uneasy pallets stretching thee,
And hush'd with buzzing night-flies to thy slumber,
Than in the perfumed chambers of the great,
Under the canopies of costly state,
And lull'd with sound of sweetest melody?
O thou dull god, why liest thou with the vile
In loathsome beds, and leavest the kingly couch
A watch-case or a common 'larum-bell?
Wilt thou upon the high and giddy mast
Seal up the ship-boy's eyes, and rock his brains
In cradle of the rude imperious surge,
And in the visitation of the winds,
Who take the ruffian billows by the top,
Curling their monstrous heads, and hanging them
With deafening clamour in the slippery clouds,
That, with the hurly, death itself awakes?
Canst thou, O partial sleep, give thy repose
To the wet sea-boy in an hour so rude;
And in the calmest and most stillest night,
With all appliances and means to boot,
Deny it to a king? Then happy low, lie down!
Uneasy lies the head that wears a crown.

VIXI: CHARLES MACKAY

I have lived and I have loved;
I have waked and I have slept;
I have sung and I have danced;
I have smiled and I have wept;
I have won and wasted treasure;
I have had my fill of pleasure;

And all these things were weariness,
And some of them were dreariness.
And all these things, but two things,
Were emptiness and pain:
And Love—it was the best of them;
And Sleep—worth all the rest of them.

SANCHO PANZA ON SLEEP

Now, blessings light on him that first invented this same sleep! it covers a man all over, thoughts and all, like a cloak; it is meat for the hungry, drink for the thirsty, heat for the cold, and cold for the hot. It is the current coin that purchases all the pleasures of the world cheap; and the balance that sets the king and the shepherd, the fool and the wise man, even.

XXX

THE CIRCUMLOCUTION OFFICE

THE Circumlocution Office was (as everybody knows without being told) the most important Department under Government. No public business of any kind could possibly be done at any time, without the acquiescence of the Circumlocution Office. Its finger was in the largest public pie, and in the smallest public tart. It was equally impossible to do the plainest right and to undo the plainest wrong without the express authority of the Circumlocution Office. If another Gunpowder Plot had been discovered half an hour before the lighting of the match, nobody would have been justified in saving the parliament until there had been half a score of boards, half a bushel of minutes, several sacks of official memoranda, and a family-vault full of ungrammatical correspondence, on the part of the Circumlocution Office.

This glorious establishment had been early in the field, when the one sublime principle involving the difficult art of governing a country was first distinctly revealed to statesmen. It had been foremost to study that bright revelation, and to carry its shining influence through the whole of the official proceedings. Whatever was required to be done, the Circumlocution Office was beforehand with all the public departments in the art of perceiving—HOW NOT TO DO IT.

Through this delicate perception, through the tact with which it invariably seized it, and through the genius with which it always acted on it, the Circumlocution Office had risen to over-top all the public departments; and the public condition had risen to be—what it was.

It is true that How not to do it was the great study and object of all public departments and professional politicians all round the Circumlocution Office. It is true that every new premier and every new government, coming in because they had upheld a certain thing as necessary to be done, were no sooner come in than they applied their utmost faculties to discover How not to do it. It is true that from the moment when a general election was over, every returned man who had been raving on hustings because it hadn't been done, and who had been asking the friends of the honourable gentleman in the opposite interest on pain of impeachment to tell him why it hadn't been done, and who had been asserting that it must be done, and who had been pledging himself that it should be done, began to devise, How it was not to be done. It is true that the debates of both Houses of Parliament the whole session through, uniformly tended to the protracted deliberation, How not to do it. It is true that the royal speech at the opening of such session virtually said, My lords and gentlemen, you have a considerable stroke of work to do, and you will please to retire to your respective chambers, and discuss, How not to do it. It is true that the royal speech, at the close of such session, virtually said, My lords and gentlemen, you have through several laborious months been considering with great loyalty and patriotism, How not to do it, and you have found out; and with the blessing of Providence upon the harvest (natural, not political), I now dismiss you. All this is true, but the Circumlocution Office went beyond it.

Because the Circumlocution Office went on mechanically, every day, keeping this wonderful, all-sufficient wheel of statesmanship, How not to do it, in motion. Because the Circumlocution Office was down upon any ill-advised public servant who was going to do it, or who appeared to be by any surprising accident in remote danger of doing it, with a minute, and a memorandum, and a letter of instructions, that extinguished him. It was this spirit of national efficiency in the Circumlocution Office that had gradually led to its having something to do with everything. Mechanicians, natural philosophers, soldiers, sailors, petitioners, memorialists, people with grievances, people who wanted to prevent grievances, people who wanted to redress grievances, jobbing people, jobbed people, people who couldn't get rewarded for merit, and people who couldn't get punished for demerit, were all indiscriminately turned up under the foolscap paper of the Circumlocution Office.

Numbers of people were lost in the Circumlocution Office. Unfortunates with wrongs, or with projects for the general welfare (and they had better have had wrongs at first, than have taken that bitter English recipe for certainly getting them), who in slow lapse of time and agony had passed safely through other public departments; who, according to rule, had been bullied in this, over-reached by that, and evaded by the other; got referred at last to the Circumlocution Office, and never reappeared in the light of day. Boards sat upon them, secretaries minuted upon them, commissioners gabbled about them, clerks registered, entered, checked, and ticked them off, and they melted away. In short, all the business of the country went through the Circumlocution Office, except the business that never came out of it; and *its* name was Legion.

Sometimes, angry spirits attacked the Circumlocution Office. Sometimes, parliamentary questions were asked about it, and even parliamentary motions made or threatened about it, by demagogues so low and ignorant as to hold that the real recipe of government was, How to do it. Then would the nobe lord, or right honourable gentleman, in whose department it was to defend the Circumlocution Office, put an orange in his pocket, and make a regular field-day of the occasion. Then would he come down to that house with a slap upon the table, and meet the honourable gentleman foot to foot. Then would he be there to tell that honourable gentleman that the Circumlocution Office not only was blameless in this matter, but was commendable in this matter, was extollable to the skies in this matter. Then would he be there to tell that honourable gentleman, that, although the Circumlocution Office was invariably right and wholly right, it never was so right as in this matter. Then would he be there to tell that honourable gentleman that it would have been more to his honour, more to his credit, more to his good taste, more to his good sense, more to half the dictionary of commonplaces, if he had left the Circumlocution Office alone, and never approached this matter. Then would he keep one eye upon a coach or crammer from the Circumlocution Office sitting below the bar, and smash the honourable gentleman with the Circumlocution Office account of this matter. And although one of two things always happened; namely, either that the Circumlocution Office had nothing to say and said it, or that it had something to say of which the noble lord, or right honourable gentleman, blundered one half and forgot the other; the Circumlocution Office was always voted immaculate by an accommodating majority.

Such a nursery of statesmen had the Department become in virtue of a long career of this nature, that several solemn lords had attained the reputation of being quite unearthly prodigies of business, solely from having practised, How not to do it, at the head of the Circumlocution Office. As to the minor priests and acolytes of that temple, the result of all this was that they stood divided into two classes, and, down to the junior messenger, either believed in the Circumlocution Office as a heaven-born institution, that had an absolute right to do whatever it liked; or took refuge in total infidelity, and considered it a flagrant nuisance.

The Barnacle family had for some time helped to

administer the Circumlocution Office. The Tite Barnacle Branch, indeed, considered themselves in a general way as having vested rights in that direction, and took it ill if any other family had much to say to it. The Barnacles were a very high family, and a very large family. They were dispersed all over the public offices, and held all sorts of public places. Either the nation was under a load of obligation to the Barnacles, or the Barnacles were under a load of obligation to the nation. It was not quite unanimously settled which; the Barnacles having their opinion, the nation theirs.

The Mr. Tite Barnacle who at the period now in question usually coached or crammed the statesman at the head of the Circumlocution Office, when that noble or right honourable individual sat a little uneasily in his saddle, by reason of some vagabond making a tilt at him in a newspaper, was more flush of blood than money. As a Barnacle he had his place, which was a snug thing enough; and as a Barnacle he had of course put in his son Barnacle Junior, in the office. But he had intermarried with a branch of the Stiltstalkings, who were also better endowed in a sanguineous point of view than with real or personal property, and of this marriage there had been issue, Barnacle Junior, and three young ladies. What with the patrician requirements of Barnacle Junior, the three young ladies, Mrs. Tite Barnacle née Stiltstalking, and himself, Mr. Tite Barnacle found the intervals between quarter day and quarter day rather longer than he could have desired; a circumstance which he always attributed to the country's parsimony.

XXXI

NELSON

THE SPIRITS OF THE GREAT

THE death of Nelson was felt in England as something more than a public calamity: men started at the intelligence, and turned pale, as if they had heard of the loss of a dear friend. An object of our admiration and affection, of our pride and of our hopes, was suddenly taken from us; and it seemed as if we had never, till then, known how deeply we loved and reverenced him. What the country had lost in its great naval hero—the greatest of our own, and of all former times, was scarcely taken into the account of grief. So perfectly, indeed, had he performed his part, that the maritime war, after the battle of Trafalgar, was considered at an end: the fleets of the enemy were not merely defeated, but destroyed: new navies must be built, and a new race of seamen reared for them, before the possibility of their invading our shores could again be contemplated. It was not, therefore, from any selfish reflection upon the magnitude of our loss that we mourned for him: the general sorrow was of a higher character. The people of England grieved that funeral ceremonies, public monuments, and posthumous rewards, were all which they could now bestow upon him whom the king, the legislature, and the nation would alike have delighted to honour; whom every tongue would have blessed; whose presence in every village through which he might have passed would have wakened the church bells, have given schoolboys a holiday, have drawn children from their sports to gaze upon him, and 'old men from the chimney corner' to look upon Nelson ere they died. The victory of Trafalgar was celebrated, indeed, with the usual forms of rejoicing, but they were without joy; for such already was the glory of the British navy, through Nelson's surpassing genius, that it scarcely seemed to receive any addition from the most signal victory that ever was achieved upon the seas; and the destruction of this mighty fleet, by which all the maritime schemes of France were totally frustrated, hardly appeared to add to our security or strength; for, while Nelson was living to watch the combined squadrons of the enemy, we felt ourselves as secure as now, when they were no longer in existence.

There was reason to suppose, from the appearances upon opening the body, that, in the course of nature, he might have attained, like his father, to a good old age. Yet he cannot be said to have fallen prematurely whose work was done; nor ought he to be lamented, who died so full of honours, and at the height of human fame. The most triumphant death is that of the martyr; the most awful, that of the martyred patriot; the most splendid, that of the hero in the hour of victory; and if the chariot and the horses of fire had been vouchsafed for Nelson's translation, he could scarcely have departed in a brighter blaze of glory. He has left us, not indeed his mantle of inspiration, but a name and an example, which are at this hour inspiring hundreds of the youth of England: a name which is our pride, and an example which will continue to be our shield and our strength. Thus it is that the spirits of the great and the wise continue to live and to act after them: verifying, in this sense, the language of the old mythologist:

For gods they are, through high Jove's counsels good,
Haunting the earth, the guardians of mankind.

LET US NOW PRAISE FAMOUS MEN

Let us now praise famous men, and our fathers that begat us.

The Lord hath wrought great glory by them through his great power from the beginning.

Such as did bear rule in their kingdoms, men renowned for their power, giving counsel by their understanding, and declaring prophecies:

Leaders of the people by their counsels, and by their knowledge of learning meet for the people, wise and eloquent in their instructions:

Such as found out musical tunes, and recited verses in writing:

Rich men furnished with ability, living peaceably in their habitations:

All these were honoured in their generations, and were the glory of their times.

There be of them, that have left a name behind them, that their praises might be reported.

And some there be, which have no memorial; who are perished, as though they had never been; and are become as though they had never been born; and their children after them.

But these were merciful men, whose righteousness hath not been forgotten.

With their seed shall continually remain a good inheritance, and their children are within the covenant.

Their seed standeth fast, and their children for their sakes.

Their seed shall remain for ever, and their glory shall not be blotted out.

Their bodies are buried in peace; but their name liveth for evermore.

The people will tell of their wisdom, and the congregation will shew forth their praise.

Enoch pleased the Lord, and was translated, being an example of repentance to all generations.

Noah was found perfect and righteous; in the time of wrath he was taken in exchange [for the world;] therefore was he left as a remnant unto the earth, when the flood came.

An everlasting covenant was made with him, that all flesh should perish no more by the flood.

Abraham was a great father of many people: in glory was there none like unto him;

Who kept the law of the most High, and was in covenant with him: he established the covenant in his flesh; and when he was proved, he was found faithful.

Therefore he assured him by an oath, that he would bless the nations in his seed, and that he would multiply him as the dust of the earth, and exalt his seed as the stars, and cause them to inherit from sea to sea, and from the river unto the utmost part of the land.

With Isaac did he establish likewise [for Abraham his father's sake] the blessing of all men, and the covenant,

And made it rest upon the head of Jacob. He acknowledged him in his blessing, and gave him an heritage, and divided his portions; among the twelve tribes did he part them.

XXXII

SCOTT IN ADVERSITY

*D*ECEMBER 18.—Ballantyne called on me this morning. *Venit illa suprema dies.* My extremity is come. Cadell has received letters from London which all but positively announce the failure of Hurst and Robinson, so that Constable & Co. must follow, and I must go with poor James Ballantyne for company. I suppose it will involve my all. But if they leave me £500, I can still make it £1,000 or £1,200 a year. And if they take my salaries of £1,300 and £300, they cannot but give me something out of them. I have been rash in anticipating funds to buy land, but then I made from £5,000 to £10,000 a year, and land was my temptation. I think nobody can lose a penny—that is one comfort. Men will think pride has had a fall. Let them indulge their own pride in thinking that my fall makes them higher, or seems so at least. I have the satisfaction to recollect that my prosperity has been of advantage to many, and that some at least will forgive my transient wealth on account of the innocence of my intentions, and my real wish to do good to the poor. This news will make sad hearts at Darnick, and in the cottages of Abbotsford, which I do not nourish the least hope of preserving. It has been my Delilah, and so I have often termed it; and now the recollection of the extensive woods I planted, and the walks I have formed, from which strangers must derive both the pleasure and profit, will excite feelings likely to sober my gayest moments. I have half resolved never to see the place again. How could I tread my hall with such a diminished crest? How live a poor indebted man where I was once the wealthy, the honoured? My children are provided; thank God for that. I was to have gone there on Saturday in joy and prosperity to receive my friends. My dogs will wait for me in vain. It is foolish—but the thoughts of parting from these dumb creatures have moved me more than any of the painful reflections I have put down. Poor things, I must get them kind masters; there may be yet those who loving me may love my dog because it has been mine. I must end this, or I shall lose the tone of mind with which men should meet distress.

What a life mine has been!—half educated, almost wholly neglected or left to myself, stuffing my head with most nonsensical trash, and undervalued in society for a time by most of my companions, getting forward and held a bold and clever fellow, contrary to the opinion of all who thought me a mere dreamer, broken-hearted for two years, my heart handsomely pieced again, but the crack will remain to my dying day. Rich and poor four or five times, once on the verge of ruin, yet opened new sources of wealth almost overflowing. Now taken in my pitch of pride, and nearly winged (unless the good news hold), because London chooses to be in an uproar and in the tumult of bulls and bears, a poor inoffensive lion like myself is pushed to the wall. And what is to be the end of it? God knows. And so ends the catechism.

Worked at Pepys in the evening, with the purpose of review for Lockhart. Notwithstanding the depressing effects of the calomel, I feel the pleasure of being alone and uninterrupted. Few men, leading a quiet life, and without any strong or highly varied change of circumstances, have seen more variety of society than I—few have enjoyed it more, or been *bored*, as it is called, less by the company of tiresome people. I have rarely, if ever, found anyone, out of whom I could not extract amusement or edification; and were I obliged to account for hints afforded on such occasions, I should make an ample deduction from my inventive powers.

Still, however, from the earliest time I can remember, I preferred the pleasure of being alone to waiting for visitors, and have often taken a bannock and a bit of cheese to the wood or hill, to avoid dining with company. As I grew from boyhood to manhood I saw this would not do; and that to gain a place in men's esteem I must mix and bustle with them. Pride and an excitation of spirits supplied the real pleasure which others seem to feel in society, and certainly upon many occasions it was real. Still, if the question was, eternal company, without the power of retiring within yourself, or solitary confinement for life, I should say, 'Turnkey, lock the cell!' My life, though not without its fits of waking and strong exertion, has been a sort of dream, spent in

'Chewing the cud of sweet and bitter fancy.'

I have worn a wishing-cap, the power of which has been to divert present griefs by a touch of the wand of imagination, and gild over the future prospect by prospects more fair than can ever be realized. Somewhere it is said that this castle-building—this wielding of the aërial trowel—is fatal to exertions in actual life. I cannot tell; I have not found it so. I cannot, indeed, say like Madame Genlis, that in the imaginary scenes in which I have acted a part I ever prepared myself for anything which actually befell me; but I have certainly fashioned out much that made the present hour pass pleasantly away, and much that has enabled me to contribute to the amusement of the public. Since I was five years old I cannot remember the time when I had not some ideal part to play for my own solitary amusement.

January 22.—I feel neither dishonoured nor broken down by the bad—now really bad news I have received. I have walked my last on the domains I have planted—sate the last time in the halls I have built. But death would have taken them from me if misfortune had spared them. My poor people whom I loved so well! There is just another die to turn up against me in this run of ill-luck; *i.e.* if I should break my magic wand in the fall from this elephant, and lose my popularity with my fortune. Then *Woodstock* and *Bony* may both go to the paper-maker, and I may take to smoking cigars and drinking grog, or turn devotee, and intoxicate the brain another way. In prospect of absolute ruin, I wonder if they would let me leave the Court of Session. I would like, methinks, to go abroad

> 'And lay my bones far from the *Tweed*.'

But I find my eyes moistening, and that will not do. I will not yield without a fight for it. It is odd, when I set myself to work *doggedly*, as Dr. Johnson would say, I am exactly the same man that I ever was, neither low-spirited nor *distrait*. In prosperous times I have sometimes felt my fancy and powers of language flag, but adversity is to me at least a tonic and bracer; the fountain is awakened from its inmost recesses, as if the spirit of affliction had troubled it in his passage.

Poor Mr. Pole the harper sent to offer me £500 or £600, probably his all. There is much good in the world, after all. But I will involve no friend, either rich or poor. My own right hand shall do it—else will I be *done* in the slang language, and *undone* in common parlance. . . .

I went to the Court for the first time to-day, and, like the man with the large nose, thought everybody was thinking of me and my mishaps. Many were, undoubtedly, and all rather regrettingly; some obviously affected. It is singular to see the difference of men's manner whilst they strive to be kind or civil in their way of addressing me. Some smile as they wish me good-day, as if to say, 'Think nothing about it, my lad; it is quite out of our thoughts.' Others greeted me with the affected gravity which one sees and despises at a funeral. The best bred—all, I believe, meaning equally well—just shook hands and went on. A foolish puff in the papers, calling on men and gods to assist a popular author, who, having choused the public of many thousands, had not the sense to keep wealth when he had it. If I am hard pressed, and measures used against me, I must use all means of legal defence, and subscribe myself bankrupt in a petition for sequestration. It is the course I would have advised a client to take, and would have the effect of saving my land, which is secured by my son's contract of marriage. I might save my library, etc., by assistance of friends, and bid my creditors defiance. But for this I would, in a court of honour, deserve to lose my spurs. No, if they permit me, I will be their vassal for life, and dig in the mine of my imagination to find diamonds (or what may sell for such) to make good my engagements, not to enrich myself. And this from no reluctance to allow myself to be called the Insolvent, which I probably am, but because I will not put out of the [power] of my creditors the resources, mental or literary, which yet remain to me.

XXXIII

FOUR POEMS BY GEORGE HERBERT

LIFE

I MADE a posie while the day ran by.
    Here will I smell my remnant out, and tie
        My life within this band.
But time did becken to the flowers, and they
By noon most cunningly did steal away
        And wither'd in my hand.

My hand was next to them, and then my heart.
I took, without more thinking, in good part
        Time's gentle admonition;
Who did so sweetly death's sad taste convey,
Making my minde to smell my fatall day,
        Yet sugring the suspicion.

Farewell deare flowers! Sweetly your time ye spent,
Fit, while ye liv'd, for smell or ornament,
        And after death for cures.
I follow straight without complaints or grief,
Since if my sent be good, I care not if
        It be as short as yours.

THE QUIP

The merrie world did on a day
　With his train-bands and mates agree
To meet together where I lay,
　And all in sport to geere at me.

First, Beautie crept into a rose;
　Which when I pluckt not, Sir, said she,
Tell me, I pray, whose hands are those?
　But thou shalt answer, Lord, for me.

Then Money came, and chinking still,
　What tune is this, poore man? said he,
I heard in Musick you had skill.
　But thou shalt answer, Lord, for me.

Then came brave Glorie puffing by
　In silks that whistled, who but he?
He scarce allow'd me half an eie.
　But thou shalt answer, Lord, for me.

Then came quick Wit and Conversation,
　And he would needs a comfort be,
And, to be short, make an oration,
　But thou shalt answer, Lord, for me.

Yet when the houre of thy designe
　To answer these fine things shall come,
Speak not at large, say, I am thine;
　And then they have their answer home.

THE PULLEY

When God at first made man,
Having a glasse of blessings standing by,
　Let us (said he) poure on him all we can.
Let the world's riches, which dispersed lie,
　　Contract into a span.

So strength first made a way,
Then beautie flow'd, then wisdome, honour, pleasure.
  When almost all was out, God made a stay,
Perceiving that alone of all his treasure
  Rest in the bottome lay.

  For if I should (said he)
Bestow this jewell also on my creature,
  He would adore my gifts instead of me,
And rest in Nature, not the God of Nature.
  So both should losers be.

  Yet let him keep the rest,
But keep them with repining restlesnesse.
  Let him be rich and wearie, that at least
If goodnesse leade him not, yet wearinesse,
  May tosse him to my breast.

MAN

  My God, I heard this day
That none doth build a stately habitation
  But he that means to dwell therein.
  What house more stately hath there been,
Or can be, then is Man? To whose creation
  All things are in decay.

  For Man is ev'ry thing,
And more. He is a tree, yet bears no fruit;
  A beast, yet is, or should be more;
  Reason and speech we onely bring.
Parrats may thank us if they are not mute,
  They go upon the score.

  Man is all symmetrie,
Full of proportions, one limbe to another,
  And all to all the world besides,
  Each part may call the farthest, brother;
For head with foot hath private amitie,
  And both with moons and tides.

Nothing hath got so farre
But Man hath caught and kept it as his prey.
  His eyes dismount the highest starre.
  He is in little all the sphere.
Herbs gladly cure our flesh, because that they
    Finde their acquaintance there.

  For us the windes do blow,
The earth doth rest, heav'n move, and fountains flow.
  Nothing we see but means our good,
  As our *delight*, or as our *treasure*;
The whole is either our cupboard of *food*
    Or cabinet of *pleasure*.

  The starres have us to bed;
Night draws the curtain, which the sunne withdraws;
  Musick and light attend our head.
  All things unto our *flesh* are kinde
In their *descent* and *being*; to our *minde*
    In their *ascent* and *cause*.

  Each thing is full of dutie:
Waters united are our navigation;
  Distinguished, our habitation;
  Below, our drink; above, our meat;
Both are our cleanlinesse. Hath one such beautie?
    Then how are all things neat?

  More servants wait on Man
Then he'l take notice of; in ev'ry path
  He treads down that which doth befriend him
  When sicknesse makes him pale and wan.
Oh mightie love! Man is one world, and hath
    Another to attend him.

  Since then, my God, thou hast
So brave a Palace built, O dwell in it,
  That it may dwell with thee at last!
  Till then afford us so much wit
That as the world serves us we may serve thee,
    And both thy servants be.

XXXIV

NORSE TALES

WHY THE SEA IS SALT

ONCE on a time, but it was a long, long time ago, there were two brothers, one rich and one poor. Now, one Christmas eve, the poor one hadn't so much as a crumb in the house, either of meat or bread, so he went to his brother to ask him for something to keep Christmas with, in God's name. It was not the first time his brother had been forced to help him, and you may fancy he wasn't very glad to see his face, but he said—

'If you will do what I ask you to do, I'll give you a whole flitch of bacon.'

So the poor brother said he would do anything, and was full of thanks.

'Well, here is the flitch,' said the rich brother, 'and now go straight to Hell.'

'What I have given my word to do, I must stick to,' said the other; so he took the flitch and set off. He walked the whole day, and at dusk he came to a place where he saw a very bright light.

'Maybe this is the place,' said the man to himself. So he turned aside, and the first thing he saw was an old, old man, with a long white beard, who stood in an outhouse, hewing wood for the Christmas fire.

'Good even,' said the man with the flitch.

'The same to you; whither are you going so late?' said the man.

'Oh! I'm going to Hell, if I only knew the right way,' answered the poor man.

'Well, you're not far wrong, for this is Hell,' said the old man; 'when you get inside they will be all for buying your flitch, for meat is scarce in Hell; but mind, you don't sell it unless you get the hand-quern which stands behind the door for it. When you come out, I'll teach you how to handle the quern, for it's good to grind almost anything.'

So the man with the flitch thanked the other for his good advice, and gave a great knock at the Devil's door.

When he got in, everything went just as the old man had said. All the devils, great and small, came swarming up to him like ants round an anthill, and each tried to outbid the other for the flitch.

'Well!' said the man, 'by rights my old dame and I ought to have this flitch for our Christmas dinner; but since you have all set your hearts on it, I suppose I must give it up to you; but if I sell it at all, I'll have for it that quern behind the door yonder.'

At first the Devil wouldn't hear of such a bargain, and chaffered and haggled with the man; but he stuck to what he said, and at last the Devil had to part with his quern. When the man got out into the yard, he asked the old woodcutter how he was to handle the quern; and after he had learned how to use it, he thanked the old man and went off home as fast as he could, but still the clock had struck twelve on Christmas eve before he reached his own door.

'Wherever in the world have you been?' said his old dame; 'here have I sat hour after hour waiting and watching, without so much as two sticks to lay together under the Christmas brose.'

'Oh!' said the man, 'I couldn't get back before, for I had to go a long way first for one thing, and then for another; but now you shall see what you shall see.'

So he put the quern on the table, and bade it first of all grind lights, then a table-cloth, then meat, then ale, and so on till they had got everything that was nice for Christmas fare. He had only to speak the word, and the quern ground out what he wanted. The old dame stood by blessing her stars, and kept on asking where he had got this wonderful quern, but he wouldn't tell her.

'It's all one where I got it from; you see the quern is a good one, and the mill-stream never freezes, that's enough.'

So he ground meat and drink and dainties enough to last

out till Twelfth Day, and on the third day, he asked all his friends and kin to his house, and gave a great feast. Now, when his rich brother saw all that was on the table, and all that was behind in the larder, he grew quite spiteful and wild, for he couldn't bear that his brother should have anything.

"'Twas only on Christmas eve,' he said to the rest, 'he was in such straits that he came and asked for a morsel of food in God's name, and now he gives a feast as if he were count or king'; and he turned to his brother and said—

'But whence, in Hell's name, have you got all this wealth?'

'From behind the door,' answered the owner of the quern, for he didn't care to let the cat out of the bag. But later on the evening, when he had got a drop too much, he could keep his secret no longer, and brought out the quern and said—'There, you see what has gotten me all this wealth'; and so he made the quern grind all kind of things. When his brother saw it, he set his heart on having the quern, and, after a deal of coaxing, he got it; but he had to pay three hundred dollars for it, and his brother bargained to keep it till hay-harvest, for he thought, if I keep it till then, I can make it grind meat and drink that will last for years. So you may fancy the quern didn't grow rusty for want of work, and when hay-harvest came, the rich brother got it, but the other took care not to teach him how to handle it.

It was evening when the rich brother got the quern home, and next morning he told his wife to go out into the hay-field and toss, while the mowers cut the grass, and he would stay at home and get the dinner ready. So, when dinner-time drew near, he put the quern on the kitchen table and said—

'Grind herrings and broth, and grind them good and fast.'

So the quern began to grind herrings and broth; first of all, all the dishes full, then all the tubs full, and so on till the kitchen floor was quite covered. Then the man twisted and twirled at the quern to get it to stop, but for all his twisting and fingering the quern went on grinding, and in a little while the broth rose so high that the man was like to drown. So he threw open the kitchen door and ran into the parlour, but it wasn't long before the quern had ground the parlour full too, and it was only at the risk of his life that the man could get hold of the latch of the house door through the stream of broth. When he got the door open, he ran out and set off down the road, with the stream of herrings and broth at his heels, roaring like a waterfall over the whole farm.

Now, his old dame, who was in the field tossing hay, thought it a long time to dinner and at last she said—

'Well! though the master doesn't call us home, we may as well go. Maybe he finds it hard work to boil the broth, and will be glad of my help.'

The men were willing enough, so they sauntered homewards; but just as they had got a little way up the hill, what should they meet but herrings, and broth, and bread, all running and dashing, and splashing together in a stream, and the master himself running before them for his life, and as he passed them he bawled out,—'Would to heaven each of you had a hundred throats! but take care you're not drowned in the broth.'

Away he went, as though the Evil One were at his heels, to his brother's house, and begged him for God's sake to take back the quern that instant; for, said he—

'If it grinds only one hour more the whole parish will be swallowed up by herrings and broth.'

But his brother wouldn't hear of taking it back till the other paid him down three hundred dollars more.

So the poor brother got both the money and the quern, and it wasn't long before he set up a farm-house far finer than the one in which his brother lived, and with the quern he ground so much gold that he covered it with plates of gold; and as the farm lay by the sea-side, the golden house gleamed and glistened far away over the sea. All who sailed by put ashore to see the rich man in the golden house, and to see the wonderful quern, the fame of which spread far and wide, till there was nobody who hadn't heard tell of it.

So one day there came a skipper who wanted to see the quern; and the first thing he asked was if it could grind salt.

'Grind salt!' said the owner; 'I should just think it could. It can grind anything.'

When the skipper heard that, he said he must have the quern, cost what it would; for if he only had it, he thought he should be rid of his long voyages across stormy seas for a lading of salt. Well, at first the man wouldn't hear of parting with the quern; but the skipper begged and prayed so hard, that at last he let him have it, but he had to pay many, many thousand dollars for it. Now, when the skipper had got the quern on his back, he soon made off with it, for he was afraid lest the man should change his mind; so he had no time to ask how to handle the quern, but got on board his ship as fast as he could, and set sail. When he had sailed a good way off, he brought the quern on deck and said—

'Grind salt, and grind both good and fast.'

Well, the quern began to grind salt so that it poured out like water; and when the skipper had got the ship full, he wished to stop the quern, but whichever way he turned it, and however much he tried, it was no good; the quern kept grinding on, and the heap of salt grew higher and higher, and at last down sunk the ship.

There lies the quern at the bottom of the sea, and grinds away at this very day; and that's why the sea is salt.

THE LAD AND THE DEIL

Once on a time there was a lad who was walking along a road cracking nuts, so he found one that was worm-eaten, and just at that very moment he met the Deil.

'Is it true, now,' said the lad, 'what they say, that the Deil can make himself as small as he chooses, and thrust himself in through a pinhole?'

'Yes, it is,' said the Deil.

'Oh! it is, is it? then let me see you do it, and just creep into this nut,' said the lad.

So the Deil did.

Now, when he had crept well into it through the worm's hole, the lad stopped it up with a pin.

'Now, I've got you safe,' he said, and put the nut into his pocket.

So when he had walked on a bit, he came to a smithy, and he turned in and asked the smith if he'd be good enough to crack that nut for him.

'Ay, that'll be an easy job,' said the smith, and took his smallest hammer, laid the nut on the anvil, and gave it a blow, but it wouldn't break.

So he took another hammer a little bigger, but that wasn't heavy enough either.

Then he took one bigger still, but it was still the same story; and so the smith got wroth, and grasped his great sledge-hammer.

'Now, I'll crack you to bits,' he said, and let drive at the nut with all his might and main. And so the nut flew to pieces with a bang that blew off half the roof of the smithy, and the whole house creaked and groaned as though it were ready to fall.

'Why! if I don't think the Deil must have been in that nut,' said the smith.

'So he was; you're quite right,' said the lad, as he went away laughing.

XXXV

THE DEFENCE OF LUCKNOW

I.

BANNER of England, not for a season, O banner of Britain, hast thou
    Floated in conquering battle or flapt to the battle-cry!
Never with mightier glory than when we had rear'd thee on high
Flying at top of the roofs in the ghastly siege of Lucknow—
Shot thro' the staff or the halyard, but ever we raised thee anew,
And ever upon the topmost roof our banner of England blew.

II.

Frail were the works that defended the hold that we held
  with our lives—
Women and children among us, God help them, our children
  and wives!
Hold it we might—and for fifteen days or for twenty at
  most.
'Never surrender, I charge you, but every man die at his
  post!'
Voice of the dead whom we loved, our Lawrence, the best
  of the brave:
Cold were his brows when we kiss'd him—we laid him that
  night in his grave,
'Every man die at his post!' and there hail'd on our houses
  and halls
Death from their rifle-bullets, and death from their cannon-
  balls,
Death in our innermost chamber, and death at our slight
  barricade,
Death while we stood with the musket, and death while we
  stoopt to the spade,
Death to the dying, and wounds to the wounded, for often
  there fell,
Striking the hospital wall, crashing thro' it, their shot and
  their shell,
Death—for their spies were among us, their marksmen were
  told of our best,
So that the brute bullet broke thro' the brain that could
  think for the rest;
Bullets would sing by our foreheads, and bullets would rain
  at our feet—
Fire from ten thousand at once of the rebels that girdled us
  round—
Death at the glimpse of a finger from over the breadth of a
  street,
Death from the heights of the mosque and the palace, and
  death in the ground!

Mine? yes, a mine! Countermine! down, down! and creep thro' the hole!
Keep the revolver in hand! you can hear him—the murderous mole!
Quiet, ah! quiet—wait till the point of the pickaxe be thro'!
Click with the pick, coming nearer and nearer again than before—
Now let it speak, and you fire, and the dark pioneer is no more;
And ever upon the topmost roof our banner of England blew!

III.

Ay, but the foe sprung his mine many times, and it chanced on a day
Soon as the blast of that underground thunderclap echo'd away,
Dark thro' the smoke and the sulphur like so many fiends in their hell—
Cannon-shot, musket-shot, volley on volley, and yell upon yell—
Fiercely on all the defences our myriad enemy fell.
What have they done? Where is it? Out yonder? Guard the Redan!
Storm at the Water-gate! storm at the Bailey-gate! storm, and it ran
Surging and swaying all round us, as ocean on every side
Plunges and heaves at a bank that is daily devour'd by the tide—
So many thousands that, if they be bold enough, who shall escape?
Kill or be kill'd, live or die, they shall know we are soldiers and men!
Ready! take aim at their leaders—their masses are gapp'd with our grape—
Backward they reel like the wave, like the wave flinging forward again,

Flying and foil'd at the last by the handful they could not subdue;
And ever upon the topmost roof our banner of England blew.

IV.

Handful of men as we were, we were English in heart and in limb,
Strong with the strength of the race to command, to obey, to endure,
Each of us fought as if hope for the garrison hung but on him;
Still—could we watch at all points? we were every day fewer and fewer.
There was a whisper among us, but only a whisper that past:
'Children and wives—if the tigers leap into the fold unawares—
Every man die at his post—and the foe may outlive us at last—
Better to fall by the hands that they love, than to fall into theirs!'
Roar upon roar in a moment two mines by the enemy sprung
Clove into perilous chasms our walls and our poor palisades.
Rifleman, true is your heart, but be sure that your hand be as true!
Sharp is the fire of assault, better aimed are your flank fusillades—
Twice do we hurl them to earth from the ladders to which they had clung,
Twice from the ditch where they shelter we drive them with hand-grenades;
And ever upon the topmost roof our banner of England blew.

V.

Then on another wild morning another wild earthquake out-tore
Clean from our lines of defence ten or twelve good paces or more.

Rifleman, high on the roof, hidden there from the light of
  the sun—
One has leapt up on the breach, crying out: 'Follow me,
  follow me!'—
Mark him—he falls! then another, and *him* too, and down
  goes he.
Had they been bold enough then, who can tell but the
  traitors had won?
Boardings and rafters and doors—an embrasure! make way
  for the gun!
Now double-charge it with grape! It is charged and we
  fire, and they run.
Praise to our Indian brothers, and let the dark face have his
  due!
Thanks to the kindly dark faces who fought with us, faithful
  and few,
Fought with the bravest among us, and drove them, and
  smote them, and slew,
That ever upon the topmost roof our banner in India blew.

VI.

Men will forget what we suffer and not what we do. We
  can fight!
But to be soldier all day and be sentinel all thro' the night—
Ever the mine and assault, our sallies, their lying alarms,
Bugles and drums in the darkness, and shoutings and sound-
  ings to arms,
Ever the labour of fifty that had to be done by five,
Ever the marvel among us that one should be left alive,
Ever the day with its traitorous death from the loopholes
  around,
Ever the night with its coffinless corpse to be laid in the
  ground,
Heat like the mouth of a hell, or a deluge of cataract skies,
Stench of old offal decaying, and infinite torment of flies,
Thoughts of the breezes of May blowing over an English
  field,

Cholera, scurvy, and fever, the wound that *would* not be heal'd,
Lopping away of the limb by the pitiful-pitiless knife,—
Torture and trouble in vain,—for it never could save us a life.
Valour of delicate women who tended the hospital bed,
Horror of women in travail among the dying and dead,
Grief for our perishing children, and never a moment for grief,
Toil and ineffable weariness, faltering hopes of relief,
Havelock baffled, or beaten, or butcher'd for all that we knew—
Then day and night, day and night, coming down on the still-shatter'd walls
Millions of musket-bullets, and thousands of cannon-balls—
But ever upon the topmost roof our banner of England blew.

VII.

Hark cannonade, fusillade! is it true what was told by the scout,
Outram and Havelock breaking their way through the fell mutineers?
Surely the pibroch of Europe is ringing again in our ears!
All on a sudden the garrison utter a jubilant shout,
Havelock's glorious Highlanders answer with conquering cheers,
Sick from the hospital echo them, women and children come out,
Blessing the wholesome white faces of Havelock's good fusileers,
Kissing the war-harden'd hand of the Highlander wet with their tears!
Dance to the pibroch!—saved! we are saved—is it you? is it you?
Saved by the valour of Havelock, saved by the blessing of Heaven!
'Hold it for fifteen days!' we have held it for eighty-seven!
And ever aloft on the palace roof the old banner of England blew.

XXXVI

CHARLES LAMB TO A FRIEND IN CHINA

January 2, 1810.

DEAR MANNING—When I last wrote to you I was in lodgings. I am now in chambers, No. 4, Inner Temple Lane, where I should be happy to see you any evening. Bring any of your friends, the Mandarins, with you. I have two sitting-rooms: I call them so *par excellence*, for you may stand, or loll, or lean, or try any posture in them, but they are best for sitting; not squatting down Japanese fashion, but the more decorous use of the posteriors which European usage has consecrated. I have two of these rooms on the third floor, and five sleeping, cooking, etc., rooms, on the fourth floor. In my best room is a choice collection of the works of Hogarth, an English painter of some humour. In my next best are shelves containing a small but well-chosen library. My best room commands a court, in which there are trees and a pump, the water of which is excellent—cold with brandy, and not very insipid without. Here I hope to set up my rest, and not quit till Mr. Powell, the undertaker, gives me notice that I may have possession of my last lodging. He lets lodgings for single gentlemen. I sent you a parcel of books by my last, to give you some idea of the state of European literature. There comes with this two volumes, done up as letters, of minor poetry, a sequel to 'Mrs. Leicester'; the best you may suppose mine; the next best are my coadjutor's. You may amuse yourself in guessing them out; but I must tell you mine are but one-third in quantity of the whole. So much for a very delicate subject. It is hard to speak of one's self, etc. Holcroft had finished his life when I wrote to you, and Hazlitt has since finished his life; I do not mean his own life, but he has finished a life of Holcroft, which is going to press. Tuthill is Dr. Tuthill. I continue Mr. Lamb. I have published a little book for children on titles of honour; and to give them some idea of the difference of rank and gradual rising, I have made a little scale, supposing myself to receive the following various accessions of dignity from the king, who is the fountain of honour—As at first, 1, Mr. C. Lamb; 2, C. Lamb, Esq.; 3, Sir C. Lamb, Bart.; 4, Baron Lamb, of Stamford; 5, Viscount Lamb; 6, Earl Lamb; 7, Marquis Lamb; 8, Duke Lamb. It would look like quibbling to carry it on further, and especially as it is not necessary for children to go beyond the ordinary titles of sub-regal dignity in our own country; otherwise I have sometimes in my dreams imagined myself still advancing, as 9th, King Lamb; 10th, Emperor Lamb; 11th, Pope Innocent; higher than which is nothing but the Lamb of God. Puns I have not made many (nor punch much) since the date of my last; one I cannot help relating. A constable in Salisbury Cathedral was telling me that eight people dined at the top of the spire of the cathedral; upon which I remarked, that they must be very sharp set. But in general I cultivate the reasoning part of my mind more than the imaginative. I am stuffed out so with eating turkey for dinner, and another turkey for supper yesterday (Turkey in Europe and Turkey in Asia), that I can't jog on. It is New Year here; that is, it was New Year half a year back, when I was writing this. Nothing puzzles me more than time and space; and yet nothing puzzles me less, for I never think about them. The Persian ambassador is the principal thing talked of now. I sent some people to see him worship the sun on Primrose Hill, at half-past six in the morning, 28th November; but he did not come, which makes me think the old fire-worshippers are a sect almost extinct in Persia. The Persian ambassador's name is Shaw Ali Mirza. The common people call him Shaw Nonsense. While I think of it, I have put three letters, besides my own three, into the India Post for you, from your brother, sister, and some gentleman whose name I forget. Will they, have they, did they come safe? The distance you are at, cuts up tenses by the root. I think you said you did not know Kate ✱✱✱✱✱✱ ✱✱✱. I express her by nine stars, though she is but one. You must have seen her at her father's. Try and remember her. Coleridge is bringing out a paper in weekly Numbers, called the *Friend*, which I would send if I could; but the difficulty I had in getting the packets of books out to you before, deters me; and you'll want something new to read when you come home. It is chiefly intended to puff off Wordsworth's poetry; but there are some noble things in it by the by. Except Kate, I have had no vision of excellence this year, and she passed by like the Queen on her coronation day; you don't know whether you saw her or not. Kate is fifteen: I go about moping, and sing the old pathetic ballad I used to like in my youth—

> 'She's sweet fifteen,
> I'm *one year more*.'

Mrs. Bland sang it in boy's clothes the first time I heard it. I sometimes think the lower notes in my voice are like Mrs. Bland's. That glorious singer, Braham, one of my lights, is fled. He was for a season. He was a rare composition of the Jew, the gentleman, and the angel; yet all these elements mixed up so kindly in him, that you could not tell which preponderated; but he is gone, and one Phillips is engaged instead. Kate is vanished, but Miss B—— is always to be met with!

'Queens drop away, while blue-legg'd Maukin thrives;
And courtly Mildred dies while country Madge survives.'

That is not my poetry, but Quarles's; but haven't you observed that the rarest things are the least obvious? Don't show anybody the names in this letter. I write confidentially, and wish this letter to be considered as *private*. Hazlitt has written a *grammar* for Godwin; Godwin sells it bound up with a treatise of his own on language; but the *gray mare is the better horse*. I don't allude to Mrs. Godwin, but to the word *grammar*, which comes near to *gray mare*, if you observe, in sound. That figure is called paronomasia in Greek. I am sometimes happy in it. An old woman begged of me for charity. 'Ah! sir,' said she, 'I have seen better days.' 'So have I, good woman,' I replied; but I meant, literally, days not so rainy and overcast as that on which she begged: she meant more prosperous days. Mr. Dawe is made associate of the Royal Academy. By what law of association I can't guess. Mrs. Holcroft, Miss Holcroft, Mr. and Mrs. Godwin, Mr. and Mrs. Hazlitt, Mrs. Martin and Louisa, Mrs. Lum, Capt. Burney, Mrs. Burney, Martin Burney, Mr. Rickman, Mrs. Rickman, Dr. Stoddart, William Dollin, Mr. Thompson, Mr. and Mrs. Norris, Mr. Fenwick, Mrs. Fenwick, Miss Fenwick, a man that saw you at our house one day, and a lady that heard me speak of you; Mrs. Buffam that heard Hazlitt mention you, Dr. Tuthill, Mrs. Tuthill, Colonel Harwood, Mrs. Harwood, Mr. Collier, Mrs. Collier, Mr. Sutton, Nurse, Mr. Fell, Mrs. Fell, Mr. Marshall, are very well, and occasionally inquire after you,

I remain yours ever,
Ch. Lamb.

XXXVII

NAVAL BALLADS

WE CONQUER TO SAVE

(A Song of the Napoleonic War)

WHEN in war on the ocean we meet the proud foe
Tho' with ardour for conquest our bosoms may glow;
Let us see on their vessels old England's flag wave,
They shall find British sailors but conquer to save.

See their tri-colour'd ensigns we view from afar,
With three cheers they are welcom'd by each British tar;
While the genius of Britain still bids us advance,
Our guns hurl in thunders defiance to France.

But mark the last broadside: she sinks, down she goes;
Quickly man all your boats, they no longer are foes;
To snatch a brave fellow from a wat'ry grave,
Is worthy of Britons—who conquer to save.

Happy land! thou hast now in defence of thy rights
Brave Nelson, who the man and the hero unites;
The friend to the wretched, the boast of the brave;
He lives but to conquer, and conquers to save.

THE ISLAND

Daddy Neptune one day to Freedom did say,
  If ever I lived upon dry land,
The spot I should hit on would be little Britain.
  Says Freedom, Why that's my own Island.
    O what a snug little Island!
    A right little, tight little Island!
      All the globe round,
      None can be found
    So happy as this little Island.

Julius Cæsar the Roman, who yielded to no man,
  Came by water—he cou'dn't come by land;
And Dane, Pict, and Saxon their homes turn'd their backs on,
  And all for the sake of our Island.
    Oh what a snug little Island!
    They'd have a touch at the Island!
      Some were shot dead,
      Some of them fled,
    And some stay'd to live in the Island.

Then a very great war-man, called Billy the Norman,
  Cried, D——n it! I never lik'd my land;
It would be much more handy to leave this Normandy
  And live on yon beautiful Island!

Says he, 'Tis a snug little Island!
Sha'n't us go visit the Island?
    Hop, skip, and jump,
    There he was plump,
And he kick'd up a dust in the Island.

But party deceit helpt the Normans to beat,
  Of traitors they manag'd to buy land;
By Dane, Saxon, or Pict we ne'er should be lick'd
  Had they stuck to the king of their Island!
    Poor Harold the king of the Island!
    He lost both his life and his Island!
      That's very true,
      What could he do?
    Like a Briton he died for his Island!

The Spanish Armada set out to invade her,
  Quite sure, if they ever came nigh land,
They cou'dn't do less than tuck up Queen Bess,
  And take their full swing in the Island.
    Oh the poor Queen and the Island!
    The Dons came to plunder the Island!
      But snug in the hive,
      The Queen was alive,
    And *buz* was the word at the Island!

These proud puff'd-up cakes thought to make ducks and drakes
Of our wealth; but they scarcely could spy land
Ere our Drake had the luck to make their pride duck,
  And stoop to the lads of the Island.
    Huzza for the lads of the island!
    The good wooden walls of the Island!
      Devil or Don,
      Let 'em come on,
    But how would they come off the Island?

Then Freedom and Neptune have hitherto kept tune
  In each saying this shall be my land;
Should the army of England, or all they could bring, land,
  We'd show 'em some play for the Island.
    We'll fight for our right to the Island!
    We'll give them enough of the Island!
      Invaders should just
      Bite at the dust,
    But not a bit more of the Island.

BLACK-EYED SUSAN

All in the Downs the fleet was moor'd,
  The streamers waving to the wind,
When black-ey'd Susan came on board:
  Oh! where shall I my true love find.
Tell me, ye jovial sailors, tell me true,
If my sweet William sails among your crew?

William, who high upon the yard,
  Rock'd with the billows to and fro,
Soon as her well-known voice he heard,
  He sigh'd and cast his eyes below;
The cords glide swiftly through his glowing hands,
And quick as lightning on the deck he stands.

So the sweet lark, high pois'd in air,
  Shuts close his pinions to his breast,
If chance his mate's shrill call he hear,
  And drops at once into her nest.
The noblest captain in the British fleet
Might envy William's lips those kisses sweet.

O Susan, Susan, lovely dear,
  My vows shall ever true remain;
Let me kiss off that falling tear,
  We only part to meet again.
Change as ye list, ye winds, my heart shall be
The faithful compass that still points to thee.

Believe not what the landmen say,
    Who tempt with doubts thy constant mind,
They'll tell thee, sailors, when away,
    In ev'ry port a mistress find.
Yes, yes, believe them when they tell thee so,
For thou art present wheresoe'er I go.

If to fair India's coast we sail,
    Thy eyes are seen in di'monds bright;
Thy breath in Afric's spicy gale,
    Thy skin in ivory so white.
Thus ev'ry beauteous object that I view,
Wakes in my soul some charm of lovely Sue.

Though battle calls me from thy arms,
    Let not my pretty Susan mourn;
Though cannons roar, yet safe from harms,
    William shall to his dear return.
Love turns aside the balls that round me fly,
Lest precious tears should drop from Susan's eye.

The boatswain gave the dreadful word,
    The sails their swelling bosom spread;
No longer must she stay aboard;
    They kiss'd, she sigh'd, he hung his head.
Her less'ning boat unwilling rows to land;
Adieu, she cries, and wav'd her lily hand!

THE ENGLISHMAN'S IDOLATRY

Our *Trimmer* is far from Idolatry in other things, in one thing only he cometh near it, his Country is in some degree his Idol; he doth not Worship the Sun, because 'tis not peculiar to us, it rambles about the World, and is less kind to us than others; but for the Earth of *England*, tho' perhaps inferior to that of many places abroad, to him there is Divinity in it, and he would rather dye, than see a spire of *English* grass trampled down by a Foreign Trespasser: He thinketh there are a great many of his mind, for all plants are apt to taste of the Soyl in which they grow, and we that grow here have a Root that produceth in us a Stalk of English Juice, which is not to be changed by grafting or foreign infusion; and I do not know whether anything less will prevail, than the Modern Experiment, by which the Blood of one Creature is transmitted into another; according to which, before the *French* blood can be let into our Bodies, every drop of our own must be drawn out of them.

XXXVIII

FROM DR. JOHNSON

JOHNSON'S DICTIONARY

IN hope of giving longevity to that which its own nature forbids to be immortal, I have devoted this book, the labour of years, to the honour of my country, that we may no longer yield the palm of philology, without a contest, to the nations of the continent. The chief glory of every people arises from its authors: whether I shall add anything by my own writings to the reputation of *English* literature, must be left to time: much of my life has been lost under the pressures of disease; much has been trifled away; and much has always been spent in provision for the day that was passing over me; but I shall not think my employment useless or ignoble, if by my assistance foreign nations, and distant ages, gain access to the propagators of knowledge, and understand the teachers of truth; if my labours afford light to the repositories of science, and add celebrity to *Bacon*, to *Hooker*, to *Milton*, and to *Boyle*.

When I am animated by this wish, I look with pleasure on my book, however defective, and deliver it to the world with the spirit of a man that has endeavoured well. That it will immediately become popular I have not promised to myself: a few wild blunders, and risible absurdities, from which no work of such multiplicity was ever free, may for a time furnish folly with laughter, and harden ignorance into contempt; but useful diligence will at last prevail, and there never can be wanting some who distinguish desert; who will consider that no dictionary of a living tongue ever can be perfect, since, while it is hastening to publication, some words are budding, and some falling away; that a whole life cannot be spent upon syntax and etymology, and that even a whole life would not be sufficient; that he, whose design includes whatever language can express, must often speak of what he does not understand; that a writer will sometimes be hurried by eagerness to the end, and sometimes faint with weariness under a task, which *Scaliger* compares to the labours of the anvil and the mine; that what is obvious is not always known, and what is known is not always present; that sudden fits of inadvertency will surprise vigilance, slight avocations will seduce attention, and casual eclipses of the mind will darken learning; and that the writer shall often in vain trace his memory at the moment of need, for that which yesterday he knew with intuitive readiness, and which will come uncalled into his thoughts to-morrow.

In this work, when it shall be found that much is omitted, let it not be forgotten that much likewise is performed; and though no book was ever spared out of tenderness to the author, and the world is little solicitous to know whence proceed the faults of that which it condemns; yet it may gratify curiosity to inform it, that the *English Dictionary* was written with little assistance of the learned, and without any patronage of the great; not in the soft obscurities of retirement, or under the shelter of academick bowers, but amidst inconvenience and distraction, in sickness and in sorrow. It may repress the triumph of malignant criticism to observe, that if our language is not here fully displayed, I have only failed in an attempt which no human powers have hitherto completed. If the lexicons of ancient tongues, now immutably fixed, and comprised in a few volumes, be yet, after the toil of successive ages, inadequate and delusive; if the aggregated knowledge, and co-operating diligence of the *Italian* academicians, did not secure them from the censure of *Beni*; if the embodied criticks of *France*, when fifty years had been spent upon their work, were obliged to change its œconomy, and give their second edition another form, I may surely be contented without the praise of perfection, which, if I could obtain, in this gloom of solitude, what would it avail me? I have protracted my work till most of those whom I wished to please have sunk into the grave, and success and miscarriage are empty sounds: I therefore dismiss it with frigid tranquillity, having little to fear or hope from censure or from praise.

JOHNSON ON PATIENCE

Patience and submission are very carefully to be distinguished from cowardice and indolence. We are not to repine, but we may lawfully struggle; for the calamities of life, like the necessities of nature, are calls to labour and exercises of diligence. When we feel any pressure of distress, we are not to conclude that we can only obey the will of heaven by languishing under it, any more than when we perceive the pain of thirst, we are to imagine that water is prohibited. Of misfortune it never can be certainly known whether, as proceeding from the hand of God, it is an act of favour or of punishment: but since all the ordinary dispensations of Providence are to be interpreted according to the general analogy of things, we may conclude that we have a right to remove one inconvenience as well as another; that we are only to take care lest we purchase ease with guilt; and that our Maker's purpose, whether of reward or severity, will be answered by the labours which he lays us under the necessity of performing.

This duty is not more difficult in any state than in diseases intensely painful, which may indeed suffer such exacerbations as seem to strain the powers of life to their utmost stretch, and leave very little of the attention vacant to precept or reproof. In this state the nature of man requires some indulgence, and every extravagance but impiety may be easily forgiven him. Yet, lest we should think ourselves too soon entitled to the mournful privileges of irresistible misery, it is proper to reflect, that the utmost anguish which human wit can contrive or human malice can inflict, has been borne with constancy; and that if the pains of disease be, as I believe they are, sometimes greater than those of artificial torture, they are therefore in their own nature shorter: the vital frame is quickly broken, or the union between soul and body is for a time suspended by insensibility, and we soon cease to feel our maladies when they once become too violent to be borne. I think there is some reason for questioning whether the body and mind are not so proportioned, that the one can bear all that can be inflicted on the other, whether virtue cannot stand its ground as long as life, and whether a soul well principled will not be separated sooner than subdued.

EPITAPH ON ROBERT LEVETT

[*Robert Levett was a doctor of medicine who practised in London, for small fees or none, among the poorest of the poor. He lived with Johnson for many years, and died in 1782. 'So ended,' wrote Johnson, 'the long life of a very useful and very blameless man.'*]

Condemn'd to Hope's delusive mine,
    As on we toil from day to day,
By sudden blast or slow decline
    Our social comforts drop away.

Well try'd through many a varying year,
    See Levett to the grave descend;
Officious, innocent, sincere,
    Of every friendless name the friend.

Yet still he fills affection's eye,
    Obscurely wise, and coarsely kind,
Nor, letter'd arrogance, deny
    Thy praise to merit unrefin'd.

When fainting Nature call'd for aid,
    And hov'ring Death prepar'd the blow,
His vigorous remedy display'd
    The power of art without the show.

In Misery's darkest caverns known,
  His ready help was ever nigh,
Where hopeless Anguish pour'd his groan,
  And lonely Want retir'd to die.

No summons mock'd by chill delay,
  No petty gains disdain'd by pride;
The modest wants of every day
  The toil of every day supply'd.

His virtues walk'd their narrow round,
  Nor made a pause, nor left a void;
And sure the eternal Master found
  His single talent well employ'd.

The busy day, the peaceful night,
  Unfelt, uncounted, glided by;
His frame was firm, his powers were bright,
  Though now his eightieth year was nigh.

Then, with no throbs of fiery pain,
  No cold gradations of decay,
Death broke at once the vital chain,
  And freed his soul the nearest way.

XXXIX

GERARD, DENYS AND THE BEAR

GERARD did not answer; for his ear was attracted by a sound behind them. It was a peculiar sound too, like something heavy, but not hard, rushing softly over the dead leaves. He turned round with some little curiosity. A colossal creature was coming down the road at about sixty paces distance.

He looked at it in a sort of calm stupor at first; but the next moment he turned ashy pale.

'Denys!' he cried. 'O God! Denys!'

Denys whirled round.

It was a bear as big as a cart-horse.

It was tearing along with its huge head down, running on a hot scent.

The very moment he saw it Denys said in a sickening whisper—

'THE CUB!'

Oh! the concentrated horror of that one word, whispered hoarsely, with dilating eyes! For in that syllable it all flashed upon them both like a sudden stroke of lightning in the dark—the bloody trail, the murdered cub, the mother upon them, *and it*. Death.

All this in a moment of time. The next, she saw them. Huge as she was, she seemed to double herself (it was her long hair bristling with rage): she raised her head big as a bull's, her swine-shaped jaws opened wide at them, her eyes turned to blood and flame, and she rushed upon them, scattering the leaves about her like a whirlwind as she came.

'Shoot!' screamed Denys, but Gerard stood shaking from head to foot, useless.

'Shoot, man! ten thousand devils, shoot! too late! Tree! tree!' and he dropped the cub, pushed Gerard across the road, and flew to the first tree and climbed it, Gerard the same on his side; and, as they fled, both men uttered inhuman howls like savage creatures grazed by death.

With all their speed one or other would have been torn to fragments at the foot of his tree; but the bear stopped a moment at the cub.

Without taking her bloodshot eyes off those she was hunting, she smelt it all round, and found—how, her Creator only knows—that it was dead, quite dead. She gave a yell such as neither of the hunted ones had ever heard, nor dreamed to be in nature ; and flew after Denys. She reared and struck at him as he climbed. He was just out of reach.

Instantly she seized the tree, and with her huge teeth tore a great piece out of it with a crash. Then she reared again, dug her claws deep into the bark, and began to mount it slowly, but as surely as a monkey.

Denys's evil star had led him to a dead tree, a mere shaft, and of no very great height. He climbed faster than his pursuer, and was soon at the top. He looked this way and that for some bough of another tree to spring to. There was none: and, if he jumped down, he knew the bear would be upon him ere he could recover the fall, and make short work of him. Moreover Denys was little used to turning his back on danger, and his blood was rising at being hunted. He turned to bay.

'My hour is come,' thought he. 'Let me meet death like a man.' He kneeled down and grasped a small shoot to steady himself, drew his long knife, and, clenching his teeth, prepared to jab the huge brute as soon as it should mount within reach.

Of this combat the result was not doubtful.

The monster's head and neck were scarce vulnerable for bone and masses of hair. The man was going to sting the bear, and the bear to crack the man like a nut.

Gerard's heart was better than his nerves. He saw his friend's mortal danger, and passed at once from fear to blindish rage. He slipped down his tree in a moment, caught up the cross-bow, which he had dropped in the road, and, running furiously up, sent a bolt into the bear's body with a loud shout. The bear gave a snarl of rage and pain, and turned its head irresolutely.

'Keep aloof!' cried Denys, 'or you are a dead man.'

'I care not;' and in a moment he had another bolt ready and shot it fiercely into the bear, screaming, 'Take that! take that!'

Denys poured a volley of oaths down at him. 'Get away, idiot!'

He was right: the bear, finding so formidable and noisy a foe behind him, slipped growling down the tree, rending deep furrows in it as she slipped. Gerard ran back to his tree and climbed it swiftly. But while his legs were dangling some eight feet from the ground, the bear came rearing and struck with her fore paw, and out flew a piece of bloody cloth from Gerard's hose. He climbed, and climbed; and presently he heard as it were in the air a voice say, 'Go out on the bough!' He looked, and there was a long massive branch before him shooting upwards at a slight angle; he threw his body across it, and by a series of convulsive efforts worked up it to the end.

Then he looked round panting.

The bear was mounting the tree on the other side. He heard her claws scrape, and saw her bulge on both sides of the massive tree. Her eye not being very quick she reached the fork and passed it, mounting the main stem. Gerard drew breath more freely. The bear either heard him, or found by scent she was wrong: she paused; presently she caught sight of him. She eyed him steadily; then quietly descended to the fork.

Slowly and cautiously she stretched out a paw and tried the bough. It was a stiff oak branch, sound as iron. Instinct taught the creature this: it crawled carefully out on the bough, growling savagely as it came.

Gerard looked wildly down. He was forty feet from the ground. Death below. Death moving slow but sure on him in a still more horrible form. His hair bristled. The sweat poured from him. He sat helpless, fascinated, tongue-tied.

As the fearful monster crawled growling towards him, incongruous thoughts coursed through his mind. Margaret: the Vulgate, where it speaks of the rage of a she-bear robbed of her whelps,—Rome,—Eternity.

The bear crawled on. And now the stupor of death fell on the doomed man; he saw the open jaws and bloodshot eyes coming, but in a mist.

As in a mist he heard a twang: he glanced down; Denys, white and silent as death, was shooting up at the bear. The bear snarled at the twang; but crawled on. Again the cross-bow twanged; and the bear snarled; and came nearer. Again the cross-bow twanged: and the next moment the bear was close upon Gerard, where he sat, with hair standing stiff on end, and eyes starting from their sockets, palsied. The bear opened her jaws like a grave; and hot blood spouted from them upon Gerard as from a pump. The bough rocked. The wounded monster was reeling; it clung, it stuck its sickles of claws deep into the wood; it toppled, its claws held firm, but its body rolled off, and the sudden shock to the branch shook Gerard forward on his stomach with his face upon one of the bear's straining paws. At this, by a convulsive effort, she raised her head up, up, till he felt her hot fetid breath. Then her huge teeth snapped together loudly close below him in the air, with a last effort of baffled hate. The ponderous carcass rent the claws out of the bough; then pounded the earth with a tremendous thump. There was a shout of triumph below, and the very next instant a cry of dismay; for Gerard had swooned, and, without an attempt to save himself, rolled headlong from the perilous height.

Denys caught at Gerard, and somewhat checked his fall: but it may be doubted whether this alone would have saved him from breaking his neck or a limb. His best friend now was the dying bear, on whose hairy carcass his head and shoulders descended. Denys tore him off her. It was needless. She panted still, and her limbs quivered, but a hare was not so harmless; and soon she breathed her last: and the judicious Denys propped Gerard up against her, being soft, and fanned him. He came to by degrees, but confused, and feeling the bear all around him, rolled away yelling.

'Courage,' cried Denys, 'le diable est mort.'

XL

THREE POEMS BY MARVELL

BERMUDAS

WHERE the remote Bermudas ride,
In the ocean's bosom unespied,
From a small boat, that rowed along,
The listening winds received this song:

'What should we do but sing His praise,
That led us through the watery maze,
Unto an isle so long unknown,
And yet far kinder than our own?
Where He the huge sea-monsters wracks,
That lift the deep upon their backs;
He lands us on a grassy stage,
Safe from the storms, and prelate's rage.
He gave us this eternal spring,
Which here enamels every thing,
And sends the fowls to us in care,
On daily visits through the air;
He hangs in shades the orange bright,
Like golden lamps in a green night,
And does in the pomegranates close
Jewels more rich than Ormus shows;
He makes the figs our mouths to meet
And throws the melons at our feet;
But apples plants of such a price,
No tree could ever bear them twice;
With cedars chosen by His hand,
From Lebanon, He stores the land,
And makes the hollow seas, that roar,
Proclaim the ambergris on shore;
He cast (of which we rather boast)
The Gospel's pearl upon our coast,
And in these rocks for us did frame
A temple where to sound His name.
Oh! let our voice His praise exalt,
Till it arrive at Heaven's vault,
Which, thence (perhaps) rebounding, may
Echo beyond the Mexique Bay.'

Thus sung they, in the English boat,
An holy and a cheerful note;
And all the way, to guide their chime,
With falling oars they kept the time.

THE GARDEN

How vainly men themselves amaze,
To win the palm, the oak, or bays;
And their incessant labours see
Crowned from some single herb, or tree,
Whose short and narrow-vergèd shade
Does prudently their toils upbraid;
While all the flowers and trees do close,
To weave the garlands of Repose!

Fair Quiet, have I found thee here,
And Innocence, thy sister dear?
Mistaken long, I sought you then
In busy companies of men.
Your sacred plants, if here below,
Only among the plants will grow;
Society is all but rude
To this delicious solitude.

No white nor red was ever seen
So amorous as this lovely green.
Fond lovers, cruel as their flame,
Cut in these trees their mistress' name:
Little, alas! they know or heed,
How far these beauties hers exceed!
Fair trees! wheres'e'er your bark I wound,
No name shall but your own be found.

When we have run our passion's heat,
Love hither makes his best retreat.
The gods, that mortal beauty chase,
Still in a tree did end their race;
Apollo hunted Daphne so,
Only that she might laurel grow;
And Pan did after Syrinx speed,
Not as a nymph, but for a reed.

What wondrous life is this I lead!
Ripe apples drop about my head;
The luscious clusters of the vine
Upon my mouth do crush their wine;
The nectarine, and curious peach,
Into my hands themselves do reach;
Stumbling on melons, as I pass,
Insnared with flowers, I fall on grass.

Meanwhile the mind, from pleasure less,
Withdraws into its happiness;
The mind, that ocean where each kind
Does straight its own resemblance find;
Yet it creates, transcending these,
Far other worlds, and other seas,
Annihilating all that's made
To a green thought in a green shade.

Here at the fountain's sliding foot,
Or at some fruit-tree's mossy root,
Casting the body's vest aside,
My soul into the boughs does glide:
There, like a bird, it sits and sings,
Then whets and combs its silver wings,
And, till prepared for longer flight,
Waves in its plumes the various light.

Such was the happy garden-state,
While man there walked without a mate:
After a place so pure and sweet,
What other help could yet be meet!
But 'twas beyond a mortal's share
To wander solitary there:
Two paradises 'twere in one,
To live in Paradise alone.

How well the skilful gardener drew
Of flowers, and herbs, this dial new;
Where, from above, the milder sun
Does through a fragrant zodiac run,
And, as it works, the industrious bee
Computes its time as well as we!
How could such sweet and wholesome hours
Be reckoned but with herbs and flowers?

A DIALOGUE BETWEEN THE RESOLVED SOUL AND CREATED PLEASURE

Courage, my soul! now learn to wield
The weight of thine immortal shield;
Close on thy head thy helmet bright;
Balance thy sword against the fight;
See where an army, strong as fair,
With silken banners spreads the air!
Now, if thou be'st that thing divine,
In this day's combat let it shine,
And show that Nature wants an art
To conquer one resolvèd heart.

Pleasure. Welcome the creation's guest,
Lord of earth, and Heaven's heir!
Lay aside that warlike crest,
And of Nature's banquet share;
Where the souls of fruits and flowers
Stand prepared to heighten yours.

Soul. I sup above, and cannot stay,
To bait so long upon the way.

Pleasure. On these downy pillows lie,
Whose soft plumes will thither fly:
On these roses, strowed so plain
Lest one leaf thy side should strain.

Soul. My gentler rest is on a thought,
Conscious of doing what I ought.

Pleasure.	If thou be'st with perfumes pleased, Such as oft the gods appeased Thou in fragrant clouds shalt show, Like another god below.
Soul.	A soul that knows not to presume, Is Heaven's, and its own, perfume.
Pleasure.	Everything does seem to vie Which should first attract thine eye; But since none deserves that grace, In this crystal view thy face.
Soul.	When the Creator's skill is prized, The rest is all but earth disguised.
Pleasure.	Hark how music then prepares For thy stay these charming airs, Which the posting winds recall, And suspend the river's fall.
Soul.	Had I but any time to lose, On this I would it all dispose. Cease, tempter! None can chain a mind, Whom this sweet cordage cannot bind.

Chorus.	Earth cannot show so brave a sight,
	   As when a single soul does fence
	   The batteries of alluring sense,
	 And Heaven views it with delight.
	   Then persevere; for still new charges sound,
	   And if thou overcom'st thou shalt be crowned.

Pleasure.	All that's costly, fair, and sweet,
	   Which scatteringly doth shine,
	 Shall within one beauty meet,
	   And she be only thine.

Soul.	If things of sight such heavens be, What heavens are those we cannot see?

Pleasure.	Whereso'er thy foot shall go
	   The minted gold shall lie,
	Till thou purchase all below,
	   And want new worlds to buy.

Soul.	We'rt not for price who'd value gold? And that's worth naught that can be sold.

Pleasure.	Wilt thou all the glory have
	   That war or peace commend?
	Half the world shall be thy slave,
	   The other half thy friend.

Soul.	What friend, if to myself untrue? What slaves, unless I captive you?

Pleasure.	Thou shalt know each hidden cause,
	   And see the future time;
	Try what depth the centre draws,
	   And then to Heaven climb.

Soul.	None thither mounts by the degree Of knowledge, but humility.

Chorus.	Triumph, triumph, victorious soul!
	   The world has not one pleasure more;
	The rest does lie beyond the pole,
	   And is thine everlasting store.

XLI

STORY OF THE FALCON

THERE once lived in Florence a young gentleman named Federigo degli Alberighi, who was reputed for courtesy and feats of arms above all the other gallants in Tuscany. He fell in love with a lady called Monna Giovanna, the fairest and most gracious lady in

STORY OF THE FALCON

Florence, and to win her favour he launched out into lavish expenses of every kind, feasts and banquets, tilts and tournaments. But she, being as virtuous as she was fair, made no account whatever of these things, nor of the giver of them. So Federigo wasted all his substance, and in the end had to retire to a single poor little farm, where he lived with no companion but his favourite hawk or falcon, one of the best in the world; and there living on what his falcon caught for him, he passed his time in poverty and obscurity.

Meantime Monna Giovanna's husband died, leaving all his property to their son, and if the son should die without issue, to Monna Giovanna herself. Being left a widow, she lived during the summer season at a country house which happened to be near Federigo's farm.

The young man, her son, who was fond of coursing and hawking, struck up a friendship with Federigo, and took especial delight in the wonderful flights of the falcon. He greatly coveted to have the falcon for his own, but seeing how dearly Federigo loved her, he forbore to make the request. After a time the youth, who was an only child, fell ill, and, in spite of his mother's care, wasted away. She cherished him night and day, and urged him to ask her for anything that he had a fancy for, promising that she would get it for him if by any means she could. So at last he said, 'If I could only have Federigo's falcon for my own, I believe I should recover.'

The lady stood still for a long time on hearing this, and thought of many things. What could she do? She remembered how Federigo loved the falcon, never letting it go far from him. She remembered how constant he had been in his affection to herself, and how she had never shown him the least token of kindness. 'How dare I send, or go,' she thought, 'and ask him for the falcon, the best that ever flew? How can I be so churlish as to try to take away from this gentleman his one remaining delight?' She knew that she had only to ask for the falcon to have it, and her mind was full of troubled thoughts. At last love for her son prevailed, and she determined, whatever might come of it, not to send, but to go herself and make the request. So she promised her son that she would bring it to him, and at once he began to amend.

The first thing in the morning she took a waiting gentlewoman with her and walked to Federigo's farm. He was in a little garden behind the house, attending to the work of the place, but when he heard that Monna Giovanna was there, he ran to welcome her. She greeted him gently, and said, 'I have come, Federigo, to recompense a part of the loss you had by me, when you offered me more love than it befitted you to give or me to take. And the recompense is this: I and this lady are willing to be your guests, and to dine with you this morning.' Federigo made reverence and said, 'Madonna, I do not remember ever to have had any loss by you, but rather so much gain that if I am worth anything at all it is by virtue of your worthiness and of the love that I bore to you. Your generous visit is more to me than it would be if I had all my riches to spend again, for now you have come to a poor house.' So he received her with diffidence, and took her into his little garden, and said, 'Madonna, since I have no other retinue, this good woman here, the wife of an honest labourer, will attend on you while I make ready the dinner.'

Though his poverty was extreme, he had never felt it till now, for in the house he found nothing to entertain the lady herself for whose sake he had in times past feasted thousands; he was beside himself with distress, and ran hither and thither, cursing his ill-fortune, but found no money, and nothing of value that he could sell for money. He could not bring himself to borrow from the labouring people who served him, much less to beg of anyone else, when suddenly his eyes fell upon his falcon, sitting on its perch in the little room in which he lived. This was his only resource; he took hold of it, and, finding it plump, thought that it would make a dish worthy of his lady. Without more ado he wrung the falcon's neck, and gave it to a little maid to pluck it, and truss it, and put it on the spit, while he laid the table with the few white napkins which were left to him. Then with a more cheerful countenance he went to the lady in the garden and told her that dinner, the best that he could provide, was served. So they sat down, and Federigo waited on them, and, without suspecting what they were eating, they ate the falcon.

When they had risen from the table and had talked pleasantly on indifferent topics for a while, it seemed to the lady that the time was come to tell her errand; so, looking kindly at Federigo, she said, 'Federigo, I daresay when I tell you what brought me here you will be amazed at my presumption, and will think of the past, and of my honourable rejection of you, which perhaps seemed to you nothing but cruelty and hardness of heart; but if you had ever had children, you would forgive me, at least in part, for you would know how strong is the love that binds us to them. Though you have none, I have an only child. I must obey the law that is laid on mothers; I am forced, against my will, to make an unseemly request and to ask you to give me something that is very dear to you, and no wonder, for your hard fortune has left you no other pleasure or comfort in life—I mean your falcon, which has so infatuated my poor boy that if I do not take it home to him he will grow worse, and if complications set in I dread that I may lose him. So I implore you, not for the love that you once felt for me—that is no obligation at all—but in the name of your own generosity, which is greater than ever I found in anyone else, to give me the falcon, so that when it has saved the life of my son he may be your debtor for ever.'

Federigo, hearing what the lady asked, and knowing that he could not help her, because he had given her the falcon to eat, stood with the tears in his eyes, and could not answer her a word. She thought that he grieved at parting with the falcon, and very nearly said she would not take it; however, she controlled herself, and waited to hear his reply. 'Madonna,' he said, when he had mastered his grief, 'since first it pleased God that I should set my love on you, I have often had to lament my fortune, which has been adverse in many things, but all that ever I suffered has been a trifle compared with this. How can I ever forgive my hard fate when I think that you have come to my poor house, where you never would condescend to come while I was rich, and have asked me for a little tiny gift, and it is out of my power to give it you. I will tell you why: When I heard that you were pleased to dine with me, for which I cannot thank you enough, I thought of your nobility and worth, and I felt it only right to honour you, so far as I could, with a dearer entertainment and choicer fare than is offered on common occasions. So I remembered my falcon, which now you ask me to give you, and I thought how splendid a creature she was, and worthy to lay before you. So this very morning you have had her roasted upon a dish, and I felt I could not have put her to a better use. But now that I know you wanted her for quite another purpose, it is so great a grief to me to be unable to serve you that I shall never have peace again for thinking of it.' To witness what he said, he sent for the feathers and talons and beak, and laid them before her.

The lady, when she saw and heard all this, at first felt that he was much to blame for having killed so noble a creature to give a woman something to eat, but when she thought of his greatness of soul, which poverty had no power to abase, she commended him in her secret heart. Having no hope now of getting the falcon, and fearing for her son's health, she took her leave in very low spirits, and returned to her son, who before many days, whether because he was disappointed about the falcon, or perhaps because his disease ran its natural course, died, and left his mother inconsolable. And she, though she continued in great sorrow, yet being rich and still in the flower of her age, was urged by her brothers to marry again. She had no mind to another marriage, yet being plagued without ceasing by her brothers, she called to mind Federigo's loftiness of character and especially the magnificence of his generosity in sacrificing so noble a falcon to do her honour, and she said to them, 'I am well content to stay as I am, if only you would leave me in peace; but if you insist on my marrying again, I must tell you that I will certainly never marry anyone unless it be Federigo degli Alberighi.' Then her brothers laughed at her, and said, 'You silly creature, do you know what you are talking about? How can you take him for a husband; he has not a farthing in the world.' But she replied, 'I know that quite well, but I think it is better to marry a man ill-provided with wealth, than to marry wealth ill-provided with a man.' The brothers, seeing that her mind was fixed, and knowing Federigo for a man of mark, poor though he was, fell in with her wishes, and gave her to him, with all that belonged to her. And he seeing that a lady of such worth, whom he had loved so long and so dearly, was now his wife, and had brought him all her wealth, became a better manager than before, and lived with her in all gladness to the end of his days.

XLII

SAVOY SONGS

THE MIKADO'S SONG

A MORE humane Mikado never
    Did in Japan exist,
      To nobody second,
   I'm certainly reckoned
A true philanthropist.
It is my very humane endeavour
   To make, to some extent,
     Each evil liver
     A running river
Of harmless merriment.

All prosy dull society sinners,
   Who chatter and bleat and bore,
     Are sent to hear sermons
     From mystical Germans
Who preach from ten to four.

The amateur tenor, whose vocal villainies
  All desire to shirk,
    Shall, during off-hours,
    Exhibit his powers
  To Madame Tussaud's waxwork.

The lady who dies a chemical yellow,
  Or stains her grey hair puce,
    Or pinches her figger,
    Is blacked like a nigger
  With permanent walnut juice.
The idiot who, in railway carriages,
  Scribbles on window panes,
    We only suffer
    To ride on a buffer
  In parliamentary trains.

The advertising quack who wearies
  With tales of countless cures,
    His teeth, I've enacted,
    Shall all be extracted
  By terrified amateurs.
The music-hall singer attends a series
  Of masses and fugues and 'ops'
    By Bach, interwoven
    With Spohr and Beethoven,
  At classical Monday Pops.

The billiard sharp whom any one catches,
  His doom's extremely hard—
    He's made to dwell—
    In a dungeon cell
  On a spot that's always barred.
And there he plays extravagant matches
  In fitless finger-stalls
    On a cloth untrue
    With a twisted cue,
  And elliptical billiard balls!

My object all sublime
I shall achieve in time—
To let the punishment fit the crime—
　　The punishment fit the crime;
And make each prisoner pent
Unwillingly represent
A source of innocent merriment,
　　Of innocent merriment!

KING GOODHEART

There lived a king, as I've been told,
In the wonder-working days of old,
When hearts were twice as good as gold
　　And twenty times as mellow.
Good-temper triumphed in his face,
And in his heart he found a place
For all the erring human race
　　And every wretched fellow.
When he had Rhenish wine to drink
It made him very sad to think
That some, at junket or at jink,
　　Must be content with toddy.
He wished all men as rich as he
(And he was rich as rich could be),
So to the top of every tree
　　Promoted everybody.

Lord Chancellors were cheap as sprats,
And Bishops in their shovel hats
Were plentiful as tabby cats—
　　In point of fact, too many.
Ambassadors cropped up like hay,
Prime Ministers and such as they
Grew like asparagus in May,
　　And Dukes were three a penny.
On every side Field Marshals gleamed,
Small beer were Lords Lieutenant deemed,

With Admirals the ocean teemed
    All round his wide dominions.
And Party Leaders you might meet,
In twos and threes in every street,
Maintaining, with no little heat,
    Their various opinions.

That King, although no one denies
His heart was of abnormal size,
Yet he'd have acted otherwise
    If he had been acuter.
The end is easily foretold,
When every blessed thing you hold
Is made of silver, or of gold,
    You long for simple pewter.
When you have nothing else to wear
But cloth of gold and satins rare,
For cloth of gold you cease to care—
    Up goes the price of shoddy.
In short, whoever you may be,
To this conclusion you'll agree,
When every one is somebodee,
    Then no one's anybody!

THE MAJOR-GENERAL'S SONG

I am the very pattern of a modern major-gineral,
I've information vegetable, animal, and mineral;
I know the kings of England, and I quote the fights historical
From Marathon to Waterloo, in order categorical;
I'm very well acquainted too with matters mathematical;
I understand equations, both the simple and quadratical;
About binomial theorem I'm teeming with a lot o' news—
With many cheerful facts about the square of the hypotenuse.
I'm very good at integral and differential calculus;
I know the scientific names of beings animalculous.
In short, in matters vegetable, animal, and mineral,
I am the very model of a modern major-gineral.
I know our mythic history, King Arthur's and Sir Caradoc's
I answer hard acrostics, I've a pretty taste for paradox,

I quote in elegiacs all the crimes of Heliogabalus,
In conics I can floor peculiarities parabolous.
I can tell undoubted Raphaels from Gerard Dows and Zoffanies;
I know the croaking chorus from the 'Frogs' of Aristophanes.
Then I can hum a fugue, of which I've heard the music's din afore,
And whistle all the airs from that confounded nonsense 'Pinafore.'
Then I can write a washing bill in Babylonic cuneiform,
And tell you every detail of Caractacus's uniform.
In short, in matters vegetable, animal, and mineral,
I am the very model of a modern major-gineral.

In fact, when I know what is meant by mamelon and ravelin,
When I can tell at sight a chassepôt rifle from a javelin,
When such affairs as sorties and surprises I'm more wary at,
And when I know precisely what is meant by commissariat,
When I have learnt what progress has been made in modern gunnery,
When I know more of tactics than a novice in a nunnery;
In short, when I've a smattering of elemental strategy,
You'll say a better major-general has never *sat* a gee!
For my military knowledge, though I'm plucky and adventury,
Has only been brought down to the beginning of the century,
But still in learning vegetable, animal, and mineral,
I am the very model of a modern major-gineral.

'IS LIFE A BOON?'

Is life a boon?
    If so, it must befal
    That Death, whene'er he call,
Must call too soon.
    Though fourscore years he give,
    Yet one would pray to live
Another moon!

What kind of plaint have I,
Who perish in July?
I might have had to die,
Perchance, in June!

Is life a thorn?
Then count it not a whit!
Man is well done with it;
Soon as he's born
He should all means essay
To put the plague away;
And I, war-worn,
Poor captured fugitive,
My life most gladly give—
I might have had to live
Another morn!

TITWILLOW

On a tree by a river a little tom-tit
    Sang, 'Willow, titwillow, titwillow!'
And I said to him, 'Dicky-bird, why do you sit
    Singing "Willow, titwillow, titwillow"?'
'Is it weakness of intellect, birdie?' I cried,
'Or a rather tough worm in your little inside?'
With a shake of his poor little head he replied,
    'Oh, willow, titwillow, titwillow!'

He slapped at his chest, as he sat on that bough,
    Singing, 'Willow, titwillow, titwillow!'
And a cold perspiration bespangled his brow,
    Oh, willow, titwillow, titwillow!
He sobbed and he sighed, and a gurgle he gave,
Then he threw himself into the billowy wave,
And an echo arose from the suicide's grave—
    'Oh, willow, titwillow, titwillow!'

Now, I feel just as sure as I'm sure that my name
    Isn't willow, titwillow, titwillow,
That 'twas blighted affection that made him exclaim,
    'Oh, willow, titwillow, titwillow!'

And if you remain callous and obdurate, I
Shall perish as he did, and you will know why,
Though I probably shall not exclaim as I die,
   'Oh, willow, titwillow, titwillow!'

XLIII

THE MIGHTY WORKS OF GOD

I

THEN the Lord answered Job out of the whirlwind,
   and said,
   Who is this that darkeneth counsel
By words without knowledge?
Gird up now thy loins like a man;
For I will demand of thee, and answer thou me.
Where wast thou when I laid the foundations of the earth?
Declare, if thou hast understanding.
Who hath laid the measures thereof, if thou knowest?
Or who hath stretched the line upon it?
Whereupon are the foundations thereof fastened?
Or who laid the corner stone thereof;
When the morning stars sang together,
And all the sons of God shouted for joy?
Or who shut up the sea with doors,
When it brake forth, as if it had issued out of the womb?
When I made the cloud the garment thereof,
And thick darkness a swaddlingband for it,
And brake up for it my decreed place,
And set bars and doors,
And said, Hitherto shalt thou come, but no further:
And here shall thy proud waves be stayed?
Hast thou commanded the morning since thy days;
And caused the dayspring to know his place;
That it might take hold of the ends of the earth,
That the wicked might be shaken out of it?
It is turned as clay to the seal;
And they stand as a garment.

And from the wicked their light is withholden,
And the high arm shall be broken.
Hast thou entered into the springs of the sea?
Or hast thou walked in the search of the depth?
Have the gates of death been opened unto thee?
Or hast thou seen the doors of the shadow of death?
Hast thou perceived the breadth of the earth?
Declare if thou knowest it all.
Where is the way where light dwelleth?
And as for darkness, where is the place thereof,
That thou shouldest take it to the bound thereof,
And that thou shouldest know the paths to the house thereof?
Knowest thou it, because thou wast then born?
Or because the number of thy days is great?
Hast thou entered into the treasures of the snow?
Or hast thou seen the treasures of the hail,
Which I have reserved against the time of trouble,
Against the day of battle and war?
By what way is the light parted,
Which scattereth the east wind upon the earth?
Who hath divided a watercourse for the overflowing of waters,
Or a way for the lightning of thunder;
To cause it to rain on the earth, where no man is;
On the wilderness, wherein there is no man;
To satisfy the desolate and waste ground;
And to cause the bud of the tender herb to spring forth?
Hath the rain a father?
Or who hath begotten the drops of dew?
Out of whose womb came the ice?
And the hoary frost of heaven, who hath gendered it?
The waters are hid as with a stone,
And the face of the deep is frozen.
Canst thou bind the sweet influences of Pleiades,
Or loose the bands of Orion?
Canst thou bring forth Mazzaroth in his season?
Or canst thou guide Arcturus with his sons?

Knowest thou the ordinances of heaven?
Canst thou set the dominion thereof in the earth?
Canst thou lift up thy voice to the clouds,
That abundance of waters may cover thee?
Canst thou send lightnings, that they may go,
And say unto thee, Here we are?
Who hath put wisdom in the inward parts?
Or who hath given understanding to the heart?
Who can number the clouds in wisdom?
Or who can stay the bottles of heaven,
When the dust groweth into hardness,
And the clods cleave fast together?
Wilt thou hunt the prey for the lion?
Or fill the appetite of the young lions,
When they couch in their dens,
And abide in the covert to lie in wait?
Who provideth for the raven his food?
When his young ones cry unto God,
They wander for lack of meat.
Knowest thou the time when the wild goats of the rock bring
    forth?
Or canst thou mark when the hinds do calve?
Canst thou number the months that they fulfil?
Or knowest thou the time when they bring forth?
They bow themselves, they bring forth their young ones,
They cast out their sorrows.
Their young ones are in good liking, they grow up with
    corn;
They go forth, and return not unto them.
Who hath sent out the wild ass free?
Or who hath loosed the bands of the wild ass?
Whose house I have made the wilderness,
And the barren land his dwellings.
He scorneth the multitude of the city,
Neither regardeth he the crying of the driver.
The range of the mountains is his pasture,
And he searcheth after every green thing.
Will the unicorn be willing to serve thee,

Or abide by thy crib?
Canst thou bind the unicorn with his band in the furrow?
Or will he harrow the valleys after thee?
Wilt thou trust him, because his strength is great?
Or wilt thou leave thy labour to him?
Wilt thou believe him, that he will bring home thy seed,
And gather it into thy barn?
Gavest thou the goodly wings unto the peacocks?
Or wings and feathers unto the ostrich?
Which leaveth her eggs in the earth,
And warmeth them in dust,
And forgetteth that the foot may crush them,
Or that the wild beast may break them.
She is hardened against her young ones, as though they were
    not hers;
Her labour is in vain without fear;
Because God hath deprived her of wisdom,
Neither hath he imparted to her understanding.
What time she lifteth up herself on high,
She scorneth the horse and his rider.
Hast thou given the horse strength?
Hast thou clothed his neck with thunder?
Canst thou make him afraid as a grasshopper?
The glory of his nostrils is terrible.
He paweth in the valley, and rejoiceth in his strength:
He goeth on to meet the armed men.
He mocketh at fear, and is not affrighted;
Neither turneth he back from the sword.
The quiver rattleth against him,
The glittering spear and the shield.
He swalloweth the ground with fierceness and rage:
Neither believeth he that it is the sound of the trumpet.
He saith among the trumpets, Ha, ha!
And he smelleth the battle afar off,
The thunder of the captains, and the shouting.
Doth the hawk fly by thy wisdom,
And stretch her wings toward the south?
Doth the eagle mount up at thy command,

And make her nest on high?
She dwelleth and abideth on the rock,
Upon the crag of the rock, and the strong place.
From thence she seeketh the prey,
And her eyes behold afar off.
Her young ones also suck up blood:
And where the slain are, there is she.

2

>The spacious firmament on high
>With all the blue ethereal sky
>And spangled heavens, a shining frame,
>Their great Original proclaim.
>Th' unwearied sun, from day to day,
>Does his Creator's power display:
>And publishes to every land
>The work of an Almighty hand.
>
>Soon as the evening shades prevail
>The moon takes up the wondrous tale,
>And nightly to the listening earth
>Repeats the story of her birth:
>Whilst all the stars that round her burn,
>And all the planets in their turn,
>Confirm the tidings as they roll
>And spread the truth from pole to pole.
>
>What though in solemn silence all
>Move round the dark terrestrial ball?
>What though no real voice nor sound
>Amidst their radiant orbs be found?—
>In Reason's ear they all rejoice
>And utter forth a glorious voice;
>For ever singing, as they shine,
>'The hand that made us is divine.'

XLIV

THE TRIAL OF FAITHFUL

THEN a convenient time being appointed, they brought them forth to their Tryal in order to their Condemnation. When the time was come, they were brought before their Enemies and arraigned; The Judge's name was Lord *Hate-good*. Their indictment was one and the same in substance, though somewhat varying in form; the Contents whereof was this.

That they were enemies to, and disturbers of their Trade; that they had made commotions and Divisions in the Town, and had won a party to their own most dangerous opinions, in contempt of the Law of their Prince.

Then *Faithful* began to answer, That he had only set himself against that which had set itself against him that is higher than the highest. And said he, As for disturbance, I make none, being myself a man of Peace; the Parties that were won to us, were won by beholding our Truth and Innocence, and they are only turned from the worse to the better. And as to the King you talk of, since he is *Beelzebub*, the Enemy of our Lord, I defy him and all his Angels.

Then Proclamation was made, that they that had ought to say for their Lord the King against the Prisoner at the Bar, should forthwith appear and give in their evidence. So there came in three Witnesses, to wit, *Envy*, *Superstition*, and *Pickthank*. They were then asked, If they knew the Prisoner at the Bar? and what they had to say for their Lord the King against him?

Then stood forth *Envy*, and said to this effect: My Lord, I have known this man a long time, and will attest upon my Oath before this honourable Bench, That he is——

JUDGE. Hold, give him his Oath;

So they sware him. Then he said, My Lord, This man, notwithstanding his plausible name, is one of the vilest men in our Country; he neither regardeth Prince nor People, Law nor Custom: but doth all that he can to possess all men with certain of his disloyal notions, which he in the general calls Principles of Faith and Holiness. And in particular, I heard him once myself affirm, *That Christianity and the Customs of our Town of* Vanity, *were Diametrically opposite, and could not be reconciled.* By which saying, my Lord, he doth at once, not only condemn all our laudable doings, but us in the doing of them.

JUDGE. Then did the Judge say to him, Hast thou any more to say?

ENVY. My Lord, I could say much more, only I would not be tedious to the Court. Yet if need be, when the other Gentlemen have given in their Evidence, rather than anything shall be wanting that will dispatch him, I will enlarge my Testimony against him. So he was bid stand by. Then they called *Superstition*, and bid him look upon the Prisoner; they also asked, What he could say for their Lord the King against him? Then they sware him, so he began.

SUPER. My Lord, I have no great acquaintance with this man, nor do I desire to have further knowledge of him. However this I know, that he is a very pestilent fellow, from some discourse that the other day I had with him in this *Town*; for then talking with him, I heard him say, That our Religion was naught, and such by which a man could by no means please God: which sayings of his, my Lord, your Lordship very well knows, what necessarily thence will follow, *to wit*, That we still do worship in vain, are yet in our Sins, and finally shall be damned; and this is that which I have to say.

Then was *Pickthank* sworn, and bid say what he knew, in behalf of their Lord the King against the Prisoner at the Bar.

PICK. My Lord, and you gentlemen all, This fellow I have known of a long time, and have heard him speak things that ought not to be spoke. For he hath railed on our noble Prince *Beelzebub*, and hath spoke contemptibly of his honourable Friends, whose names are the Lord *Oldman*, the Lord *Carnal-delight*, the Lord *Luxurious*, the Lord *Desire of Vainglory*, my old Lord *Lechery*, Sir *Having Greedy*, with all the rest of our Nobility; and he hath said moreover, that if all men were of his mind, if possible, there is not one of these Noblemen should have any longer a being in this Town. Besides, he hath not been afraid to rail on you, my Lord, who are now appointed to be his Judge, calling you an ungodly Villain, with many other such like vilifying terms, with which he hath bespattered most of the Gentry of our Town. When this *Pickthank* had told his tale, the Judge directed his speech to the Prisoner at the Bar, saying, Thou Runagate, Heretick, and Traitor, hast thou heard what these honest Gentlemen have witnessed against thee?

FAITH. *May I speak a few words in my own defence?*

JUDGE. Sirrah, Sirrah, thou deservest to live no longer, but to be slain immediately upon the place; yet that all men may see our gentleness towards thee, let us see what thou hast to say.

FAITH. 1. I say then in answer to what Mr. *Envy* hath spoken, I never said ought but this, *That what Rule, or Laws, or Custom, or People, were flat against the Word of God, are diametrically opposite to Christianity.* If I have said amiss in this, convince me of my error, and I am ready here before you to make my recantation.

2. As to the second, to wit, Mr. *Superstition*, and his charge against me, I said only this, *That in the worship of God there is required a divine Faith; but there can be no divine Faith without a divine Revelation of the will of God: therefore whatever is thrust into the worship of God, that is not agreeable to divine Revelation, cannot be done but by an human Faith; which Faith will not be profit to Eternal life.*

3. As to what Mr. *Pickthank* hath said, I say (avoiding terms, as that I am said to rail, and the like), That the Prince of this Town, with all the Rabblement his Attendants, by this Gentleman named, are more fit for a being in Hell, than in this Town and Country; *and so the Lord have mercy upon me.*

Then the Judge called to the Jury (who all this while stood by, to hear and observe), Gentlemen of the Jury, you see this man about whom so great an uproar hath been made in this Town: you have also heard what these worthy

Gentlemen have witnessed against him; also you have heard his reply and confession: It lieth now in your breasts to hang him, or save his life, But yet I think meet to instruct you into our Law.

There was an Act made in the days of *Pharaoh* the Great, Servant to our Prince, That lest those of a contrary Religion should multiply and grow too strong for him, their Males should be thrown into the River. There was also an Act made in the days of *Nebuchadnezzar* the Great, another of his Servants, that whoever would not fall down and worship his golden Image, should be thrown into a fiery Furnace. There was also an Act made in the days of *Darius*, That whoso, for some time, called upon any God but him, should be cast into the Lions' Den. Now the substance of these Laws this Rebel has broken, not only in thought (which is not to be borne) but also in word and deed; which must therefore needs be intolerable.

For that of *Pharaoh*, his Law was made upon a supposition, to prevent mischief, no Crime being yet apparent; but here is a Crime apparent. For the second and third, you see he disputeth against our Religion; and for the Treason he hath confessed, he deserveth to die the death.

Then went the Jury out, whose names were, Mr. *Blindman*, Mr. *No-good*, Mr. *Malice*, Mr. *Love-lust*, Mr. *Live-loose*, Mr. *Heady*, Mr. *High-mind*, Mr. *Enmity*, Mr. *Lyar*, Mr. *Cruelty*, Mr. *Hate-light*, and Mr. *Implacable*, who every one gave in his private Verdict against him among themselves, and afterwards unanimously concluded to bring him in guilty before the Judge, And first Mr. *Blind-man* the Foreman, said: *I see clearly that this man is an Heretick.* Then said Mr. *No-good, Away with such a fellow from the Earth. Ay*, said Mr. *Malice, for I hate the very looks of him.* Then said Mr. *Love-lust, I could never endure him. Nor I,* said Mr. *Live-loose, for he would always be condemning my way. Hang him, hang him,* said Mr. *Heady. A sorry Scrub,* said Mr. *High-mind. My heart riseth against him,* said Mr. *Enmity. He is a Rogue,* said Mr. *Lyar. Hanging is too good for him,* said Mr. *Cruelty. Let's dispatch him out of the way,* said Mr. *Hate-light.* Then said Mr. *Implacable, Might I have all the World given me, I could not be reconciled to him, therefore let us forthwith bring him in guilty of death;* And so they did, therefore he was presently condemned, To be had from the place where he was, to the place from whence he came, and there to be put to the most cruel death that could be invented.

They therefore brought him out, to do with him according to their Law; and first they Scourged him, then they Buffeted him, then they Lanced his flesh with Knives; after that, they Stoned him with Stones, then prickt him with their Swords, and last of all they burned him to Ashes at the Stake. Thus came *Faithful* to his end. Now, I saw that there stood behind the multitude, a Chariot and a couple of Horses, waiting for *Faithful*, who (so soon as his adversaries had dispatched him) was taken up into it, and straightway was carried up through the Clouds, with sound of Trumpet, the nearest way to the Cœlestial Gate.

XLV

FROM SIR WALTER RALEIGH

THE END OF ALL THINGS

NOW these great kings and conquering nations have been the subject of those ancient histories which have been preserved and yet remain among us; and withal of so many tragical poets as in the persons of powerful princes and other mighty men have complained against infidelity, time, destiny, and most of all against the variable success of worldly things and instability of fortune. To these undertakings the greatest lords of the world have been stirred up rather by the desire of fame, which ploughteth up the air and soweth in the wind, than by the affection of bearing rule, which draweth after it so much vexation and so many cares. And that this is true the good advice of Cineas to Pyrrhus proves. And certainly, as fame hath often been dangerous to the living, so it is to the dead of no use at all because separate from knowledge. Which were it otherwise, and the extreme ill bargain of buying this lasting discourse understood by them which are dissolved, they themselves would then rather have wished to have stolen out of the world without noise than to be put in mind that they have purchased the report of their actions in the world by rapine, oppression and cruelty, by giving in spoil the innocent and labouring soul to the idle and insolent, and by having emptied the cities of the world of their ancient inhabitants and filled them again with so many and so variable sorts of sorrows. . . .

For the rest, if we seek a reason of the succession and continuance of this boundless ambition in mortal men, we may add to that which hath been already said that the kings and princes of the world have always laid before them the actions, but not the ends, of those great ones which preceded them. They are always transported with the glory of the one, but they never mind the misery of the other till they find the experience in themselves. They neglect the advice of God, while they enjoy life, or hope it; but they follow the counsel of Death upon his first approach. It is he that puts into man all the wisdom of the world, without speaking a word, which God with all the words of His law, promises or threats doth not infuse. Death, which hateth and destroyeth man, is believed; God, which hath made him and loves him, is always deferred: *I have considered*, saith Solomon, *all the works that are under the sun, and, behold, all is vanity and vexation of spirit*; but who believes it, till Death tells it us? It was Death which, opening the conscience of Charles the Fifth, made him enjoin his son Philip to restore Navarre: and King Francis the First of France to command that justice should be done upon the murderers of the Protestants in Merindol and Cabrieres, which till then he neglected. It is therefore Death alone that can suddenly make man to know himself. He tells the proud and insolent that they are but abjects, and humbles them at the instant, makes them cry, complain and repent, yea, even to hate their forepast happiness. He takes the account of the rich and proves him a beggar, a naked beggar, which hath interest in nothing but in the gravel that fills his mouth. He holds a glass before the eyes of the most beautiful, and makes them see therein their deformity and rottenness, and they acknowledge it.

O eloquent, just and mighty Death! whom none could advise, thou hast persuaded; what none hath dared, thou hast done; and whom all the world hath flattered, thou only hast cast out of the world and despised; thou hast drawn together all the far-stretched greatness, all the pride, cruelty and ambition of man, and covered it all over with these two narrow words, *Hic jacet*!

'EVEN SUCH IS TIME'
(Written the night before his death)

Even such is time, that takes on trust
   Our youth, our joys, our all we have,
And pays us but with age and dust;
   Who in the dark and silent grave,
When we have wandered all our ways,
Shuts up the story of our days!
But from this earth, this grave, this dust,
The Lord shall raise me up, I trust!

XLVI

THE JUST MAN

SOCRATES TO HIS JUDGES

NOT much time will be gained, O Athenians, in return for the evil name which you will get from the detractors of the city, who will say that you killed Socrates, a wise man; for they will call me wise, even although I am not wise, when they want to reproach you. If you had waited a little while, your desire would have been fulfilled in the course of nature. For I am far advanced in years, as you may perceive, and not far from death. I am speaking now only to those of you who have condemned me to death. And I have another thing to say to them: You think that I was convicted because I had no words of the sort which would have procured my acquittal—I mean, if I had thought fit to leave nothing undone or unsaid. Not so; the deficiency which led to my conviction was not of words— certainly not! But I had not the boldness or impudence or inclination to address you as you would have liked me to address you, weeping and wailing and lamenting, and saying and doing many things which you have been accustomed to hear from others, and which, as I maintain, are unworthy of me. I thought at the time that I ought not to do anything common or mean when in danger: nor do I now repent of the manner of my defence, and I would rather die having spoken after my manner, than speak in your manner and live. For neither in war nor yet at law ought I or any man to use every way of escaping death. Often in battle there can be no doubt that if a man will throw away his arms, and fall on his knees before his pursuers, he may escape death; and in other dangers there are other ways of escaping death, if a man is willing to say and do anything. The difficulty, my friends, is not in avoiding death, but in avoiding unrighteousness; for that runs faster than death. I am old and move slowly, and the slower runner has overtaken me, and my accusers are keen and quick, and the faster runner, who is unrighteousness, has overtaken them. And now I depart hence condemned by you to suffer the penalty of death, and they too go their ways condemned by the truth to suffer the penalty of villainy and wrong; and I must abide by my award—let them abide by theirs. I suppose that these things may be regarded as fated,—and I think that they are well.

And now, O men who have condemned me, I would fain prophesy to you; for I am about to die, and that is the hour in which men are gifted with prophetic power. And I prophesy to you who are my murderers, that immediately after my death punishment far heavier than you have inflicted on me will surely await you. Me you have killed because you wanted to escape the accuser, and not to give an account of your lives. But that will not be as you suppose: far otherwise. For I say that there will be more accusers of you than there are now; accusers whom hitherto I have restrained: and as they are younger they will be more inconsiderate with you, and you will be more offended at them. If you think that by killing men you can prevent some one from censuring your evil lives, you are mistaken; that is not a way of escape which is either possible or honourable; the easiest and the noblest way is not to be disabling others, but to be improving yourselves. This is the prophecy which I utter before my departure to the judges who have condemned me.

Friends, who would have acquitted me, I would like also to talk with you about this thing which has happened, while the magistrates are busy, and before I go to the place at which I must die. Stay then awhile, for we may as well talk with one another while there is time. You are my friends, and I should like to show you the meaning of this event which has happened to me. O my judges—for you I may truly call judges—I should like to tell you of a wonderful circumstance. Hitherto the familiar oracle within me has constantly been in the habit of opposing me even about trifles, if I was going to make a slip or error in any matter; and now as you see there has come upon me that which may be thought, and is generally believed to be, the last and worst evil. But the oracle made no sign of opposition, either as I was leaving my house and going out in the morning, or when I was going up into this court, or while I was speaking, at anything which I was going to say; and yet I have often been stopped in the middle of a speech, but now in nothing I either said or did touching this matter has the oracle opposed me. What do I take to be the explanation of this? I will tell you. I regard this as a great proof that what has happened to me is a good, and that those of us who think that death is an evil are in error. For the customary sign would surely have opposed me had I been going to evil and not to good.

Let us reflect in another way, and we shall see that there is great reason to hope that death is a good; for one of two things—either death is a state of nothingness and utter unconsciousness, or, as men say, there is a change and migration of the soul from this world to another. Now if you suppose that there is no consciousness, but a sleep like the sleep of him who is undisturbed even by the sight of dreams, death will be an unspeakable gain. For if a person were to select the night in which his sleep was undisturbed even by dreams, and were to compare with this the other days and nights of his life, and then were to tell us how many days and nights he had passed in the course of his life better and more pleasantly than this one, I think that any man, I will not say a private man, but even the great king will not find many such days or nights, when compared with the others. Now if death is like this, I say that to die is gain; for eternity is then only a single night. But if death is the journey to another place, and there, as men say, all the dead are, what good, O my friends and judges, can be greater than this? If indeed when the pilgrim arrives in the world below, he is delivered from the professors of justice in this world, and finds the true judges who are said to give judgment there, Minos and Rhadamanthus and Aeacus and Triptolemus, and other sons of God who were righteous in their own life, that pilgrimage will be worth making. What would not a man give if he might converse with Orpheus and Musaeus and Hesiod and Homer? Nay, if this be true, let me die again and again. I myself, too, shall have a wonderful interest in there meeting and conversing with Palamedes, and Ajax the son of Telamon, and other heroes of old, who have suffered death through an unjust judgment; and there will be no small pleasure, as I think, in comparing my own sufferings with theirs. Above all I shall then be able to continue my search into true and false knowledge; as in this world, so also in that; and I shall find out who is wise, and who pretends to be wise and is not. What would not a man give, O judges, to be able to examine the leader of the great Trojan expedition; or Odysseus or Sisyphus, or numberless others, men and women too! What infinite delight would there be in conversing with them and asking them questions! In another world they do not put a man to death for asking questions; assuredly not. For besides being happier in that world than in this, they will be immortal, if what is said is true.

Wherefore, O judges, be of good cheer about death, and know of a certainty, that no evil can happen to a good man, either in life or after death. He and his are not neglected by the gods; nor has my own approaching end happened by mere chance. But I see clearly that to die and be released was better for me; and therefore the oracle gave no sign. For which reason, also, I am not angry with my condemners, or with my accusers; they have done me no harm, although they did not mean to do me any good; and for this I may gently blame them.

Still I have a favour to ask of them. When my sons are grown up, I would ask you, O my friends, to punish them; and I would have you trouble them, as I have troubled you, if they seem to care about riches, or anything, more than about virtue; or if they pretend to be something when they are really nothing,—then reprove them, as I have reproved you, for not caring about that for which they ought to care, and thinking that they are something when they are really nothing. And if you do this, I and my sons will have received justice at your hands.

The hour of departure has arrived, and we go our ways— I to die, and you to live. Which is better God only knows.

LINES BY W. S. LANDOR

Death stands above me, whispering low
I know not what into my ear:
Of his strange language all I know
    Is, there is not a word of fear.

XLVII
THE PUNISHMENT OF KHIPIL

THEY relate that Shahpesh, the Persian, commanded the building of a palace, and Khipil was his builder. The work lingered from the first year of the reign of Shahpesh even to his fourteenth. One day Shahpesh went to the river-side where it stood, to inspect it. Khipil

THE PUNISHMENT OF KHIPIL

was sitting on a marble slab among the stones and blocks; round him stretched lazily the masons and stonecutters and slaves of burden; and they with the curve of humorous enjoyment on their lips, for he was reciting to them adventures, interspersed with anecdotes and recitations and poetic instances, as was his wont. They were like pleased flocks whom the shepherd hath led to a pasture freshened with brooks, there to feed indolently; he, the shepherd, in the midst.

Now, the King said to him, 'O Khipil, show me my palace where it standeth, for I desire to gratify my sight with its fairness.'

Khipil abased himself before Shahpesh, and answered, "'T is even here, O King of the age, where thou delightest the earth with thy foot and the ear of thy slave with sweetness. Surely a site of vantage, one that dominateth earth, air, and water, which is the builder's first and chief requisition for a noble palace, a palace to fill foreign kings and sultans with the distraction of envy; and it is, O Sovereign of the time, a site, this site I have chosen, to occupy the tongues of travellers and awaken the flights of poets!'

Shahpesh smiled and said, 'The site is good! I laud the site! Likewise I laud the wisdom of Ebn Busrac, where he exclaims:

> "Be sure, where Virtue faileth to appear,
> For her a gorgeous mansion men will rear;
> And day and night her praises will be heard,
> Where never yet she spake a single word." '

Then said he, 'O Khipil, my builder, there was once a farm-servant that, having neglected in the seed-time to sow, took to singing the richness of his soil when it was harvest, in proof of which he displayed the abundance of weeds that coloured the land everywhere. Discover to me now the completeness of my halls and apartments, I pray thee, O Khipil, and be the excellence of thy construction made visible to me!'

Quoth Khipil, 'To hear is to obey.'

He conducted Shahpesh among the unfinished saloons and

imperfect courts and roofless rooms, and by half-erected obelisks, and columns pierced and chipped, of the palace of his building. And he was bewildered at the words spoken by Shahpesh; but now the King exalted him, and admired the perfection of his craft, the greatness of his labour, the speediness of his construction, his assiduity; feigning not to behold his negligence.

Presently they went up winding balusters to a marble terrace, and the King said, 'Such is thy devotion and constancy in toil, O Khipil, that thou shalt walk before me here.'

He then commanded Khipil to precede him, and Khipil was heightened with the honour. When Khipil had paraded a short space he stopped quickly, and said to Shahpesh, 'Here is, as it chanceth, a gap, O King! and we can go no further this way.'

Shahpesh said, 'All is perfect, and it is my will thou delay not to advance.'

Khipil cried, 'The gap is wide, O mighty King, and manifest, and it is the one incomplete part of thy palace.'

Then said Shahpesh, 'O Khipil, I see no distinction between one part and another; excellent are all parts in beauty and proportion, and there can be no part incomplete in this palace that occupieth the builder fourteen years in its building: so advance, and do my bidding.'

Khipil yet hesitated, for the gap was of many strides, and at the bottom of the gap was a deep water, and he one that knew not the motion of swimming. But Shahpesh ordered his guard to point their arrows in the direction of Khipil, and Khipil stepped forward hurriedly, and fell in the gap, and was swallowed by the water below. When he rose the second time, succour reached him, and he was drawn to land trembling, his teeth chattering. And Shahpesh praised him, and said, 'This is an apt contrivance for a bath, Khipil O my builder! well conceived; one that taketh by surprise; and it shall be thy reward daily when much talking hath fatigued thee.'

Then he bade Khipil lead him to the hall of state. And when they were there Shahpesh said, 'For a privilege, and as a mark of my approbation, I give thee permission to sit in the marble chair of yonder throne, even in my presence, O Khipil.'

Khipil said, 'Surely, O King, the chair is not yet executed.'

And Shahpesh exclaimed, 'If this be so, thou art but the length of thy measure on the ground, O talkative one!'

Khipil said, 'Nay, 't is not so, O King of splendours! blind that I am! yonder 's indeed the chair.'

And Khipil feared the King, and went to the place where, the chair should be, and bent his body in a sitting posture, eyeing the King, and made pretence to sit in the chair of Shahpesh as in conspiracy to amuse his master.

Then said Shahpesh, 'For a token that I approve thy execution of the chair, thou shalt be honoured by remaining seated in it one day and one night; but move thou to the right or to the left, showing thy soul insensible of the honour done thee, transfixed thou shalt be with twenty arrows and five'

The King then left him with a guard of twenty-five of his body-guard; and they stood around him with bent bows. so that Khipil dared not move from his sitting posture. And the masons and the people crowded to see Khipil sitting on his master's chair, for it became rumoured about. When they beheld him sitting upon nothing, and he trembling to stir for fear of the loosening of the arrows, they laughed so that they rolled upon the floor of the hall, and the echoes of laughter were a thousandfold. Surely the arrows of the guards swayed with the laughter that shook them.

Now, when the time had expired for his sitting in the chair, Shahpesh returned to him, and he was cramped, pitiable to see; and Shahpesh said, 'Thou hast been exalted above men, O Khipil! for that thou didst execute for thy master has been found fitting for thee.'

Then he bade Khipil lead the way to the noble gardens of dalliance and pleasure that he had planted and contrived. And Khipil went in that state described by the poet, when we go draggingly, with remonstrating members,

> Knowing a dreadful strength behind,
> And a dark fate before.

They came to the gardens, and behold, these were full of weeds and nettles, the fountains dry, no tree to be seen—a desert. And Shahpesh cried, 'This is indeed of admirable design, O Khipil! Feelest thou not the coolness of the fountains?—their refreshingness? Truly I am grateful to thee! And these flowers, pluck me now a handful, and tell me of their perfume.'

Khipil plucked a handful of the nettles that were there in the place of flowers, and put his nose to them before Shahpesh, till his nose was reddened; and desire to rub it waxed in him, and possessed him, and became a passion, so that he could scarce refrain from rubbing it even in the King's presence. And the King encouraged him to sniff and enjoy their fragrance, repeating the poet's words:

> Methinks I am a lover and a child,
> A little child and happy lover, both!
> When by the breath of flowers I am beguiled
> From sense of pain, and lulled in odorous sloth.
> So I adore them, that no mistress sweet
> Seems worthier of the love which they awake:
> In innocence and beauty more complete,
> Was never maiden cheek in morning lake.
> Oh, while I live, surround me with fresh flowers!
> Oh, when I die, then bury me in their bowers.

And the King said, 'What sayest thou, O my builder? that is a fair quotation, applicable to thy feelings, one that expresseth them?'

Khipil answered, "'T is eloquent, O great King! comprehensiveness would be its portion, but that it alludeth not to the delight of chafing.'

Then Shahpesh laughed, and cried, 'Chafe not! it is an ill thing and a hideous! This nosegay, O Khipil, it is for thee to present to thy mistress. Truly she will receive thee well after its presentation! I will have it now sent in thy name, with word that thou followest quickly. And for thy nettled nose, surely if the whim seize thee that thou desirest its chafing, to thy neighbour is permitted what to thy hand is refused.'

So the King set a guard upon Khipil to see that his orders were executed, and appointed a time for him to return to the gardens.

At the hour indicated Khipil stood before Shahpesh again. He was pale, saddened; his tongue drooped like the tongue of a heavy bell, that when it soundeth giveth forth mournful sounds only: he had also the look of one battered with many beatings. So the King said, 'How of the presentation of the flowers of thy culture, O Khipil?'

He answered, 'Surely, O King, she received me with wrath, and I am shamed by her.'

And the King said, 'How of my clemency in the matter of the chafing?'

Khipil answered, 'O King of splendours! I made petition to my neighbours whom I met, accosting them civilly and with imploring, for I ached to chafe, and it was the very raging thirst of desire to chafe that was mine, devouring intensity of eagerness for solace of chafing. And they chafed me, O King; yet not in those parts which throbbed for the chafing, but in those which abhorred it.'

Then Shahpesh smiled and said, "'T is certain that the magnanimity of monarchs is as the rain that falleth, the sun that shineth: and in this spot it fertilizeth richness; in that encourageth rankness. So art thou but a weed, O Khipil! and my grace is thy chastisement.'

Now, the King ceased not persecuting Khipil, under pretence of doing him honour and heaping favours on him. Three days and three nights was Khipil gasping without water, compelled to drink of the drought of the fountain, as an honour at the hands of the King. And he was seven days and seven nights made to stand with stretched arms, as they were the branches of a tree, in each hand a pomegranate. And Shahpesh brought the people of his court to regard the wondrous pomegranate-shoot planted by Khipil, very wondrous, and a new sort, worthy the gardens of a King. So the wisdom of the King was applauded, and men wotted he knew how to punish offences in coin, by the punishment inflicted on Khipil the builder.

XLVIII

INSPIRED MOMENTS

THERE are in our existence spots of time,
    That with distinct pre-eminence retain
    A renovating virtue, whence, depressed
By false opinion and contentious thought,
Or aught of heavier or more deadly weight,
In trivial occupations, and the round
Of ordinary intercourse, our minds
Are nourished and invisibly repaired;
A virtue, by which pleasure is enhanced,
That penetrates, enables us to mount,
When high, more high, and lifts us up when fallen.
This efficacious spirit chiefly lurks
Among those passages of life that give
Profoundest knowledge to what point, and how,
The mind is lord and master—outward sense
The obedient servant of her will. Such moments
Are scattered everywhere, taking their date
From our first childhood. I remember well,
That once, while yet my inexperienced hand
Could scarcely hold a bridle, with proud hopes
I mounted, and we journeyed towards the hills:
An ancient servant of my father's house
Was with me, my encourager and guide:
We had not travelled long, ere some mischance
Disjoined me from my comrade; and, through fear
Dismounting, down the rough and stony moor
I led my horse, and, stumbling on, at length
Came to a bottom; where in former times
A murderer had been hung in iron chains.
The gibbet-mast had mouldered down, the bones
And iron case were gone; but on the turf,
Hard by, soon after that fell deed was wrought,
Some unknown hand had carved the murderer's name.

The monumental letters were inscribed
In times long past; but still, from year to year,
By superstition of the neighbourhood,
The grass is cleared away, and to this hour
The characters are fresh and visible:
A casual glance had shown them, and I fled,
Faltering and faint, and ignorant of the road:
Then, reascending the bare common, saw
A naked pool that lay beneath the hills,
The beacon on the summit, and, more near,
A girl, who bore a pitcher on her head,
And seemed with difficult steps to force her way
Against the blowing wind. It was, in truth,
An ordinary sight; but I should need
Colours and words that are unknown to man,
To paint the visionary dreariness
Which, while I looked all round for my lost guide,
Invested moorland waste, and naked pool,
The beacon crowning the lone eminence,
The female and her garments vexed and tossed
By the strong wind. When, in the blessed hours
Of early love, the loved one at my side,
I roamed, in daily presence of this scene,
Upon the naked pool and dreary crags,
And on the melancholy beacon, fell
A spirit of pleasure and youth's golden gleam;
And think ye not with radiance more sublime
For these remembrances, and for the power
They had left behind? So feeling comes in aid
Of feeling, and diversity of strength
Attends us, if but once we have been strong.
Oh! mystery of man, from what a depth
Proceed thy honours. I am lost, but see
In simple childhood something of the base
On which thy greatness stands; but this I feel,
That from thyself it comes, that thou must give,
Else never canst receive. The days gone by
Return upon me almost from the dawn

Of life: the hiding-places of man's power
Open; I would approach them, but they close.
I see by glimpses now; when age comes on,
May scarcely see at all; and I would give,
While yet we may, as far as words can give,
Substance and life to what I feel, enshrining,
Such is my hope, the spirit of the past
For future restoration.—Yet another
Of these memorials:—

        One Christmas-time,
On the glad eve of its dear holidays,
Feverish, and tired, and restless, I went forth
Into the fields, impatient for the sight
Of those led palfreys that should bear us home;
My brothers and myself. There rose a crag,
That from the meeting-point of two highways
Ascending, overlooked them both, far stretched;
Thither, uncertain on which road to fix
My expectation, thither I repaired,
Scout-like, and gained the summit; 'twas a day
Tempestuous, dark, and wild, and on the grass
I sate half-sheltered by a naked wall;
Upon my right hand couched a single sheep,
Upon my left a blasted hawthorn stood;
With those companions at my side, I watched,
Straining my eyes intensely, as the mist
Gave intermitting prospect of the copse
And plain beneath. Ere we to school returned,—
That dreary time,—ere we had been ten days
Sojourners in my father's house, he died,
And I and my three brothers, orphans then,
Followed his body to the grave. The event,
With all the sorrow that it brought, appeared
A chastisement; and when I called to mind
That day so lately past, when from the crag
I looked in such anxiety of hope;
With trite reflections of morality,

Yet in the deepest passion, I bowed low
To God, Who thus corrected my desires:
And, afterwards, the wind and sleety rain,
And all the business of the elements,
The single sheep, and the one blasted tree,
And the bleak music from that old stone wall,
The noise of wood and water, and the mist
That on the line of each of those two roads
Advanced in such indisputable shapes;
All these were kindred spectacles and sounds
To which I oft repaired, and thence would drink,
As at a fountain; and on winter nights,
Down to this very time, when storm and rain
Beat on my roof, or, haply, at noon-day,
While in a grove I walk, whose lofty trees,
Laden with summer's thickest foliage, rock
In a strong wind, some working of the spirit,
Some inward agitations thence are brought,
Whate'er their office, whether to beguile
Thoughts over busy in the course they took,
Or animate an hour of vacant ease.

XLIX

AT A WESTERN HOTEL

THERE was a wonderful chandelier in the hotel dining-room. Fine bronze it was made of, with mermaids and Tritons and dolphins flourishing their tails up towards the dingy ceiling-paper. James, the hotel waiter, knew the family history of the chandelier, as he knew that of most people and things in the county. I commented upon it to a young gentleman with a pointed beard, who sat next to me at dinner, and said that it looked to me like Renaissance. The young gentleman suggested, alternatively, that it looked more like bronze. I did not dispute the point, but I think he found the subject precarious, as he turned to the young lady on his left, and I heard him embark upon a new theme.

'I was half dead with the toothache all day,' he observed.

The young lady replied sympathetically that toothache was a fright.

'Well, indeed, that's true,' said James, smoothly entering the conversation from behind my chair. 'I got my own share of it. Sure, there was one time I used to be roaring like a Banshee all night with it.'

'Were you so?' said the gentleman, with a wink at me. 'That must have been a long time ago, James.'

'Well, indeed, it is too, Doctor,' replied James meditatively, 'going on forty years, I daresay. I went to Dublin, and I went to a great dentist that was in it that time, and he pulled all the teeth I had, and he gave me a new set entirely.'

'Oh, my!' said the young lady, 'that must have been very expensive.'

'It was so,' said James, not without pride. 'Twenty pounds I gave him.'

'That was awful,' said the young lady feelingly; 'it was well to be you that had it to spend.'

'Well, it wasn't all out so bad,' said James; 'sure I only wore them a few times—I wouldn't be bothered with them, and a doctor that was a friend of mine gave me ten pounds for them.'

'I suppose they were a fit for a patient of his?' said the doctor.

'They were a bad fit for me, anyway,' returned James, glancing over his shoulder at the clattering operations of his two female subordinates, with the eye of the sergeant-major —the eye that always contains a grievance.

The meal wore slowly on. A sea fish, of a genus unknown to me, and amazingly endowed with bones, was consumed in distracted silence.

'I hear you have a fish shop opened in Ballinagar, Mrs. M'Evoy,' remarked the Doctor, taking his last fish bone out of action with professional adroitness, and addressing the mother of the young lady. 'That's very up-to-date. There wasn't one I met from Ballinagar but was bragging of it.'

'It was the Hoolahanes that had it,' said Mrs. M'Evoy. 'It's closed.'

'Oh, dear, why so?' said the Doctor. 'Why did they do that, I wonder?'

'They said that morning, noon, and night people were bothering them for fish,' returned Mrs. M'Evoy, to whom this triumph of the artistic temperament presented no exceptional feature.

It was somewhere in the reposeful period that came with the cheese that Dr. Hickey ordered a bottle of port, of which he very handsomely invited the ladies and me to partake. He leaned back in his chair.

'Was this in the cellar the time of the flood?' he said, putting down his glass. 'I don't mean Noah's flood. James —you mightn't remember that—but the time the river came up in the town here.'

'If it was Noah's flood itself,' said James, instantly accepting combat, 'it couldn't get into *our* cellars. But, faith, it was up in this room you're sitting in, and I had to get up on the table from it, and it ruz to the table, and I had to hang out of the chandelier, and a boat came into the room then and took me out. Sure, that was the time that the porpoise came up the river, with the dint of the flood, and she was in it for a week, in front of the hotel.'

'In compliment to the visitors, I suppose,' said the Doctor. 'And what happened her, James?'

'She was in it till a whale came up the river,' replied James, with the simplicity of Holy Writ, 'and b'Jove he banished her!'

'It's a wonder you'd let him treat a lady that way, James,' said Dr. Hickey.

It was still twilight when we left the dining-room, and strayed to the open hall door, and out into the September evening. We sat with Mrs. and Miss M'Evoy in the summer-house, and drank something that was unearthly black in the red light, and was singularly unsuggestive of coffee. Presently a railway whistle made a thin bar of sound somewhere out under the low moon, that had now lifted herself clear of the haze.

'There's the night-mail,' said Mrs. M'Evoy, 'and it half an hour late!'

'She had pigs to shunt,' said James, re-entering with a plate of biscuits, adorned with pink and white sugar.

'Ah! what signifies half an hour here or there on this line!' said Dr. Hickey. 'I'm told there was a lady travelling on it last week, and she had a canary in a cage, and the canary got loose and flew out of the window, and by George! the lady pulled the communication cord, and stopped the train!'

'Well, now, she showed her sense,' said Mrs. M'Evoy, with an utterance slightly muffled in pink biscuit.

'She and the guard went then trying to catch the canary,' continued Dr. Hickey, 'and he'd sit till they'd get near him, and then he'd fly on another piece. Everyone that was in the train was hanging out of it, and betting on it, from one carriage to another, and some would back the lady and some would back the bird, and everyone telling them what to do.'

'It's a pity *you* weren't in it,' said Miss M'Evoy, 'they'd have been all right then.'

'It was that bare bit of bog near Bohirmeen,' pursued Dr. Hickey, without a stagger, 'not a tree in it. "If he have a fly left in him at all," says a chap out of a third smoker, "ye'll get him in Mike Doogan's bush." That was the only bush in the country.'

''Twas true for him,' said James.

'Well, they got him in the bush,' proceeded Dr. Hickey, 'singing away for himself; but they had some trouble crossing the drains. I'm told the guard said the lady lepped like a horse!'

'You had it right, all to the singing,' commented Mrs. M'Evoy, advancing as it were to the footlights. 'I have the little bird upstairs this minute, and she never sang a note yet!'

'Well, now, I thought it was a nice idea, the canary to be singing,' said Dr. Hickey, emerging from the situation as from a football scrimmage, in which he had retained possession of the ball. 'The next time I tell the story, I'll leave that out, and I can say that the lady that lepped like a horse was Mrs. M'Evoy. They'll believe me then.'

'Why wouldn't you say the canary was an eagle?' said Miss M'Evoy. 'There used to be plenty eagles in these mountains back here.'

'Well, indeed, I might too,' said Dr. Hickey. 'I remember it was somewhere in these parts that an uncle of mine was staying one time, and a man came to the hotel with an eagle to sell to the tourists. My uncle was like Mrs. M'Evoy here, he was very fond of birds; and the man said the eagle'd be a lovely pet. Whatever way it was, he bought it.' He paused to light a cigarette, and James pretended to collect the coffee cups.

'He gave the eagle to the Boots to mind for him,' resumed the Doctor, 'and the Boots put it into an empty bedroom. It wasn't more than seven o'clock next morning when my uncle was wakened up, and the waiter came in. "There's a man in the kitchen, your honour," says he, "and he has a great fighting aigle, and he says he'll fight your honour's aigle in the passage." They had a grand fight between the two o' them in the spare room, and in the end my uncle's eagle went up the chimney, and the man's eagle went out through the glass in the window. My uncle had a nice bill to pay for all that was broken in the room and in the end he gave the eagle to the Zoo.'

'Faith, he did not!' shouted James suddenly. 'He left him stuck in the chimbley! And sure it was I that got him out, and meself that sold him to a gentleman that was going to Ameriky. Sure, I was the waiter!'

Dr. Hickey threw himself back in his rustic chair.

'Holy smoke! This is no place for me,' he said; 'every story I have is true in spite of me.'

L

TAM O' SHANTER

A TALE

WHEN chapman billies leave the street,
And drouthy neebors neebors meet;
As market days are wearing late,
An' folk begin to tak the gate;
While we sit bousing at the nappy,
An' gettin fou and unco happy,
We think na on the lang Scots miles,
The mosses, waters, slaps, and stiles,
That lie between us and our hame,
Whare sits our sulky sullen dame,
Gathering her brows like gathering storm,
Nursing her wrath to keep it warm.

This truth fand honest Tam o' Shanter,
As he frae Ayr ae night did canter;
(Auld Ayr, wham ne'er a town surpasses
For honest men and bonny lasses.)

O Tam! hadst thou but been sae wise
As taen thy ain wife Kate's advice!
She tauld thee weel thou was a skellum,
A blethering, blustering, drunken blellum;
That frae November till October
Ae market-day thou was na sober;
That ilka melder wi' the miller
Thou sat as lang as thou had siller;
That every naig was ca'd a shoe on
The smith and the gat roaring fou on;
That at the L—d's house, ev'n on Sunday,
Thou drank wi' Kirkton Jean till Monday.
She prophesy'd that, late or soon,
Thou wad be found deep drown'd in Doon;
Or catch'd wi' warlocks in the mirk
By Alloway's auld haunted kirk.

Ah, gentle dames! it gars me greet
To think how mony counsels sweet,
How mony lengthen'd, sage advices
The husband from the wife despises!

But to our tale:— Ae market night,
Tam had got planted unco right;
Fast by an ingle, bleezing finely,
Wi' reaming swats, that drank divinely;
And at his elbow, Souter Johnny,
His ancient, trusty, drouthy crony;
Tam lo'ed him like a very brither;
They had been fou for weeks thegither.
The night drave on wi' sangs and clatter;
And ay the ale was growing better:
The Landlady and Tam grew gracious
Wi' favours secret, sweet and precious:
The Souter tauld his queerest stories;
The landlord's laugh was ready chorus:
The storm without might rair and rustle,
Tam did na mind the storm a whistle.

Care, mad to see a man sae happy,
E'en drown'd himself amang the nappy,
As bees flee hame wi' lades o' treasure,
The minutes wing'd their way wi' pleasure;
Kings may be blest, but Tam was glorious,
O'er a' the ills o' life victorious!

But pleasures are like poppies spread,
You seize the flow'r, its bloom is shed;
Or like the snow falls in the river,
A moment white—then melts for ever;
Or like the borealis race
That flit ere you can point their place;
Or like the rainbow's lovely form
Evanishing amid the storm.

Nae man can tether time or tide;
The hour approaches Tam maun ride;
That hour, o' night's black arch the key-stane,
That dreary hour he mounts his beast in;
And sic a night he taks the road in
As ne'er poor sinner was abroad in.

The wind blew as 'twad blawn its last;
The rattling show'rs rose on the blast;
The speedy gleams the darkness swallow'd;
Loud, deep, and lang, the thunder bellow'd;
That night a child might understand
The Deil had business on his hand.

Weel mounted on his gray mare, Meg,
A better never lifted leg,
Tam skelpit on thro' dub and mire,
Despising wind, and rain, and fire;
Whiles holding fast his gude blue bonnet;
Whiles crooning o'er some auld Scots sonnet,
Whiles glow'ring round wi' prudent cares
Lest bogles catch him unawares:
Kirk-Alloway was drawing nigh,
Whare ghaists and houlets nightly cry.

By this time he was 'cross the ford,
Whare in the snaw the chapman smoor'd;
And past the birks and meikle stane
Whare drunken Charlie brak's neck-bane;
And thro' the whins, and by the cairn
Whare hunters fand the murder'd bairn;
And near the thorn, aboon the well,
Whare Mungo's mither hang'd hersel.
Before him Doon pours all his floods,
The doubling storm roars thro' the woods;
The lightnings flash frae pole to pole;
Near and more near the thunders roll:

TAM O' SHANTER

When, glimmering thro' the groaning trees,
Kirk-Alloway seem'd in a bleeze;
Thro' ilka bore the beams were glancing;
And loud resounded mirth and dancing.

　Inspiring bold John Barleycorn!
What dangers thou canst make us scorn!
Wi' tippenny, we fear nae evil;
Wi' usquabae, we'll face the devil!
The swats sae ream'd in Tammie's noddle,
Fair play, he car'd na deils a boddle.
But Maggie stood right sair astonish'd,
Till, by the heel and hand admonish'd,
She ventur'd forward on the light;
And, wow! Tam saw an unco sight!

　Warlocks and witches in a dance;
Nae cotillion brent new frae France,
But hornpipes, jigs, strathspeys and reels,
Put life and mettle in their heels.
A winnock-bunker in the east,
There sat auld Nick, in shape o' beast;
A towzie tyke, black, grim and large,
To gie them music was his charge:
He screw'd the pipes and gart them skirl
Till roof and rafters a' did dirl.
Coffins stood round, like open presses,
That shaw'd the dead in their last dresses;
And, by some devilish cantraip sleight,
Each in its cauld hand held a light—
By which heroic Tam was able
To note upon the haly table
A murderer's banes, in gibbet-airns;
Twa span-lang, wee, unchristen'd bairns;
A thief, new-cutted frae a rape,
Wi' his last gasp his gab did gape;
Five tomahawks wi' blude red-rusted;
Five scymitars wi' murder crusted;

A garter which a babe had strangled;
A knife a father's throat had mangled—
Whom his ain son o' life bereft—
The grey hairs yet stack to the heft;
Wi' mair of horrible and awefu',
Which ev'n to name wad be unlawfu'.

As Tammie glowr'd, amaz'd and curious,
The mirth and fun grew fast and furious:
The piper loud and louder blew,
The dancers quick and quicker flew:
They reel'd, they set, they cross'd, they cleekit,
Till ilka carlin swat and reekit,
And coost her duddies to the wark,
And linket at it in her sark!

Now Tam, O Tam! had thae been queans,
A' plump and strapping in their teens!
Their sarks, instead o' creeshie flainen,
Been snaw-white seventeen-hunder linen!—
Thir breeks o' mine, my only pair,
That ance were plush, o' gude blue hair,
I wad hae gi'en them off my hurdies
For ae blink o' the bonie burdies!

But wither'd beldams, auld and droll,
Rigwoodie hags wad spean a foal,
Lowping and flinging on a crummock,
I wonder didna turn thy stomach.

But Tam kend what was what fu' brawlie:
There was ae winsome wench and wawlie
That night enlisted in the core,
Lang after kend on Carrick shore:
(For mony a beast to dead she shot,
And perish'd mony a bonny boat,
And shook baith meikle corn and bear,
And held the country-side in fear).

Her cutty sark, o' Paisley harn,
That while a lassie she had worn,
In longitude tho' sorely scanty,
It was her best, and she was vauntie.—
Ah! little kend thy reverend grannie,
That sark she coft for her wee Nannie,
Wi' twa pund Scots ('twas a' her riches),
Wad ever grac'd a dance of witches!

But here my Muse her wing maun cour,
Sic flights are far beyond her pow'r;
To sing how Nannie lap and flang
(A souple jade she was and strang),
And how Tam stood like ane bewitch'd
And thought his very een enrich'd;
Even Satan glowr'd, and fidg'd fu' fain,
And hotch'd and blew wi' might and main,
Till first ae caper, syne anither,
Tam tint his reason a' thegither
And roars out 'Weel done, Cutty-sark!'
And in an instant all was dark;
And scarcely had he Maggie rallied,
When out the hellish legion sallied.

As bees bizz out wi' angry fyke,
When plundering herds assail their byke;
As open pussie's mortal foes,
When, pop! she starts before their nose;
As eager runs the market-crowd,
When 'Catch the thief!' resounds aloud;
So Maggie runs—the witches follow,
Wi' mony an eldritch skreech and hollow.

Ah, Tam! Ah, Tam! thou'll get thy fairin!
In hell they'll roast thee like a herrin!
In vain thy Kate awaits thy comin!
Kate soon will be a woefu' woman!
Now, do thy speedy utmost, Meg,
And win the key-stane of the brig;

There, at them thou thy tail may toss:
A running stream they dare na cross.
But ere the key-stane she could make,
The fient a tail she had to shake!
For Nannie, far before the rest,
Hard upon noble Maggie prest,
And flew at Tam wi' furious ettle:
But little wist she Maggie's mettle—
Ae spring brought off her master hale
But left behind her ain grey tail:
The carlin claught her by the rump,
And left poor Maggie scarce a stump.

Now, wha this tale o' truth shall read,
Ilk man and mother's son, take heed:
Whene'er to drink you are inclin'd,
Or cutty sarks run in your mind,
Think! ye may buy the joys o'er dear,
Remember Tam o' Shanter's mare.

LI

THE MARRIED STATE

THERE are several persons who have many pleasures and entertainments in their possession which they do not enjoy. It is therefore a kind and good office to acquaint them with their own happiness, and turn their attention to such instances of their good fortune which they are apt to overlook. Persons in the married state often want such a monitor, and pine away their days, by looking upon the same condition in anguish and murmur which carries with it in the opinion of others a complication of all the pleasures of life, and a retreat from its inquietudes. I am led into this thought by a visit I made an old friend who was formerly my school-fellow. He came to town last week with his family for the winter, and yesterday morning sent me word his wife expected me to dinner. I am as it were at home at that house, and every member of it knows me for their well-wisher. I cannot indeed express the pleasure it is, to be met by the children with so much joy as I am when I go thither: the boys and girls strive who shall come first, when they think it is I that am knocking at the door; and that child which loses the race to me, runs back again to tell the father it is Mr. Bickerstaff. This day I was led in by a pretty girl, that we all thought must have forgot me; for the family has been out of town these two years. Her knowing me again was a mighty subject with us, and took up our discourse at the first entrance. After which they began to rally me upon a thousand little stories they heard in the country about my marriage to one of my neighbour's daughters: upon which the gentleman my friend said, 'Nay, if Mr. Bickerstaff marries a child of any of his old companions, I hope mine shall have the preference; there's Mrs. Mary is now sixteen, and would make him as fine a widow as the best of them: but I know him too well; he is so enamoured with the very memory of those who flourished in our youth, that he will not so much as look upon the modern beauties. I remember, old gentleman, how often you went home in a day to refresh your countenance and dress, when Teraminta reigned in your heart. As we came up in the coach, I repeated to my wife some of your verses on her.' With such reflections on little passages which happened long ago, we passed our time during a cheerful and elegant meal. After dinner, his lady left the room, as did also the children. As soon as we were alone, he took me by the hand; 'Well, my good friend,' says he, 'I am heartily glad to see thee; I was afraid you would never have seen all the company that dined with you to-day again. Do not you think the good woman of the house a little altered, since you followed her from the play-house, to find out who she was, for me?' I perceived a tear fall down his cheek as he spoke, which moved me not a little. But to turn the discourse, said I, 'She is not indeed quite that creature she was when she returned me the letter I carried from you; and told me, she hoped, as I was a gentleman, I would be employed no more to trouble her who had never offended me, but would be so much the gentleman's friend as to dissuade him from a pursuit which he could never succeed in. You may remember, I thought her in earnest, and you were forced to employ your cousin Will, who made his sister get acquainted with her for you. You cannot expect her to be for ever fifteen.' 'Fifteen?' replied my good friend: 'ah! you little understand, you that have lived a bachelor, how great, how exquisite a pleasure there is in being really beloved! It is impossible that the most beauteous face in nature should raise in me such pleasing ideas as when I look upon that excellent woman. That fading in her countenance is chiefly caused by her watching with me in my fever. This was followed by a fit of sickness, which had like to have carried her off last winter. I tell you sincerely, I have so many obligations to her, that I cannot with any sort of moderation think of her present state of health. But as to what you say of fifteen, she gives me every day pleasures beyond what I ever knew in the possession of her beauty when I was in the vigour of youth. Every moment of her life brings me fresh instances of her complacency to my inclinations, and her prudence in regard to my fortune. Her face is to me much more beautiful than when I first saw it; there is no decay in any feature which I cannot trace from the very instant it was occasioned by some anxious concern for my welfare and interests. Thus at the same time, methinks, the love I conceived towards her for what she was, is heightened by my gratitude for what she is. The love of a wife is as much above the idle passion commonly called by that name, as the loud laughter of buffoons is inferior to the elegant mirth of gentlemen. Oh! she is an inestimable jewel. In her examination of her household affairs, she shows a certain fearfulness to find a fault, which makes her servants obey her like children; and the meanest we have, has an ingenuous shame for an offence, not always to be seen in children in other families. I speak freely to you, my old friend; ever since her sickness, things that gave me the quickest joy before, turn now to a certain anxiety. As the children play in the next room, I know the poor things by their steps, and am considering what they must do, should they lose their mother in their tender years. The pleasure I used to take in telling my boy stories of the battles, and asking my girl questions about the disposal of her baby, and the gossiping of it, is turned into inward reflection and melancholy.' He would have gone on in this tender way, when the good lady entered, and with an inexpressible sweetness in her countenance told us, she had been searching her closet for something very good to treat such an old friend as I was. Her husband's eyes sparkled with pleasure at the cheerfulness of her countenance; and I saw all his fears vanish in an instant. The lady observing something in our looks which showed we had been more serious than ordinary, and seeing her husband receive her with great concern under a forced cheerfulness, immediately guessed at what we had been talking of; and applying herself to me, said, with a smile, 'Mr. Bickerstaff, don't believe a word of what he tells you. I shall still live to have you for my second, as I have often promised you, unless he takes more care of himself than he has done since his coming to town. You must know, he tells me, that he finds London is a much more healthy place than the country; for he sees several of his old acquaintance and schoolfellows are here, young fellows with fair full-bottomed periwigs. I could scarce keep him this morning from going out open-breasted.' My friend, who is always extremely delighted with her agreeable humour, made her sit down with us. She did it with that easiness which is peculiar to women of sense; and to keep up the good humour she had brought in with her, turned her raillery upon me. 'Mr. Bickerstaff, you remember you followed me one night from the play-house; supposing you should carry me thither tomorrow night, and lead me into the front box.' This put us into a long field of discourse about the beauties, who were mothers to the present, and shone in the boxes twenty years ago. I told her, I was glad she had transferred so many of her charms, and I did not question but her eldest daughter was within half a year of being a toast. We were pleasing ourselves with this fantastical preferment of the young lady, when on a sudden we were alarmed with the noise of a drum, and immediately entered my little godson to give me a point of war. His mother, between laughing and chiding, would have put him out of the room; but I would not part with him so. I found, upon conversation with him, though he was a little noisy in his mirth, that the child had excellent parts, and was a great master of all the learning on the other side eight years old. I perceived him a very great historian in Æsop's fables; but he frankly declared to me his mind, that he did not delight in that learning, because he did not believe they were true; for which reason, I found he had very much turned his studies, for about a twelvemonth past, into the lives and adventures of Don Bellianis of Greece, Guy of Warwick, the Seven Champions, and other historians of that age. I could not but observe the satisfaction the father took in the forwardness of his son; and that these diversions might turn to some profit, I found the boy had made remarks, which might be of service to him during the course of his whole life. He would tell you the mismanagements of John Hickathrift, find fault with the passionate temper in Bevis of Southampton, and loved St. George for being the champion of England; and by this means, had his thoughts insensibly moulded into the notions of discretion, virtue, and honour. I was extolling his accomplishments, when the mother told me, that the little girl who led me in this morning was in her way a better scholar than he. 'Betty,' says she, 'deals chiefly in fairies and sprites; and sometimes in a winter night, will terrify the maids with her accounts, till they are afraid to go up to bed.'

I sat with them till it was very late, sometimes in merry, sometimes in serious discourse, with this particular pleasure, which gives the only true relish to all conversation, a sense that every one of us liked each other. I went home, considering the different conditions of a married life and that of a bachelor; and I must confess, it struck me with a secret concern, to reflect, that whenever I go off, I shall leave no traces behind me. In this pensive mood I returned to my family; that is to say, to my maid, my dog and my cat, who only can be the better or worse for what happens to me.

LII

THE TEMPTATION OF CYMOCHLES

A HARDER lesson, to learne Continence
  In joyous pleasure, than in grievous paine:
  For sweetnesse doth allure the weaker sence
So strongly, that uneathes it can refraine
From that, which feeble nature covets faine;
But griefe and wrath, that be her enemies,
And foes of life, she better can restraine;
  Yet vertue vauntes in both their victories,
And *Guyon* in them all shewes goodly maisteries.

Whom bold *Cymochles* travelling to find,
  With cruell purpose bent to wreake on him
  The wrath, which *Atin* kindled in his mind,
  Came to a river, by whose utmost brim
  Wayting to passe, he saw whereas did swim
  Along the shore, as swift as glaunce of eye,
  A litle Gondelay, bedecked trim
  With boughes and arbours woven cunningly,
That like a litle forrest seemed outwardly.

And therein sate a Ladie fresh and faire,
  Making sweet solace to her selfe alone;
  Sometimes she sung, as loud as larke in aire,
  Sometimes she laught, that nigh her breth was gone,
  Yet was there not with her else any one,
  That might to her move cause of meriment:
  Matter of merth enough, though there were none,
  She could devise, and thousand waies invent,
To feede her foolish humour, and vaine jolliment.

Which when farre off *Cymochles* heard, and saw,
  He loudly cald to such, as were abord,
  The little barke unto the shore to draw,
  And him to ferrie over that deepe ford:

The merry marriner unto his word
Soone hearkned, and her painted bote streight way
Turnd to the shore, where that same warlike Lord
She in receiv'd; but *Atin* by no way
She would admit, albe the knight her much did pray.

Eftsoones her shallow ship away did slide,
  More swift, than swallow sheres the liquid skie,
Withouten oare or Pilot it to guide,
Or winged canvas with the wind to flie,
Only she turn'd a pin, and by and by
It cut away upon the yielding wave,
Ne cared she her course for to apply:
For it was taught the way, which she would have,
And both from rocks and flats it selfe could wisely save.

And all the way, the wanton Damzell found
  New merth, her passenger to entertaine:
For she in pleasant purpose did abound,
And greatly ioyed merry tales to faine,
Of which a store-house did with her remaine,
Yet seemed, nothing well they her became;
For all her words she drownd with laughter vaine,
And wanted grace in utt'ring of the same,
That turned all her pleasance to a scoffing game.

And other whiles vaine toyes she would devize
  As her fantasticke wit did most delight,
Sometimes her head she fondly would aguize
With gaudie garlands, or fresh flowrets dight
About her necke, or rings of rushes plight;
Sometimes to doe him laugh, she would assay
To laugh at shaking of the leaves light,
Or to behold the water worke, and play
About her litle frigot, therein making way.

THE TEMPTATION OF CYMOCHLES

Her light behaviour, and loose dalliaunce
   Gave wondrous great contentment to the knight,
That of his way he had no sovenaunce,
Nor care of vow'd revenge, and cruell fight,
But to weake wench did yeeld his martiall might,
So easie was to quench his flamed mind
With one sweet drop of sensuall delight,
So easie is, t'appease the stormie wind
Of malice in the calme of pleasant womankind.

Diverse discourses in their way they spent,
   Mongst which *Cymochles* of her questioned,
Both what she was, and what that usage ment,
Which in her cot she daily practised.
Vaine man (said she) that wouldest be reckoned
A straunger in thy home, and ignoraunt
Of *Phædria* (for so my name is red)
Of *Phædria*, thine owne fellow servaunt;
For thou to serve *Acrasia* thy selfe doest vaunt.

In this wide Inland sea, that hight by name
   The *Idle lake*, my wandring ship I row,
That knowes her port, and thither sailes by ayme,
Ne care, ne feare I, how the wind do blow,
Or whether swift I wend, or whether slow:
Both slow and swift a like do serve my tourne,
Ne swelling *Neptune*, ne loud thundring *Ioue*
Can chaunge my cheare, or make me ever mourne;
My litle boat can safely passe this perilous bourne.

Whiles thus she talked, and whiles thus she toyd,
   They were farre past the passage, which he spake,
And come unto an Island, waste and voyd,
That floted in the midst of that great lake,
There her small Gondelay her port did make,
And that gay paire issuing on the shore
Disburdned her. Their way they forward take
Into the land, that lay them faire before,
Whose pleasaunce she him shew'd, and plentifull great store.

It was a chosen plot of fertile land.
  Emongst wide waves set, like a litle nest,
  As if it had by Natures cunning hand
  Bene choisely picked out from all the rest,
  And laid forth for ensample of the best:
  No daintie flowre or herbe, that growes on ground,
  No arboret with painted blossomes drest,
  And smelling sweet, but there it might be found
To bud out faire, and her sweet smels throw all around.

No tree, whose braunches did not bravely spring;
  No braunch, whereon a fine bird did not sit:
  No bird, but did her shrill notes sweetly sing;
  No song but did containe a lovely dit:
  Trees, braunches, birds, and songs were framed fit,
  For to allure fraile mind to carelesse ease.
  Carelesse the man soone woxe, and his weake wit
  Was overcome of thing that did him please;
So pleased, did his wrathful purpose faire appease.

Thus when she had his eyes and senses fed
  With false delights, and fild with pleasures vaine,
  Into a shadie dale she soft him led,
  And laid him downe vpon a grassie plaine;
  And her sweet selfe without dread, or disdaine,
  She set beside, laying his head disarm'd
  In her loose lap, it softly to sustaine,
  Where soone he slumbred, fearing not be harm'd,
The whiles with a loud lay she thus him sweetly charm'd.

Behold, O man, that toilesome paines doest take,
  The flowres, the fields, and all that pleasant growes,
  How they themselves doe thine ensample make,
  Whiles nothing envious nature them forth throwes
  Out of her fruitfull lap; how, no man knowes,
  They spring, they bud, they blossome fresh and faire,
  And deck the world with their rich pompous showes;
  Yet no man for them taketh paines or care,
Yet no man to them can his carefull paines compare.

The lilly, Ladie of the flowring field,
  The Flowre-deluce, her lovely Paramoure,
  Bid thee to them thy fruitlesse labours yield,
  And soone leave off this toylesome wearie stoure;
  Loe loe how brave she decks her bounteous boure,
  With silken curtens and gold coverlets,
  Therein to shrowd her sumptuous Belamoure,
  Yet neither spinnes nor cardes, ne cares nor frets,
But to her mother Nature all her care she lets.

Why then dost thou, O man, that of them all
  Art Lord, and eke of nature Soveraine,
  Wilfully make thy selfe a wretched thrall,
  And wast thy joyous houres in needlesse paine,
  Seeking for daunger and adventures vaine?
  What bootes it all to have, and nothing use?
  Who shall him rew, that swimming in the maine,
  Will die for thirst, and water doth refuse?
Refuse such fruitlesse toile, and present pleasures chuse.

LIII

DIE VERNON

FROM the summit of an eminence I had already had a distant view of Osbaldistone Hall, a large and antiquated edifice, peeping out from a Druidical grove of huge oaks; and I was directing my course towards it, as straightly and as speedily as the windings of a very indifferent road would permit, when my horse, tired as he was, pricked up his ears at the enlivening notes of a pack of hounds in full cry, cheered by the occasional bursts of a French horn, which in those days was a constant accompaniment to the chase. I made no doubt that the pack was my uncle's and drew up my horse with the purpose of suffering the hunters to pass without notice, aware that a hunting-field was not the proper scene to introduce myself to a keen sportsman, and determined, when they had passed on, to proceed to the mansion-house at my own pace, and there to await the return of the proprietor from his sport. I paused, therefore, on a rising ground, and, not unmoved by the sense of interest which that species of silvan sport is so much calculated to inspire (although my mind was not at the moment very accessible to impressions of this nature), I expected with some eagerness the appearance of the huntsmen.

The fox, hard run, and nearly spent, first made his appearance from the copse which clothed the right-hand side of the valley. His drooping brush, his soiled appearance, and jaded trot, proclaimed his fate impending; and the carrion crow, which hovered over him, already considered poor Reynard as soon to be his prey. He crossed the stream which divides the little valley, and was dragging himself up a ravine on the other side of its wild banks, when the headmost hounds, followed by the rest of the pack in full cry, burst from the coppice, followed by the huntsman, and three or four riders. The dogs pursued the trace of Reynard with unerring instinct; and the hunters followed with reckless haste, regardless of the broken and difficult nature of the ground. They were tall, stout young men, well mounted, and dressed in green and red, the uniform of a sporting association, formed under the auspices of old Sir Hildebrand Osbaldistone. My cousins! thought I, as they swept past me. The next reflection was, what is my reception likely to be among these worthy successors of Nimrod? and how improbable is it, that I, knowing little or nothing of rural sports, shall find myself at ease, or happy, in my uncle's family. A vision that passed me interrupted these reflections.

It was a young lady, the loveliness of whose very striking features was enhanced by the animation of the chase and the glow of exercise, mounted on a beautiful horse, jet black, unless where he was flecked by spots of the snow-white foam which embossed his bridle. She wore, what was then somewhat unusual, a coat, vest, and hat, resembling those of a man, which fashion has since called a riding-habit. The mode had been introduced while I was in France, and was perfectly new to me. Her long black hair streamed on the breeze, having in the hurry of the chase escaped from the ribbon which bound it. Some very broken ground, through which she guided her horse with the most admirable address and presence of mind, retarded her course, and brought her closer to me than any of the other riders had passed. I had, therefore, a full view of her uncommonly fine face and person, to which an inexpressible charm was added by the wild gaiety of the scene, and the romance of her singular dress and unexpected appearance. As she passed me, her horse made, in his impetuosity, an irregular movement, just while, coming once more upon open ground, she was again putting him to his speed. It served as an apology for me to ride close up to her, as if to her assistance. There was, however, no cause for alarm; it was not a stumble, nor a false step; and, if it had been, the fair Amazon had too much self-possession to have been deranged by it. She thanked my good intentions, however, by a smile, and I felt encouraged to put my horse to the same pace, and to keep in her immediate neighbourhood. The clamour of 'Whoop, dead, dead!' and the corresponding flourish of the French horn, soon announced to us that there was no more occasion for haste, since the chase was at a close. One of the young men whom we had seen approached us, waving the brush of the fox in triumph, as if to upbraid my fair companion.

'I see,' she replied,—'I see; but make no noise about it; if Phœbe,' she said, patting the neck of the beautiful animal on which she rode, 'had not got among the cliffs, you would have had little cause for boasting.'

They met as she spoke, and I observed them both look at me and converse a moment in an undertone, the young lady apparently pressing the sportsman to do something which he declined shyly, and with a sort of sheepish sullenness. She instantly turned her horse's head towards me, saying,—'Well, well, Thornie, if you won't I must, that's all.—Sir,' she continued, addressing me, 'I have been endeavouring to persuade this cultivated young gentleman to make inquiry of you whether, in the course of your travels in these parts, you have heard anything of a friend of ours, one Mr. Francis

Osbaldistone, who has been for some days expected at Osbaldistone Hall?'

I was too happy to acknowledge myself to be the party inquired after, and to express my thanks for the obliging inquiries of the young lady.

'In that case, sir,' she rejoined, 'as my kinsman's politeness seems to be still slumbering, you will permit me (though I suppose it is highly improper) to stand mistress of ceremonies, and to present to you young Squire Thorncliff Osbaldistone, your cousin, and Die Vernon, who has also the honour to be your accomplished cousin's poor kinswoman.'

There was a mixture of boldness, satire, and simplicity in the manner in which Miss Vernon pronounced these words. My knowledge of life was sufficient to enable me to take up a corresponding tone as I expressed my gratitude to her for her condescension, and my extreme pleasure at having met with them. To say the truth, the compliment was so expressed, that the lady might easily appropriate the greater share of it, for Thorncliff seemed an arrant country bumpkin, awkward, shy, and somewhat sulky withal. He shook hands with me, however, and then intimated his intention of leaving me that he might help the huntsman and his brothers to couple up the hounds, a purpose which he rather communicated by way of information to Miss Vernon than as apology to me.

'There he goes,' said the young lady, following him with eyes in which disdain was admirably painted,—'the prince of grooms, and cock-fighters, and blackguard horse-coursers. But there is not one of them to mend another.—Have you read Markham?' said Miss Vernon.

'Read whom, ma'am?—I do not even remember the author's name.'

'O lud! on what a strand are you wrecked!' replied the young lady. 'A poor forlorn and ignorant stranger, unacquainted with the very Alcoran of the savage tribe whom you are come to reside among—Never to have heard of Markham, the most celebrated author on farriery! then I fear you are equally a stranger to the more modern names of Gibson and Bartlett?'

'I am, indeed, Miss Vernon.'

'And do you not blush to own it?' said Miss Vernon. 'Why, we must forswear your alliance. Then, I suppose, you can neither give a ball, nor a mash, nor a horn?'

'I confess I trust all these matters to an ostler, or to my groom.'

'Incredible carelessness!—And you cannot shoe a horse, or cut his mane and tail; or worm a dog, or crop his ears, or cut his dew-claws; or reclaim a hawk, or give him his casting-stones, or direct his diet when he is sealed; or——'

'To sum up my insignificance in one word,' replied I, 'I am profoundly ignorant in all these rural accomplishments.'

'Then, in the name of Heaven, Mr. Francis Osbaldistone, what *can* you do?'

'Very little to the purpose, Miss Vernon; something, however, I can pretend to—When my groom has dressed my horse, I can ride him, and when my hawk is in the field I can fly him.'

'Can you do this?' said the young lady, putting her horse to a canter.

There was a sort of rude overgrown fence crossed the path before us, with a gate, composed of pieces of wood rough from the forest; I was about to move forward to open it, when Miss Vernon cleared the obstruction at a flying leap. I was bound, in point of honour, to follow, and was in a moment again at her side.

'There are hopes of you yet,' she said. 'I was afraid you had been a very degenerate Osbaldistone.'

LIV

THE WONDERS OF THE WORLD

SIR JOHN MANDEVILLE

AND now will I tell you of lands and countries and isles that are beyond the land of Cathay. And therefore he that will go from Cathay to Inde the less and the more, he shall go through a kingdom that is called Cadhilhe, the which is a great land. And there groweth a manner of fruit great as gourds, and when it is ripe they open it and find therein a beast with flesh and blood and bone, and it is like to a little lamb without wool. And men of that country eat that beast and the fruit also. And that is a great marvel. Nevertheless I said them that methought it no great marvel, for in my country, I said them, were trees bearing a fruit that becometh birds flying, the which men call Bernakes, and there is good meat of them; and those that fall in the water live and fly forth, and those that fall on the land die. And when I had told them this they marvelled them greatly thereof. In this land also are great apples of noble smell and noble savour, and men may find of them on a cluster an hundred and more, and the leaves of the trees are two foot long and some longer. And in that country are trees bearing gariofles and nutmegs, and great nuts of Inde, and other divers spiceries. And there are vines that bear so great bobbs of grapes that a strong man may hardly bear one of them.

In this same land are the hills of Caspy which men call Uber. And among those hills are the Jews of the ten kindreds enclosed, which men call Gog and Magog, and they may come out at no side. For King Alexander chased them thither, for he weened to have enclosed them there through working of man; and when he saw that he might not he prayed to God that he would fulfil that he had begun. And, for all he were a heathen man, God of his special grace heard his prayer and closed the hills together, the which are so great and so high that no man may pass them. . . . And nevertheless some time it happens that some of them climb over those hills and go out, but there may no great number of them climb over them together by cause of the great height of them and the ill climbing. And there is none other passage out but a narrow sty which was made through slight and working of men. And that passage is but four mile long, and then is there a great desert where men may find no water nor no dwelling for man by reason of dragons and nadders and other venomous beasts, so that no man may pass there away but if it be in the winter. . . . From this land men shall go to the land of Bachary, where are many wicked men and fell. In this land are trees that bear wool, as it were of sheep, of which they make cloth. In this land also are many ypotams that dwell some time upon land and some time on the water, and they are half man and half horse. And they eat men whereso they may get them, no meat gladlier. And in that land are many griffins, more than in any country else. And some men say that they have the shape of an eagle before, and behind the shape of a lion, and sikerly they say sooth. Nevertheless the griffin is more and stronger than eight lions of these countries, and greater and stalworther than an hundred eagles. For certainly he will bear to his nest flying a great horse and a man upon him, or two oxen yoked together as they go together at the plough. For he has nails upon his feet as great and as long as they were oxen horns, but they are wondrous sharp. And of these nails men make cups for to drink of, as we do of the horns of oxen, and of the backs of his feathers they make strong bows for to shoot with.

PIP AND JOE

'Now, boy! What was she a doing of, when you went in to-day?' asked Mr. Pumblechook. 'She was sitting,' I answered, 'in a black velvet coach.' Mr. Pumblechook and Mrs. Joe stared at one another—as they well might—and both repeated, 'In a black velvet coach?' 'Yes,' said I. 'And Miss Estella—that's her niece, I think—handed her in cake and wine at the coach-window, on a gold plate. And we all had cake and wine on gold plates. And I got up behind the coach to eat mine, because she told me to.' 'Was anybody else there?' asked Mr. Pumblechook. 'Four dogs,' said I. 'Large or small?' 'Immense,' said I, 'And they fought for veal-cutlets out of a silver basket.' Mr. Pumblechook and Mrs. Joe stared at one another again, in utter amazement. I was perfectly frantic—a reckless witness under the torture—and would have told them anything. 'Where *was* this coach, in the name of gracious?' asked my sister. 'In Miss Havisham's room.' They stared again. 'But there weren't any horses to it.' I added this saving clause, in the moment of rejecting four richly caparisoned coursers, which I had had wild thoughts of harnessing. 'Can this be possible, uncle?' asked Mrs. Joe. 'What can the boy mean?' 'I'll tell you, Mum,' said Mr. Pumblechook. 'My opinion is, it's a sedan-chair. She's flighty, you know—very flighty—quite flighty enough to pass her days in a sedan-chair.' 'Did you ever see her in it, uncle?' asked Mrs. Joe. 'How could I,' he returned, forced to the admission, 'when I never see her in my life? Never clapped eyes upon her!' 'Goodness, uncle! And yet you have spoken to her?' 'Why, don't you know,' said Mr. Pumblechook, testily, 'that when I have been there, I have been took up to the outside of her door, and the door has stood ajar, and she has spoken to me that way. Don't say you don't know *that*, Mum. However, the boy went there to play. What did you play at, boy?' 'We played with flags,' I said. (I beg to observe that I think of myself with amazement, when I recall the lies I told on this occasion.) 'Flags!' echoed my sister. 'Yes,' said I. 'Estella waved a blue flag, and I waved a red one, and Miss Havisham waved one sprinkled all over with little gold stars, out at the coach-window. And then we all waved our swords and hurrahed.' 'Swords!' repeated my sister. 'Where did you get swords from?' 'Out of a cupboard,' said I. 'And I saw pistols in it—and jam—and pills. And there was no daylight in the room, but it was all lighted up with candles.' 'That's true, Mum,' said Mr. Pumblechook, with a grave nod. 'That's the state of the case, for that much I've seen myself.' And then they both stared at me, and I, with an obtrusive show of artlessness on my countenance, stared at them, and plaited the right leg of my trousers with my right hand. If they had asked me any more questions I should undoubtedly have betrayed myself, for I was even then on the point of mentioning that there was a balloon in the yard, and should have hazarded the statement but for my invention being divided between that phenomenon and a bear in the brewery. They were so much occupied, however, in discussing the marvels I had already presented for their consideration, that I escaped.

After Mr. Pumblechook had driven off, and when my sister was washing up, I stole into the fòrge to Joe, and remained by him until he had done for the night. Then I said, 'Before the fire goes out, Joe, I should like to tell you something.' 'Should you, Pip?' said Joe, drawing his shoeing-stool near the forge. 'Then tell us. What is it, Pip?' 'Joe,' said I, taking hold of his rolled-up shirt sleeve, and twisting it between my finger and thumb, 'you remember all that about Miss Havisham's?' 'Remember?' said Joe. 'I believe you! Wonderful!' 'It's a terrible thing, Joe; it ain't true.' 'What are you telling of, Pip?' cried Joe, falling back in the greatest amazement. 'You don't mean to say it's——' 'Yes, I do; it's lies, Joe.' 'But not all of it? Why sure you don't mean to say, Pip, that there was no black welwet co———ch?' For, I stood shaking my head. 'But at least there was dogs, Pip? Come, Pip,' said Joe, persuasively, 'if there warn't no weal-cutlets, at least there was dogs?' 'No, Joe.' 'A dog?' said Joe. 'A puppy? Come!' 'No, Joe, there was nothing at all of the kind.' As I fixed my eyes hopelessly on Joe, Joe contemplated me in dismay. 'Pip, old chap! This won't do, old fellow! I say! Where do you expect to go to?'

'There's one thing you may be sure of, Pip,' said Joe, after some rumination, 'namely, that lies is lies. Howsever they come, they didn't ought to come, and they come from the father of lies, and work round to the same. Don't you tell no more of 'em, Pip. *That* ain't the way to get out of being common, old chap. And as to being common, I don't make it out at all clear. You are oncommon in some things. You're oncommon small. Likewise you're a oncommon scholar.' 'No, I am ignorant and backward, Joe.' 'Why, see what a letter you wrote last night! Wrote in print even! I've seen letters—Ah! and from gentlefolks!—that I'll swear weren't wrote in print,' said Joe. 'I have learnt next to nothing, Joe. You think much of me. It's only that.' 'Well, Pip,' said Joe, 'be it so, or be it son't, you must be a common scholar afore you can be a oncommon one, I should hope! The king upon his throne, with his crown upon his 'ed, can't sit and write his Acts of Parliament in print, without having begun, when he were a unpromoted Prince, with the alphabet—Ah!' added Joe, with a shake of the head that was full of meaning, 'and begun at A too, and worked his way to Z. And *I* know what that is to do, though I can't say I've exactly done it.' There was some hope in this piece of wisdom, and it rather encouraged me. 'Whether common ones as to callings and earnings,' pursued Joe, reflectively, 'mightn't be the better of continuing for to keep company with common ones, instead of going out to play with oncommon ones—which reminds me to hope that there were a flag, perhaps?' 'No, Joe.' '(I'm sorry there weren't a flag, Pip.) Whether that might be, or mightn't be, is a thing as can't be looked into now, without putting your sister on the Rampage; and that's a thing not to be thought of, as being done intentional. Lookee here, Pip, at what is said to you by a true friend. Which this to you the true friend say. If you can't get to be oncommon through going straight, you'll never get to do it through going crooked. So don't tell no more on 'em, Pip, and live well and die happy.'

LV

ST. PAUL'S VOYAGE AND SHIPWRECK

AND when it was determined that we should sail into Italy, they delivered Paul and certain other prisoners unto one named Julius, a centurion of Augustus' band. And entering into a ship of Adramyttium, we launched, meaning to sail by the coasts of Asia; one Aristarchus, a Macedonian of Thessalonica, being with us. And the next day we touched at Sidon. And Julius courteously entreated Paul, and gave him liberty to go unto his friends to refresh himself. And when we had launched from thence, we sailed under Cyprus because the winds were contrary. And when we had sailed over the sea of Cilicia and Pamphylia, we came to Myra, a city of Lycia. And there the centurion found a ship of Alexandria sailing into

Italy; and he put us therein. And when we had sailed slowly many days, and scarce were come over against Cnidus, the wind not suffering us, we sailed under Crete, over against Salmone; and, hardly passing it, came unto a place which is called The Fair Havens; nigh whereunto was the city of Lasea.

Now when much time was spent, and when sailing was now dangerous, because the fast was now already past, Paul admonished them, and said unto them, Sirs, I perceive that this voyage will be with hurt and much damage, not only of the lading and ship, but also of our lives. Nevertheless the centurion believed the master and the owner of the ship, more than those things which were spoken by Paul. And because the haven was not commodious to winter in, the more part advised to depart thence also, if by any means they might attain to Phenice, and there to winter; which is an haven of Crete, and lieth toward the south west and north west. And when the south wind blew softly, supposing that they had obtained their purpose, loosing thence, they sailed close by Crete. But not long after there arose against it a tempestuous wind, called Euroclydon. And when the ship was caught, and could not bear up into the wind, we let her drive. And running under a certain island which is called Clauda, we had much work to come by the boat: which when they had taken up, they used helps, undergirding the ship; and, fearing lest they should fall into the quicksands, strake sail, and so were driven. And we being exceedingly tossed with a tempest, the next day they lightened the ship; and the third day we cast out with our own hands the tackling of the ship. And when neither sun nor stars in many days appeared, and no small tempest lay on us, all hope that we should be saved was then taken away.

But after long abstinence Paul stood forth in the midst of them, and said, Sirs, ye should have hearkened unto me, and not have loosed from Crete, and to have gained this harm and loss. And now I exhort you to be of good cheer: for there shall be no loss of any man's life among you, but of the ship. For there stood by me this night the angel of God, whose I am, and whom I serve, saying, Fear not, Paul; thou must be brought before Cæsar: and, lo, God hath given thee all them that sail with thee. Wherefore, sirs, be of good cheer: for I believe God, that it shall be even as it was told me. Howbeit we must be cast upon a certain island.

But when the fourteenth night was come, as we were driven up and down in Adria, about midnight the shipmen deemed that they drew near to some country; and sounded, and found it twenty fathoms: and when they had gone a little further, they sounded again, and found it fifteen fathoms. Then fearing lest we should have fallen upon rocks, they cast four anchors out of the stern, and wished for the day. And as the shipmen were about to flee out of the ship, when they had let down the boat into the sea, under colour as though they would have cast anchors out of the foreship, Paul said to the centurion and to the soldiers, Except these abide in the ship, ye cannot be saved. Then the soldiers cut off the ropes of the boat, and let her fall off. And while the day was coming on, Paul besought them all to take meat, saying, This day is the fourteenth day that ye have tarried and continued fasting, having taken nothing. Wherefore I pray you to take some meat: for this is for your health: for there shall not an hair fall from the head of any of you. And when he had thus spoken, he took bread, and gave thanks to God in presence of them all: and when he had broken it, he began to eat. Then were they all of good cheer, and they also took some meat. And we were in all in the ship two hundred threescore and sixteen souls. And when they had eaten enough, they lightened the ship, and cast out the wheat into the sea.

And when it was day, they knew not the land: but they discovered a certain creek with a shore, into the which they were minded, if it were possible, to thrust in the ship. And when they had taken up the anchors, they committed themselves unto the sea, and loosed the rudder bands, and hoised up the mainsail to the wind, and made toward shore. And falling into a place where two seas met, they ran the ship aground; and the forepart stuck fast, and remained unmoveable, but the hinder part was broken with the violence of the waves. And the soldiers' counsel was to kill the prisoners, lest any of them should swim out, and escape. But the centurion, willing to save Paul, kept them from their purpose; and commanded that they which could swim should cast themselves first into the sea, and get to land: and the rest, some on boards, and some on broken pieces of the ship. And so it came to pass, that they escaped all safe to land.

'THEY THAT GO DOWN TO THE SEA'

They that go down to the sea in ships,
That do business in great waters;
These see the works of the Lord,
And his wonders in the deep,
For he commandeth, and raiseth the stormy wind,
Which lifteth up the waves thereof.
They mount up to the heaven, they go down again to the depths:
Their soul is melted because of trouble.
They reel to and fro, and stagger like a drunken man,
And are at their wit's end.
Then they cry unto the Lord in their trouble,
And he bringeth them out of their distresses.
He maketh the storm a calm,
So that the waves thereof are still.
Then are they glad because they be quiet;
So he bringeth them unto their desired haven.
Oh that men would praise the Lord for his goodness,
And for his wonderful works to the children of men!

LVI

AN IDEAL OF EMPIRE

MY hold of the colonies is in the close affection which grows from common names, from kindred blood, from similar privileges, and equal protection. These are ties, which, though light as air, are as strong as links of iron. Let the colonies always keep the idea of their civil rights associated with your government;—they will cling and grapple to you; and no force under heaven will be of power to tear them from their allegiance. But let it be once understood, that your government may be one thing, and their privileges another; that these two things may exist without any mutual relation; the cement is gone; the cohesion is loosened; and everything hastens to decay and dissolution. As long as you have the wisdom to keep the sovereign authority of this country as the sanctuary of liberty, the sacred temple consecrated to our common faith, wherever the chosen race and sons of England worship freedom, they will turn their faces towards you. The more they multiply, the more friends you will have; the more ardently they love liberty, the more perfect will be their obedience. Slavery they can have anywhere. It is a weed that grows in every soil. They may have it from Spain, they may have it from Prussia. But until you become lost to all feeling of your true interest and your natural dignity, freedom they can have from none but you. This is the commodity of price, of which you have the monopoly. This is the true act of navigation, which binds to you the commerce of the colonies, and through them secures to you the wealth of the world. Deny them this participation of freedom, and you break that sole bond which originally made, and must still preserve, the unity of the empire. Do not entertain so weak an imagination, as that your registers and your bonds, your affidavits and your sufferances, your cockets and your clearances, are what form the great securities of your commerce. Do not dream that your letters of office, and your instructions, and your suspending clauses are the things that hold together the great contexture of this mysterious whole. These things do not make your government. Dead instruments, passive tools as they are, it is the spirit of the English communion that gives all their life and efficacy to them. It is the spirit of the English constitution which, infused through the mighty mass, pervades, feeds, unites, invigorates, vivifies every part of the empire, even down to the minutest member.

Is it not the same virtue which does every thing for us

here in England? Do you imagine then, that it is the land tax act which raises your revenue? that it is the annual vote in the committee of supply, which gives you your army? or that it is the mutiny bill which inspires it with bravery and discipline? No! surely no! It is the love of the people; it is their attachment to their government from the sense of the deep stake they have in such a glorious institution, which gives you your army and your navy, and infuses into both that liberal obedience without which your army would be a base rabble and your navy nothing but rotten timber.

All this, I know well enough, will sound wild and chimerical to the profane herd of those vulgar and mechanical politicians, who have no place among us; a sort of people who think that nothing exists but what is gross and material; and who therefore, far from being qualified to be directors of the great movement of empire, are not fit to turn a wheel in the machine. But to men truly initiated and rightly taught, these ruling and master principles, which, in the opinion of such men as I have mentioned, have no substantial existence, are in truth every thing, and all in all. Magnanimity in politicks is not seldom the truest wisdom; and a great empire and little minds go ill together. If we are conscious of our situation, and glow with zeal to fill our places as becomes our station and ourselves, we ought to auspicate all our publick proceedings on America, with the old warning of the church, *Sursum corda*! We ought to elevate our minds to the greatness of that trust to which the order of Providence has called us.

LVII

THE HAPPY WARRIOR

WHO is the happy Warrior? Who is he
That every man in arms should wish to be?
—It is the generous Spirit, who when brought
Among the tasks of real life, hath wrought
Upon the plan that pleased his boyish thought:

Whose high endeavours are an inward light
That makes the path before him always bright:
Who, with a natural instinct to discern
What knowledge can perform, is diligent to learn;
Abides by this resolve, and stops not there,
But makes his moral being his prime care;
Who, doomed to go in company with Pain,
And Fear, and Bloodshed, miserable train!
Turns his necessity to glorious gain;
In face of these doth exercise a power
Which is our human nature's highest dower;
Controls them and subdues, transmutes, bereaves
Of their bad influence, and their good receives:
By objects, which might force the soul to abate
Her feeling, rendered more compassionate;
Is placable—because occasions rise
So often that demand such sacrifice;
More skilful in self-knowledge, even more pure,
As tempted more; more able to endure,
As more exposed to suffering and distress;
Thence, also, more alive to tenderness.
—'Tis he whose law is reason; who depends
Upon that law as on the best of friends;
Whence, in a state where men are tempted still
To evil for a guard against worse ill,
And what in quality or act is best
Doth seldom on a right foundation rest,
He labours good on good to fix, and owes
To virtue every triumph that he knows:
—Who, if he rise to station of command,
Rises by open means; and there will stand
On honourable terms, or else retire,
And in himself possess his own desire;
Who comprehends his trust, and to the same
Keeps faithful with a singleness of aim;
And therefore does not stoop, nor lie in wait
For wealth, or honours, or for worldly state;
Whom they must follow; on whose head must fall,

Like showers of manna, if they come at all:
Whose powers shed round him in the common strife,
Or mild concerns of ordinary life,
A constant influence, a peculiar grace;
But who, if he be called upon to face
Some awful moment to which Heaven has joined
Great issues, good or bad for human kind,
Is happy as a Lover; and attired
With sudden brightness, like a Man inspired;
And, through the heat of conflict, keeps the law
In calmness made, and sees what he foresaw;
Or if an unexpected call succeed,
Come when it will, is equal to the need:
—He who, though thus endued as with a sense
And faculty for storm and turbulence,
Is yet a Soul whose master-bias leans
To homefelt pleasures and to gentle scenes;
Sweet images! which, wheresoe'er he be,
Are at his heart; and such fidelity
It is his darling passion to approve;
More brave for this, that he hath much to love:——
'Tis, finally, the Man, who, lifted high,
Conspicuous object in a Nation's eye,
Or left unthought-of in obscurity,—
Who, with a toward or untoward lot,
Prosperous or adverse, to his wish or not—
Plays, in the many games of life, that one
Where what he most doth value must be won:
Whom neither shape of danger can dismay,
Nor thought of tender happiness betray;
Who, not content that former worth stand fast,
Looks forward, persevering to the last,
From well to better, daily self-surpast:
Who, whether praise of him must walk the earth
For ever, and to noble deeds give birth,
Or he must fall, to sleep without his fame,
And leave a dead unprofitable name—
Finds comfort in himself and in his cause;

And, while the mortal mist is gathering, draws
His breath in confidence of Heaven's applause:
This is the happy Warrior; this is He
That every Man in arms should wish to be.

THE VIRTUOUS MAN

He that derives his high nobility
Not from the mention of a pedigree;
Who thinks it not his praise that others know
His ancestors were gallant long ago;
Who scorns to boast the glories of his blood,
And thinks he can't be great that is not good;
Who knows the world, and what we pleasure call,
Yet cannot sell one conscience for them all;
Who hates to hoard that gold with an excuse
For which he can find out a nobler use;
Who dares not keep that life that he can spend
To serve his God, his country, and his friend;
Who flattery and falsehood doth so hate,
He would not buy ten lives at such a rate;
Whose soul, than diamonds more rich and clear,
Naked and open as his face doth wear;
Who dares be good, alone, in such a time
When virtue's held and punished as a crime;
Who thinks dark crooked plots a mean defence,
And is both safe and wise in innocence;
Who dares both fight and die, but dares not fear;
Whose only doubt is, if his cause be clear;
Whose courage and his justice, equal worn,
Can dangers grapple, overcome, and scorn,
Yet not insult upon a conquered foe,
But can forgive him and oblige him too;
Whose friendship is congenial with his soul,
Who, when he gives a heart, bestows it whole;
Whose other ties and titles here do end,
Or buried or completed in the friend;
Who ne'er resumes the soul he once did give
While his friend's honesty and honour live,

And if his friend's content could cost the price,
Would count himself a happy sacrifice;
Whose happy days no pride infects, nor can
His other titles make him slight the man,
(No dark ambitious thoughts do cloud his brow,
Nor restless cares when to be great, and how;)
Who scorns to envy wealth where'er it be,
But pities such a golden slavery;
With no mean fawnings can the people court,
Nor wholly slight a popular report;
Whose house no orphan groans do shake or blast,
Nor any riot help to serve his taste;
Who from the top of his prosperities
Can take a fall, and yet without surprise;
Who with the same august and even state
Can entertain the best and worst of fate;
Whose suffering's sweet, if honour once adorn it;
Who slights revenge, yet does not fear, but scorn it;
Whose happiness in every fortune lives,
For that no fortune either takes or gives;
Who no unhandsome ways can bribe his fate,
Nay out of prison marches through the gate;
Who, losing all his titles and his pelf,
Nay, all the world, can never lose himself;
This person shines indeed; and he that can
Be virtuous is the great immortal man.

LVIII

THE FUSILIER BRIGADE AT ALBUERA

DURING this first unhappy effort of the second division, so great was the disorder, that the Spaniards in one part fired without cessation, though the British troops were before them; in another part, flying before the lancers, they would have broken through the twenty-ninth, then advancing to succour Colborne, but with a stern resolution that regiment smote friends and foes without distinction in their onward progress. Meanwhile Beresford, finding the main body of the Spaniards would not advance, seized an ensign by the breast and bore him and his colours by main force to the front; yet the troops did not follow, and the coward ran back when released from the marshal's iron grasp. In this crisis the weather, which had ruined Colborne's brigade, saved the day. Soult could not see the whole field of battle, and kept his heavy columns inactive when the decisive blow might have been struck. His cavalry indeed began to hem in that of the allies, yet the fire of the horse-artillery enabled Lumley, covered as he was by the bed of the Aroya and supported by the fourth division, to check them on the plain; Colborne still remained on the height with the thirty-first regiment, the British artillery, under Julius Hartman, was coming fast into action, and William Stewart, who had escaped the charge of the lancers, was again mounting the hill with Houghton's brigade, which he brought on with equal vehemence, but in a juster order of battle. The day then cleared and a dreadful fire poured into the thickest of the French columns convinced Soult that the fight was yet to be won.

Houghton's regiments reached the height under a heavy cannonade, and the twenty-ninth, after breaking through the fugitive Spaniards, was charged in flank by the French lancers; yet two companies, wheeling to the right, foiled this attack with a sharp fire, and then the third brigade of the second division came up on the left, and the Spanish troops under Zayas and Ballesteros at last moved forward. Hartman's artillery was now in full play, and the enemy's infantry recoiled, but, soon recovering, renewed the fight with greater violence than before. The cannon on both sides discharged showers of grape at half range, the peals of musketry were incessant, often within pistol-shot, yet the close formation of the French embarrassed their battle, and the British line would not yield them an inch of ground or a moment of time to open their ranks. Their fighting was however fierce and dangerous. Stewart was twice wounded, colonel Duckworth was slain, and the intrepid Houghton, having received

FUSILIER BRIGADE AT ALBUERA

many wounds without shrinking, fell and died in the very act of cheering on his men. Still the struggle continued with unabated fury. Colonel Inglis, twenty-two officers, and more than four hundred men, out of five hundred and seventy who had mounted the hill, fell in the fifty-seventh alone; the other regiments were scarcely better off, not one-third were standing in any: ammunition failed, and as the English fire slackened a French column was established in advance upon the right flank. The play of the guns checked them a moment, but in this dreadful crisis Beresford wavered! Destruction stared him in the face, his personal resources were exhausted, and the unhappy thought of a retreat rose in his agitated mind. He had before brought Hamilton's Portuguese into a situation to cover a retrograde movement; he now sent Alten orders to abandon the bridge and village of Albuera, and to take, with his Germans and the Portuguese artillery, a position to cover a retreat by the Valverde road. But while the commander was thus preparing to resign the contest, colonel Hardinge had urged Cole to advance with the fourth division; and then riding to the third brigade of the second division, which, under the command of colonel Abercrombie, had hitherto been only slightly engaged, directed him also to push forward into the fight. The die was thus cast, Beresford acquiesced, Alten received orders to retake the village, and this terrible battle was continued.

The fourth division was composed of two brigades: one of Portuguese under general Harvey; the other, under Sir William Myers, consisting of the seventh and twenty-third regiments, was called the fuzileer brigade: Harvey's Portuguese were immediately pushed in between Lumley's dragoons and the hill, where they were charged by some French cavalry, whom they beat off, and meantime Cole led his fuzileers up the contested height. At this time, six guns were in the enemy's possession, the whole of Werlé's reserves were coming forward to reinforce the front column of the French, the remnant of Houghton's brigade could no longer maintain its ground, the field was heaped with carcasses, the lancers were riding furiously about the captured artillery on the upper parts of the hill, and behind all, Hamilton's Portuguese and Alten's Germans, now withdrawing from the bridge, seemed to be in full retreat. Soon however Cole's fuzileers, flanked by a battalion of the Lusitanian legion under colonel Hawkshawe, mounted the hill, drove off the lancers, recovered five of the captured guns and one colour, and appeared on the right of Houghton's brigade, precisely as Abercrombie passed it on the left.

Such a gallant line, issuing from the midst of the smoke and rapidly separating itself from the confused and broken multitude, startled the enemy's masses, which were increasing and pressing onwards as to an assured victory; they wavered, hesitated, and then vomiting forth a storm of fire, hastily endeavoured to enlarge their front, while a fearful discharge of grape from all their artillery whistled through the British ranks. Myers was killed, Cole and the three colonels, Ellis, Blakeney and Hawkshawe, fell wounded, and the fuzileer battalions, struck by the iron tempest, reeled and staggered like sinking ships; but suddenly and sternly recovering they closed on their terrible enemies, and then was seen with what a strength and majesty the British soldier fights. In vain did Soult with voice and gesture animate his Frenchmen, in vain did the hardiest veterans break from the crowded columns and sacrifice their lives to gain time for the mass to open out on such a fair field; in vain did the mass itself bear up, and, fiercely striving, fire indiscriminately upon friends and foes, while the horsemen hovering on the flank threatened to charge the advancing line. Nothing could stop that astonishing infantry. No sudden burst of undisciplined valour, no nervous enthusiasm weakened the stability of their order, their flashing eyes were bent on the dark columns in their front, their measured tread shook the ground, their dreadful volleys swept away the head of every formation, their deafening shouts overpowered the dissonant cries that broke from all parts of the tumultuous crowd, as slowly and with a horrid carnage it was pushed by the incessant vigour of the attack to the farthest edge of the hill. In vain did the French reserves mix with the struggling multitude to sustain the fight, their efforts only increased the irremediable confusion, and the mighty mass, breaking off like a loosened cliff, went headlong down the steep: the rain flowed after in streams discoloured with blood, and eighteen hundred unwounded men, the remnant of six thousand unconquerable British soldiers, stood triumphant on the fatal hill!

LIX

A TRIANGULAR DUEL

'THIS is the gentleman whom you have insulted, Mr. Easy,' replied the boatswain, pointing to the purser's steward.

'Yes, Mr. Heasy, quite as good a gentleman as yourself although I av ad misfortunes—I ham of as old a family as hany in the country,' replied Mr. Easthupp, now backed by the boatswain; 'many the year did I valk Bond Street, and I ave as good blood in my weins as you, Mr. Heasy, halthough I have been misfortunate—I've had hadmirals in my family.'

'You have grossly insulted this gentleman,' said Mr. Biggs, in continuation; 'and notwithstanding all your talk of equality, you are afraid to give him satisfaction—you shelter yourself under your quarter-deck.'

'Mr. Biggs,' replied our hero, who was now very wroth, 'I shall go on shore directly we arrive at Malta. Let you and this fellow put on plain clothes, and I will meet you both—and then I'll show you whether I am afraid to give satisfaction.'

'One at a time,' said the boatswain.

'No, sir, not one at a time, but both at the same time—I will fight both, or none. If you are my superior officer, you must *descend*,' replied Jack, with an ironical sneer, 'to meet me, or I will not descend to meet that fellow, whom I believe to have been little better than a pickpocket.'

This accidental hit of Jack's made the purser's steward turn pale as a sheet, and then equally red. . . .

'Now, Mr. Biggs, is this to be understood, or do you shelter yourself under your *forecastle*?' 'I'm no dodger,' replied the boatswain, 'and we will settle the affair at Malta.'

The second day after they had been anchored in Valette harbour the parties all went on shore, and put up at one of the small inns to make the necessary arrangements.

Mr. Tallboys then addressed Mr. Gascoigne, taking him apart while the boatswain amused himself with a glass of grog, and our hero sat outside teasing a monkey.

'Mr. Gascoigne,' said the gunner, 'I have been very much puzzled how this duel should be fought, but I have at last found it out. You see that there are *three* parties to fight; had there been two or four there would have been no difficulty, as the right line or square might guide us in that instance; but we must arrange it upon the *triangle* in this.'

Gascoigne stared; he could not imagine what was coming.

'Are you aware, Mr. Gascoigne, of the properties of an equilateral triangle?'

'Yes,' replied the midshipman, 'that it has three equal sides—but what the devil has that to do with the duel?'

'Everything, Mr. Gascoigne,' replied the gunner; 'it has resolved the great difficulty indeed, the duel between three can only be fought upon that principle. You observe,' said the gunner, taking a piece of chalk out of his pocket, and making a triangle on the table, 'in this figure we have three points, each equidistant from each other: and we have three combatants—so that, placing one at each point, it is all fair play for the three: Mr. Easy, for instance, stands here, the boatswain here, and the purser's steward at the third corner. Now, if the distance is fairly measured, it will be all right.'

'But then,' replied Gascoigne, delighted at the idea, 'how are they to fire?'

'It certainly is not of much consequence,' replied the gunner, 'but still, as sailors, it appears to me that they should fire with the sun; that is, Mr. Easy fires at Mr. Biggs, Mr. Biggs fires at Mr. Easthupp, and Mr. Easthupp fires at Mr. Easy; so that you perceive that each party has his shot at one, and at the same time receives the fire of another. . . .'

'Upon my word, Mr. Tallboys, I give you great credit;

you have a profound mathematical head, and I am delighted with your arrangement. . . .'

Gascoigne went out, and pulling Jack away from the monkey, told him what the gunner had proposed, at which Jack laughed heartily.

The gunner also explained it to the boatswain, who did not very well comprehend, but replied—'I dare say it's all right —shot for shot, and d—n all favours.'

The parties then repaired to the spot with two pairs of ship's pistols, which Mr. Tallboys had smuggled on shore; and, as soon as they were on the ground, the gunner called Mr. Easthupp out of the cooperage. In the meantime, Gascoigne had been measuring an equilateral triangle of twelve paces—and marked it out. Mr. Tallboys, on his return with the purser's steward, went over the ground, and finding that it was 'equal angles subtended by equal sides,' declared that it was all right. Easy took his station, the boatswain was put into his, and Mr. Easthupp, who was quite in a mystery, was led by the gunner to the third position.

'But, Mr. Tallboys,' said the purser's steward, 'I don't understand this. Mr. Easy will first fight Mr. Biggs, will he not?'

'No,' replied the gunner, 'this is a duel of three. You will fire at Mr. Easy, Mr. Easy will fire at Mr. Biggs, and Mr. Biggs will fire at you. It is all arranged, Mr. Easthupp.'

'But,' said Mr. Easthupp, 'I do not understand it. Why is Mr. Biggs to fire at me? I have no quarrel with Mr. Biggs.'

'Because Mr. Easy fires at Mr. Biggs, and Mr. Biggs must have his shot as well.'

'If you have ever been in the company of gentlemen, Mr. Easthupp,' observed Gascoigne, 'you must know something about duelling.'

'Yes, yes, I've kept the best company, Mr. Gascoigne, and I can give a gentleman satisfaction; but——'

'Then, sir, if that is the case, you must know that your honour is in the hands of your second, and that no gentleman appeals.'

'Yes, yes, I know that Mr. Gascoigne; but still I've no quarrel with Mr. Biggs, and therefore, Mr. Biggs, of course you will not aim at me.'

'Why you don't think that I am going to be fired at for nothing,' replied the boatswain; 'no, no, I'll have my shot anyhow.'

'But at your friend, Mr. Biggs?'

'All the same, I shall fire at somebody; shot for shot, and hit the luckiest.'

'Vel, gentlemen, I purtest against these proceedings,' replied Mr. Easthupp; 'I came here to have satisfaction from Mr. Easy, and not to be fired at by Mr. Biggs.'

'Don't you have satisfaction when you fire at Mr. Easy?' replied the gunner; 'what more would you have?'

'I purtest against Mr. Biggs firing at me.'

'So you would have a shot without receiving one,' cried Gascoigne: 'the fact is that this fellow's a confounded coward, and ought to be kicked into the cooperage again.'

At this affront Mr. Easthupp rallied, and accepted the pistol offered by the gunner.

'You ear those words, Mr. Biggs; pretty language to use to a gentleman. You shall ear from me, sir, as soon as the ship is paid off. I purtest no longer, Mr. Tallboys; death before dishonour. I'm a gentleman, damme!'

At all events, the swell was not a very courageous gentleman, for he trembled most exceedingly as he pointed his pistol.

The gunner gave the word, as if he were exercising the great guns on board ship.

'Cock your locks!'—'Take good aim at the object!'—'Fire!'—'Stop your vents!'

The only one of the combatants who appeared to comply with the latter supplementary order was Mr. Easthupp, who clapped his hand to his trousers behind, gave a loud yell, and then dropped down; the bullet having passed clean through his seat of honour, from his having presented his broadside as a target to the boatswain as he faced towards our hero. Jack's shot had also taken effect, having passed through both the boatswain's cheeks, without further mischief than extracting two of his best upper double teeth, and forcing through the hole of the further cheek the boatswain's own quid of tobacco. As for Mr. Easthupp's ball, as he was very unsettled, and shut his eyes before he fired, it had gone the Lord knows where.

The purser's steward lay on the ground and screamed— the boatswain spit his double teeth and two or three mouthfuls of blood out, and then threw down his pistols in a rage.

'A pretty business, by God,' sputtered he; 'he's put my pipe out. How the devil am I to pipe to dinner when I'm ordered, all my wind 'scaping through the cheeks?'

In the meantime, the others had gone to the assistance of the purser's steward, who continued his vociferations. They examined him, and considered a wound in that part not to be dangerous.

'Hold your confounded bawling,' cried the gunner, 'or you'll have the guard down here: you're not hurt.'

'Han't hi?' roared the steward: 'Oh, let me die, let me die; don't move me!'

'Nonsense,' cried the gunner, 'you must get up and walk down to the boat; if you don't we'll leave you—hold your tongue, confound you.' . . .

'I do not think he can move, Mr. Tallboys,' said Gascoigne; 'I should think the best plan would be to call up two of the men from the cooperage, and let them take him at once to the hospital.'

The gunner went down to the cooperage to call the men. Mr. Biggs, who had bound up his face as if he had a toothache, for the bleeding had been very slight, came up to the purser's steward.

'What the hell are you making such a howling about? Look at me, with two shot-holes through my figure head, while you have only got one in your stern: I wish I could change with you, by heavens, for I could use my whistle then—now if I attempt to pipe there will be such a wasteful expenditure of his Majesty's stores of wind, that I never shall get out a note. A wicked shot of yours, Mr. Easy.'

'I really am very sorry,' replied Jack, with a polite bow, 'and I beg to offer my best apology.'

During this conversation, the purser's steward felt very faint, and thought he was going to die. 'Oh dear! oh dear! what a fool I was; I never was a gentleman—only a swell: I shall die; I never will pick a pocket again—never—never —God forgive me!'

'Why, confound the fellow,' cried Gascoigne, 'so you were a pickpocket, were you?'

'I never will again,' replied the fellow in a faint voice. 'Hi'll hamend and lead a good life—a drop of water—oh! *lagged* at last!'

Then the poor wretch fainted away: and Mr. Tallboys coming up with the men, he was taken on their shoulders and walked off to the hospital, attended by the gunner and also the boatswain, who thought he might as well have a little medical advice before he went on board.

'Well, Easy,' said Gascoigne, collecting the pistols and tying them up in his handkerchief, 'I'll be shot but we're in a pretty scrape; there's no hushing this up. I'll be hanged if I care, it's the best piece of fun I ever met with.'

LX

THE ISLE OF WIGHT

I SHOULD like now to transport the reader to a wholly different scene, that we may consider together some of the more obvious features in the landscapes of the south coast of England. At the western end of the Isle of Wight, a long ridge of chalk-down, which stretches completely across the island, runs out to sea, and terminates in the well-known white pinnacles of the Needles. From the highest part of the ridge, when the air is clear, the eye ranges southward over a vast expanse of open sea. To the west and north the breadth of water is bounded by the blue hills of Dorsetshire, the white cliffs of Swanage Bay, and then the long low brown heights which are crowned with the spires of Bournemouth and Christchurch. Eastward we note how the ridge on which we stand sinks down into the hollow of Freshwater Gap, but rises again on the farther side, and then striking inland for some miles, sweeps round to form the heights of St. Catharine's, nearly 800 feet high, whence it descends once more in white cliffs to the sea.

On a summer noon, when a fresh westerly breeze roughens the sea into deepest azure, and keeps a continual murmur of plashing waves at the foot of the cliffs, few pieces of English coast scenery offer more attractions than this. From the verge of the short green sward of the down, the chalk plunges in a sheer precipice of dazzling whiteness, that contrasts well with the mingled blue and emerald-green of the sea below. Projecting massive buttresses, that catch the full blaze of sunlight, throw into delicate violet shadow the recesses and alcoves into which the face of chalk has been worn. On the great ocean highway in front, vessels of every size and rig sail past on their outward or homeward voyage. Though our perch above the precipice is solitary, we yet feel within sight and touch of the living world. Across the bay we mark the smoke of distant villages and towns, and the fields and woodlands that separate the scattered hamlets. Just below, at the northern foot of the ridge, sheltered and concealed among its woods, lies that home so dear to lovers of English literature, where—

> 'Groves of pine on either hand,
> To break the blast of winter, stand,
> And further on, the hoary channel
> Tumbles a breaker on chalk and sand.'

Nor are memorials of the past wanting to throw over the scene the priceless charm of old memory and tradition. The down is roughened here and there with 'the grassy barrows of the happier dead.' The steeples and towers of the country churches dotted over the landscape, mark still, as they have done for centuries, the heart of each parish and its quiet graveyard. It is a typically English scene, full of that hallowed, historic interest, and of that subdued, unobtrusive beauty, where the lineaments of nature are everywhere more or less concealed by the labours of man, which constitute so chief a source of pleasure in the landscapes of England.

Here, surely, our literary censor may claim that no room can be found for the foot of science. What can we pretend to add to the charm of such scenery; or what can we do, if we touch it at all, but lessen that charm? Again, I accept the challenge, though with perhaps somewhat more diffidence; not that I think the contribution from science is here less available or less appropriate, but because I so fully share in the feeling that a scene, in itself and to the ordinary eye so full of everything that can give pleasure, needs no addition from any source.

Let me suppose that we are placed upon the extreme western verge of the down, with the Needles in front of us. The chalk that forms these white faces of rock is shown by science to be made up entirely of the mouldered remains of creatures that gathered on the sea-bottom, ages before the species of animals living at the present day came into existence. Sponges, crinoids, corals, shells, fishes, reptiles, mingled their remains with those of the minuter forms of life that accumulated on the floor of that ancient ocean. And now, hardened into stone, the ooze of that sea-bed has been upraised into land. The 'long backs of the bushless downs,' which for many successive centuries have remained as we see them, were originally parts of the sea-bed, and are entirely built up of the vestiges of dead organisms.

But this is not all. Look at one of those noble faces of rock which shoot up from the restless breakers, and take note of the parallel lines of dark flints which, as if traced with a pencil, sweep in such graceful curves from base to crest of the cliffs. Alike on buttress and recess, from headland to headland, no matter how irregularly the chalk has been sculptured, these parallel lines may be followed. A feature so conspicuous in the architecture of the precipices could not escape the attention of the most casual visitor; but he only vaguely marvels at it, until geology tells him that these dark lines mark successive floors of that ancient sea—floors that gathered one over another, as generation after generation of marine creatures left their crumbling remains upon the bottom. But now they are bent up and placed on end, like books on the shelves of a library. And thus we learn that not only has this ancient sea-bed been turned into dry land, but its layers of hardened ooze have been tilted up vertically, and that it is the worn ends of these upturned layers which form the long ridges of the downs.

But science further makes known to us that beyond the cliffy margin on which we stand, there once stretched an ampler land that has long disappeared. Far over the English Channel the chalk downs once extended with their undulating summits, their smooth grassy slopes, their deep coombs and quiet bournes. That vanished land ran southward, until it ended off in a range of white precipices. The rain that fell on its surface gathered into a river that flowed northward through Freshwater Gap into the Solent. Strange to tell, perched on the top of the present cliffs, to the east of Freshwater, lie fragments of the bed of that ancient stream, consisting of gravel and silt which, as the cliffs are undermined by the waves, tumble to the beach and mingle with the gravel of to-day. In these ancient deposits are found teeth of the long-extinct mammoths which browsed the herbage on slopes that rose southward, where for many a long age the Atlantic has rolled its restless tides and breakers.

Musing on these records of a dim forgotten past, we once more turn to the last spurs of chalk and the isolated Needles. There, with eye quickened to recognize what science has to reveal, we trace on every feature of the rocky foreground, inscribed in characters that cannot be mistaken, the story of that process of destruction which has reduced the Isle of Wight to its present diminished proportions. The rains, frosts, and tempests splinter the chalk above and the waves gnaw it away below. Year by year fresh slices are cut off and strewn in fragments over the sea-floor by the unwearying surge. The Needles, once part of the down, are perceptibly less than they were a generation ago. The opposite white cliffs and downs of Dorset were at one time continuous with those of the Isle of Wight. They too, by their shattered precipices, tunnelled caverns, and isolated stacks of rock, tell the same tale of disintegration. And, thus, impressive though the scenery was before, it now acquires a new interest and significance, when every cliff and pinnacle becomes eloquent to us of a past so strange, so remote, and yet so closely linked with our own day by a chain of slow and unbroken causation.

'GREEN FIELDS OF ENGLAND'

Green fields of England! wheresoe'er
Across this watery waste we fare,
Your image at our hearts we bear,
Green fields of England, everywhere.

Sweet eyes in England, I must flee
Past where the waves' last confines be,
Ere your loved smile I cease to see,
Sweet eyes in England, dear to me.

Dear home in England, safe and fast
If but in thee my lot lie cast,
The past shall seem a nothing past
To thee, dear home, if won at last;
Dear home in England, won at last.

LXI

THE DRAMA AND THE CRUMMLES COMPANY

'AN uncommon snug little box this,' said Mr. Lenville, stepping into the front room, and taking his hat off, before he could get in at all. 'Pernicious snug.'
'For a man at all particular in such matters, it might be a trifle too snug,' said Nicholas. . . .
'It isn't a bit too confined for a single man,' returned Mr. Lenville. 'That reminds me,—my wife, Mr. Johnson,— I hope she'll have some good part in this piece of yours?'

'I glanced at the French copy last night,' said Nicholas. 'It looks very good, I think.'

'What do you mean to do for me, old fellow?' asked Mr. Lenville, poking the struggling fire with his walking-stick, and afterwards wiping it on the skirt of his coat. 'Anything in the gruff and grumble way?'

'You turn your wife and child out of doors,' said Nicholas, 'and in a fit of rage and jealousy stab your eldest son in the library.'

'Do I though!' exclaimed Mr. Lenville. 'That's very good business.'

'After which,' said Nicholas, 'you are troubled with remorse till the last act, and then you make up your mind to destroy yourself. But, just as you are raising the pistol to your head, a clock strikes—ten.'

'I see,' cried Mr. Lenville. 'Very good.'

'You pause,' said Nicholas; 'you recollect to have heard a clock strike ten in your infancy. The pistol falls from your hand—you are overcome—you burst into tears, and become a virtuous and exemplary character for ever afterwards.'

'Capital!' said Mr. Lenville: 'that's a sure card, a sure card. Get the curtain down with a touch of nature like that, and it'll be a triumphant success.'

'Is there anything good for me?' inquired Mr. Folair, anxiously.

'Let me see,' said Nicholas. 'You play the faithful and attached servant; you are turned out of doors with the wife and child.'

'Always coupled with that infernal phenomenon,' sighed Mr. Folair; 'and we go into poor lodgings, where I won't take any wages, and talk sentiment, I suppose?'

'Why—yes,' replied Nicholas: 'that is the course of the piece.'

'I must have a dance of some kind, you know,' said Mr. Folair. 'You'll have to introduce one for the phenomenon, so you'd better make a *pas de deux*, and save time.'

'There's nothing easier than that,' said Mr. Lenville, observing the disturbed looks of the young dramatist.

'Upon my word I don't see how it's to be done,' rejoined Nicholas.

'Why, isn't it obvious?' reasoned Mr. Lenville. 'Gadzooks, who can help seeing the way to do it?—you astonish me! You get the distressed lady, and the little child, and the attached servant, into the poor lodgings, don't you?—Well, look here. The distressed lady sinks into a chair and buries her face in her pocket-handkerchief—'What makes you weep, mama,' says the child. 'Don't weep, mama, or you'll make me weep too!'—'And me!' says the faithful servant, rubbing his eyes with his arm. 'What can we do to raise your spirits, dear mama?' says the little child. 'Aye, what *can* we do?' says the faithful servant. 'Oh, Pierre!' says the distressed lady; 'would that I could shake off these painful thoughts.'—'Try, ma'am, try,' says the faithful servant; 'rouse yourself, ma'am; be amused.'—'I will,' says the lady, 'I will learn to suffer with fortitude. Do you remember that dance, my honest friend, which, in happier days, you practised with this sweet angel? It never failed to calm my spirits then. Oh! let me see it once again before I die!'—There it is—cue for the band, *before I die,*—and off they go. That's the regular thing; isn't it, Tommy?'

'That's it,' replied Mr. Folair. 'The distressed lady, overpowered by old recollections, faints at the end of the dance and you close in with a picture.'

Profiting by these and other lessons, Nicholas worked very hard all day, and did not leave his room until the evening, when he went down to the theatre, whither Smike had repaired before him to go on with another gentleman as a general rebellion.

Here all the people were so much changed, that he scarcely knew them. False hair, false colour, false calves, false muscles—they had become different beings. Mr. Lenville was a blooming warrior of most exquisite proportions; Mr. Crummles, his large face shaded by a profusion of black hair, a Highland outlaw of most majestic bearing; one of the old gentlemen a gaoler, and the other a venerable patriarch; the comic countryman, a fighting-man of great valour, relieved by a touch of humour; each of the Master Crummleses a prince in his own right; and the low-spirited lover, a desponding captive. There was a gorgeous banquet ready spread for the third act, consisting of two pasteboard vases, one plate of biscuits, a black bottle, and a vinegar cruet; and, in short, everything was on a scale of the utmost splendour and preparation. . . .

'Been in front to-night?' said Mr. Crummles.

'No,' replied Nicholas, 'not yet. I am going to see the play.'

'We've had a pretty good Let,' said Mr. Crummles. 'Four front places in the centre, and the whole of the stage-box.'

'Oh, indeed!' said Nicholas; 'a family, I suppose?'

'Yes,' replied Mr. Crummles, 'yes. It's an affecting thing. There are six children, and they never come unless the phenomenon plays.'

It would have been difficult for any party, family or otherwise, to have visited the theatre on a night when the phenomenon did *not* play, inasmuch as she always sustained one, and not uncommonly two or three characters, every night; but Nicholas, sympathizing with the feelings of a father, refrained from hinting at this trifling circumstance, and Mr. Crummles continued to talk, uninterrupted by him.

'Six,' said that gentleman; 'Pa and Ma eight, aunt nine, governess ten, grandfather and grandmother twelve. Then, there's the footman, who stands outside, with a bag of oranges and a jug of toast-and-water, and sees the play for nothing through the little pane of glass in the box-door—it's cheap at a guinea; they gain by taking a box.'

'I wonder you allow so many,' observed Nicholas.

'There's no help for it,' replied Mr. Crummles; 'it's always expected in the country. If there are six children, six people come to hold them in their laps. A family-box carries double always. Ring in the orchestra, Grudden!'

That useful lady did as she was requested, and shortly afterwards the tuning of three fiddles was heard. Which process having been protracted as long as it was supposed that the patience of the audience could possibly bear it, was put a stop to by another jerk of the bell, which, being the signal to begin in earnest, set the orchestra playing a variety of popular airs, with involuntary variations.

If Nicholas had been astonished at the alteration for the better which the gentlemen displayed, the transformation of the ladies was still more extraordinary. When, from a snug corner of the manager's box, be beheld Miss Snevellicci in all the glories of white muslin with a golden hem, and Mrs. Crummles in all the dignity of the outlaw's wife, and Miss Bravassa in all the sweetness of Miss Snevellicci's confidential friend, and Miss Belvawney in the white silks of a page doing duty everywhere and swearing to live and die in the service of everybody, he could scarcely contain his admiration, which testified itself in great applause, and the closest possible attention to the business of the scene. The plot was most interesting. It belonged to no particular age, people, or country, and was perhaps the more delightful on that account, as nobody's previous information could afford the remotest glimmering of what would ever come of it. An outlaw had been very successful in doing something somewhere, and came home, in triumph, to the sound of shouts and fiddles, to greet his wife—a lady of masculine mind, who talked a good deal about her father's bones, which it seemed were unburied, though whether from a peculiar taste on the part of the old gentleman himself, or the reprehensible neglect of his relations, did not appear. The outlaw's wife was, somehow or other, mixed up with a patriarch, living in a castle a long way off, and this patriarch was the father of several of the characters, but he didn't exactly know which, and was uncertain whether he had brought up the right ones in his castle, or the wrong ones; he rather inclined to the latter opinion, and, being uneasy, relieved his mind with a banquet, during which solemnity somebody in a cloak said 'Beware!' which somebody was known by nobody (except the audience) to be the outlaw himself, who had come there, for reasons unexplained, but possibly with an eye to the spoons. There was an agreeable little surprise in the way of certain love passages between the desponding captive and Miss Snevellicci, and the comic fighting-man and Miss Bravassa; besides which, Mr. Lenville had several very tragic scenes in the dark, while on throat-cutting expeditions, which were all baffled by the skill and bravery of the comic fighting-man (who overheard whatever was said all through the piece) and the intrepidity of Miss Snevellicci, who adopted tights, and therein repaired to the prison of her captive lover, with a small basket of refreshments and a dark lantern. At last, it came out that the patriarch was the man who had treated the bones of the outlaw's father-in-law with so much disrespect, for which cause and reason the outlaw's wife repaired to his castle to kill him, and so got into a dark room, where, after a good deal of groping in the dark, everybody got hold of everybody else, and took them for somebody besides, which occasioned a vast quantity of confusion, with some pistolling, loss of life, and torchlight; after which, the patriarch came forward, and observing, with a knowing look, that he knew all about his children now, and would tell them when they got inside, said that there could not be a more appropriate occasion for marrying the young people than that; and therefore he joined their hands, with the full consent of the indefatigable page, who (being the only other person surviving) pointed with his cap into the clouds, and his right hand to the ground; thereby invoking a blessing and giving the cue for the curtain to come down, which it did, amidst general applause.

LXII

A SAVAGE PEOPLE

IN the morning the Captain sent a party to communicate with the Fuegians. When we came within hail, one of the four natives who were present advanced to receive us, and began to shout most vehemently, wishing to direct us where to land. When we were on shore the party looked rather alarmed, but continued talking and making gestures with great rapidity. It was without exception the most curious and interesting spectacle I ever beheld: I could not have believed how wide was the difference between savage and civilized man; it is greater than between a wild and domesticated animal, inasmuch as in man there is a greater power of improvement. The chief spokesman was old, and appeared to be the head of the family; the three others were powerful young men, about six feet high. The women and children had been sent away. These Fuegians are a very different race from the stunted, miserable wretches farther westward; and they seem closely allied to the famous Patagonians of the Strait of Magellan. Their only garment consists of a mantle made of guanaco skin, with the wool outside; this they wear just thrown over their shoulders, leaving their persons as often exposed as covered. Their skin is of a dirty coppery-red colour.

The old man had a fillet of white feathers tied round his head, which partly confined his black, coarse, and entangled hair. His face was crossed by two broad transverse bars; one, painted bright red, reached from ear to ear and included the upper lip; the other, white like chalk, extended above and parallel to the first, so that even his eyelids were thus coloured. The other two men were ornamented by streaks of black powder, made of charcoal. The party altogether closely resembled the devils which come on the stage in plays like 'Der Freischutz.'

Their very attitudes were abject, and the expression of their countenances distrustful, surprised, and startled. After we had presented them with some scarlet cloth, which they immediately tied round their necks, they became good friends. This was shown by the old man patting our breasts, and making a chuckling kind of noise, as people do when feeding chickens. I walked with the old man, and this demonstration of friendship was repeated several times; it was concluded by three hard slaps, which were given me on the breast and back at the same time. He then bared his bosom for me to return the compliment, which being done, he seemed highly pleased. The language of these people, according to our notions, scarcely deserves to be called articulate. Captain Cook has compared it to a man clearing his throat, but certainly no European ever cleared his throat with so many hoarse, guttural, and clicking sounds.

They are excellent mimics: as often as we coughed or yawned, or made any odd motion, they immediately imitated us. Some of our party began to squint and look awry; but one of the young Fuegians (whose face was painted black, excepting a white band across his eyes) succeeded in making far more hideous grimaces. They could repeat with perfect correctness each word in any sentence we addressed them, and they remembered such words for some time. Yet we Europeans all know how difficult it is to distinguish apart the sounds in a foreign language. Which of us, for instance, could follow an American Indian through a sentence of more than three words? All savages appear to possess, to an uncommon degree, this power of mimicry. I was told, almost in the same words, of the same ludicrous habit among the Caffres: the Australians, likewise, have long been notorious for being able to imitate and describe the gait of any man, so that he may be recognized. How can this faculty be explained? Is it a consequence of the more practised habits of perception and keener senses, common to all men in a savage state, as compared with those long civilized?

When a song was struck up by our party I thought the Fuegians would have fallen down with astonishment. With equal surprise they viewed our dancing; but one of the young men, when asked, had no objection to a little waltzing. Little accustomed to Europeans as they appeared to be, yet they knew and dreaded our firearms; nothing would tempt them to take a gun in their hands. They begged for knives, calling them by the Spanish word 'cuchilla.' They explained also what they wanted, by acting as if they had a piece of blubber in their mouth, and then pretending to cut instead of tear it.

I have not as yet noticed the Fuegians whom we had on board. During the former voyage of the *Adventure* and *Beagle* in 1826 to 1830, Captain Fitz Roy seized on a party of natives, as hostages for the loss of a boat, which had been stolen, to the great jeopardy of a party employed on the survey; and some of these natives, as well as a child whom he bought for a pearl-button, he took with him to England, determining to educate them and instruct them in religion at his own expense. To settle these natives in their own country was one chief inducement to Captain Fitz Roy to undertake our present voyage; and before the Admiralty had resolved to send out this expedition, Captain Fitz Roy had generously chartered a vessel, and would himself have taken them back. The natives were accompanied by a missionary, R. Matthews; of whom and of the natives, Captain Fitz Roy has published a full and excellent account. Two men, one of whom died in England of the small-pox, a boy, and a little girl, were originally taken; and we had now on board, York Minster, Jemmy Button (whose name expresses his purchase-money), and Fuegia Basket. York Minster was a fullgrown, short, thick, powerful man; his disposition was reserved, taciturn, morose, and when excited violently passionate; his affections were very strong towards a few friends on board; his intellect good. Jemmy Button was a universal favourite, but likewise passionate; the expression of his face at once showed his nice disposition. He was merry and often laughed, and was remarkably sympathetic with anyone in pain; when the water was rough, I was often a little seasick, and he used to come to me and say in a plaintive voice, 'Poor, poor fellow!' but the notion, after his aquatic life, of a man being sea-sick, was too ludicrous, and he was generally obliged to turn on one side to hide a smile or laugh, and then he would repeat his 'Poor, poor fellow!' He was of a patriotic disposition; and he liked to praise his own tribe and country, in which he truly said there were 'plenty of trees,' and he abused all the other tribes; he stoutly declared that there was no devil in his land. Jemmy was short, thick, and fat, but vain of his personal appearance; he used always to wear gloves, his hair was neatly cut, and he was distressed if his well-polished shoes were dirtied. He was fond of admiring himself in a looking-glass; and a merry faced little Indian boy from the Rio Negro whom we had for some months on board, soon perceived this, and used to mock him; Jemmy, who was always rather jealous of the attention paid to this little boy, did not at all like this, and used to say, with rather a contemptuous twist of his head, 'Too much skylark.' It seems yet wonderful to me, when I think over all his many good qualities, that he should have been of the same race, and doubtless partaken of the same character, with the miserable, degraded savages whom we first met here. Lastly, Fuegia Basket was a nice, modest, reserved young girl, with a rather pleasing but sometimes sullen expression, and very quick in learning anything, especially languages. This she showed in picking up some Portuguese and Spanish, when left on shore for only a short time at Rio de Janeiro and Monte Video, and in her knowledge of English. York Minster was very jealous of any attention paid to her; for it was clear he determined to marry her as soon as they were settled on shore.

Although all three could both speak and understand a good deal of English, it was singularly difficult to obtain much information from them concerning the habits of their countrymen; this was partly owing to their apparent difficulty in understanding the simplest alternative. Every one accustomed to very young children knows how seldom one can get an answer even to so simple a question as whether a thing is black *or* white; the idea of black or white seems alternately to fill their minds. So it was with these Fuegians, and hence it was generally impossible to find out, by cross-questioning, whether one had rightly understood anything which they had asserted. Their sight was remarkably acute; it is well known that sailors, from long practice, can make out a distant object much better than a landsman; but both York and Jemmy were much superior to any sailor on board; several times they have declared what some distant object has been, and though doubted by every one, they have proved right, when it has been examined through a telescope. They were quite conscious of this power; and Jemmy, when he had any little quarrel with the officer on watch, would say, 'Me see ship, me no tell.'

It was interesting to watch the conduct of the savages, when we landed, towards Jemmy Button; they immediately perceived the difference between him and ourselves, and held much conversation one with another on the subject. The old man addressed a long harangue to Jemmy, which it seems was to invite him to stay with them. But Jemmy understood very little of their language, and was, moreover, thoroughly ashamed of his countrymen. When York Minster afterwards came on shore, they noticed him in the same way, and told him he ought to shave; yet he had not twenty dwarf hairs on his face, whilst we all wore our untrimmed beards. They examined the colour of his skin, and compared it with ours. One of our arms being bared, they expressed the liveliest surprise and admiration at its whiteness, just in the same way in which I have seen the ourang-outang do at the Zoological Gardens. We thought that they mistook two or three of the officers, who were rather shorter and fairer, though adorned with large beards, for the ladies of our party. The tallest amongst the Fuegians was evidently much pleased at his height being noticed. When placed back to back with the tallest of the boat's crew, he tried his best to edge on higher ground, and to stand on tip-toe. He opened his mouth to show his teeth, and turned his face for a side view; and all this was done with such alacrity, that I daresay he thought himself the handsomest man in Tierra del Fuego. After our first feeling of grave astonishment was over, nothing could be more ludicrous than the odd mixture of surprise and imitation which these savages every moment exhibited.

LXIII

THE DONCASTER ST. LEGER

THE sun is bright, the sky is clear,
    Above the crowded course,
  As the mighty moment draweth near
Whose issue shows *the horse*.

The fairest of the land are here
To watch the struggle of the year,
The dew of beauty and of mirth,
Lies on the living flowers of earth,
And blushing cheek and kindling eye
Lend brightness to the sun on high:
And every corner of the north
Has poured her hardy yeomen forth;
The dweller by the glistening rills
That sound among the Craven hills;
The stalwart husbandman who holds
His plough upon the eastern wolds;
The sallow shrivelled artisan,
Twisted below the height of man,
Whose limbs and life have mouldered down,
Within some foul and clouded town,
Are gathered thickly on the lea,
Or streaming from far homes to see
If Yorkshire keeps her old renown;
Of if the dreaded Derby horse
Can sweep in triumph o'er her course;
With the same look in every face,
The same keen feeling, they retrace
The legends of each ancient race:
Recalling Reveller in his pride,
Or Blacklock of the mighty stride,
Or listening to some grey-haired sage
Full of the dignity of age;
How Hambletonian beat of yore
Such rivals as are seen no more;
How his old father loved to tell
Of that long struggle—ended well,
When, strong of heart, the Wentworth Bay
From staggering Herod strode away:
How Yorkshire racers, swift as they,
Would leave this southern horse half way,
But that the creatures of to-day
Are cast in quite a different mould
From what he recollects of old.

Clear peals the bell; at that known sound,
Like bees, the people cluster round;
On either side upstarting then,
One close dark wall of breathless men,
Far down as eye can stretch, is seen
Along yon vivid strip of green,
Where keenly watched by countless eyes,
'Mid hopes, and fears, and prophecies,
Now fast, now slow, now here, now there,
With hearts of fire, and limbs of air,
Snorting and prancing—sidling by
With arching neck, and glancing eye,
In every shape of strength and grace,
The horses gather for the race;
Soothed for a moment all, they stand
Together like a sculptured band,
Each quivering eyelid flutters thick,
Each face is flushed, each heart beats quick;
And all around dim murmurs pass,
Like low winds moaning on the grass.
Again—the thrilling signal sound—
And off at once, with one long bound,
Into the speed of thought they leap,
Like a proud ship rushing to the deep.
A start! a start! they're off, by heaven,
Like a single horse, though twenty-seven,
And 'mid the flash of silks we scan
A Yorkshire jacket in the van;
  Hurrah! for the bold bay mare!

I'll pawn my soul her place is there
 Unheaded to the last,
For a thousand pounds, she wins unpast—
 Hurrah! for the matchless mare!

A hundred yards have glided by,
 And they settle to the race,
More keen becomes each straining eye,
 More terrible the pace.

Unbroken yet o'er the gravel road
Like maddening waves the troop has flowed,
  But the speed begins to tell;
And Yorkshire sees, with eye of fear,
The Southron stealing from the rear.
  Ay! mark his action well!
Behind he is, but what repose!
How steadily and clean he goes!
What latent speed his limbs disclose!
What power in every stride he shows!
They see, they feel, from man to man
The shivering thrill of terror ran,
And every soul instinctive knew
It lay between the mighty two.
The world without, the sky above,
  Have glided from their straining eyes—
Future and past, and hate and love,
  The life that wanes, the friend that dies,
E'en grim remorse, who sits behind
Each thought and motion of the mind,
These now are nothing, Time and Space
Lie in the rushing of the race;
As with keen shouts of hope and fear
They watch it in its wild career.
Still far ahead of the glittering throng,
Dashes the eager mare along,
And round the turn, and past the hill,
Slides up the Derby winner still.
The twenty-five that lay between
Are blotted from the stirring scene,
And the wild cries which rang so loud
Sink by degrees throughout the crowd
To one deep humming, like the tremulous roar
Of seas remote along a northern shore.
In distance dwindling to the eye
Right opposite the stand they lie,
  And scarcely seem to stir.

Though an Arab scheich his wives would give
For a single steed, that with them could live
  Three hundred yards, without the spur.
But though so indistinct and small,
You hardly see them move at all,
There are not wanting signs, which show
Defeat is busy as they go.
Look how the mass, which rushed away
As full of spirit as the day,
So close compacted for a while,
Is lengthening into single file.
Now inch by inch it breaks, and wide
And spreading gaps the line divide.
As forward still and far away
Undulates on the tired array.
Gay colours, momently less bright,
Fade flickering on the gazer's sight,
Till keenest eyes can scarcely trace
The homeward ripple of the race.
Care sits on every lip and brow.
'Who leads? who fails? how goes it now?'
One shooting spark of life intense,
One throb of refluent suspense,
And a far rainbow-coloured light
Trembles again upon the sight.
Look to yon turn! Already there
Gleams the pink and black of the fiery mare,
And through *that*, which was but now a gap,
Creeps on the terrible white cap.
Half-strangled in each throat, a shout
Wrung from their fevered spirits out,
Booms through the crowd like muffled drums,
'His jockey moves on him. He comes!'
Then momently like gusts, you heard,
'He's sixth—he's fifth—he's fourth—he's third;'
And on, like some glancing meteor-flame,
The stride of the Derby winner came.

And during all that anxious time,
(Sneer as it suits you at my rhyme)
The earnestness became sublime;
Common and trite as is the scene,
At once so thrilling and so mean,
To him who strives his heart to scan
And feels the brotherhood of man
That needs *must* be a mighty minute,
When a crowd has but one soul within it.
As some bright ship with every sail
Obedient to the urging gale
Darts by vext hulls, which side by side
Dismasted on the raging tide,
Are struggling onward wild and wide,
Thus, through the reeling field he flew,
And near, and yet more near he drew;
Each leap seems longer than the last,
Now—now—the second horse is past,
And the keen rider of the mare,
With haggard looks of feverish care,
Hangs forward on the speechless air,
By steady stillness nursing in
The remnant of her speed to win.
One other bound—one more—'tis done;
Right up to her the horse has run,
And head to head, and stride for stride,
Newmarket's hope and Yorkshire's pride,
Like horses harnessed side by side,
   Are struggling to the goal.
Ride! gallant son of Ebor, ride!
For the dear honour of the north,
Stretch every bursting sinew forth,
   Put out thy inmost soul,—
And with knee, and thigh, and tightened rein,
Lift in the mare by might and main;
The feelings of the people reach,
What lies beyond the springs of speech,
So that there rises up no sound

From the wide human life around;
One spirit flashes from each eye,
One impulse lifts each heart throat-high,
One short and panting silence broods
O'er the wildly-working multitudes;
As on the struggling coursers press,
So deep the eager silentness,
That underneath their feet the turf
Seems shaken, like the eddying surf
  When it tastes the rushing gale,
And the singing fall of the heavy whips,
Which tear the flesh away in strips,
  As the tempest tears the sail,
On the throbbing heart and quivering ear,
Strike vividly distinct, and near.
But mark what an arrowy rush is there,
'He's beat! he's beat!'—by heaven, the mare!
Just on the post, her spirit rare,
When Hope herself might well despair,
When Time had not a breath to spare,
With bird-like dash shoots clean away
And by half a length has gained the day,
Then how to life that silence wakes!
Ten thousand hats thrown up on high
Send darkness to the echoing sky,
And like the crash of hill-pent lakes,
Out-bursting from their deepest fountains
Among the rent and reeling mountains,
At once, from thirty thousand throats
  Rushes the Yorkshire roar,
And the name of their northern winner floats
  A league from the course, and more.

LXIV

SOME EARLY NATURAL HISTORY
OF ELEPHANTS

YOU may know yong elephants by the whiteness of their teeth; and a speciall care and regard have these beasts of them above all. They looke to one of them alwaies, that the point be sharpe, and therefore they forbeare to occupie it, least it should be blunt against they come to fight; the other they use ordinarily, either to get up roots out of the earth, or to cast down any banks or mures, that stand in their way. When they chance to be environed and compassed round with hunters, they set formost in the rank to be seen those of the heard that have the least teeth; to the end that, their price might not be thought worth the hazard and venture in chase of them. But afterwards, when they see the hunters eager, and themselves overmatched and weary, they breake them with running against the hard trees, and leaving them behind, escape by this ransome, as it were, out of the hunters' hands.

Covered their skin is neither with haire nor bristle, no not so much as in their taile, which might serve them in good stead to drive away the busie and troublesome flie (for as vast and huge a beast as he is, the flie hunteth and stingeth him); but ful their skin is of crosse wrinkles latticewise, and besides that, the smell thereof is able to draw and allure such vermin to it; and therefore when they are laid stretched along, and perceive the flies by whole swarms settled on their skin, suddenly they draw those crannies and crevises together close, and so crush them all to death.

OF THE TYGER AND HIS NATURE

Tygers are bred in Hircania and India; this beast is most dreadfull for incomparable swiftnesse, and most of all seen it is in the taking of her yong; for her litter (whereof there is a great number) by the hunter is stolne and carried away at once, upon a most swifte horse for the purpose, lying in wait to espy when the dam is abroad; and shifteth this booty upon one fresh horse to another, riding away upon the spur as hard as they can. But when the tygresse comes and finds her den and nest empty (for the male tyger hath no care nor regard at all of the yong) she runs on end after her yong ones, following them that carried them awaie by the scent of the horse footing. They perceiving the tygresse to approach, by the noise she maketh, let fall or cast from them one of her whelps; up she taketh it in her mouth, and away she runneth towards her den, swifter for the burden that she carrieth. And presently she setteth out again, followeth the quest after her Fawnes, and overtaketh the Hunter that had them away. Thus runneth she to and fro, until she see that they be embarqued and gone; and then for very anger that she hath not sped of her purpose, she rageth upon the shore and the sands for the losse of her Fawnes.

To come again to our Lions, the signe of their intent and disposition is their taile; like as in horses their eares; for these two marks and tokens certainly hath Nature given to the most couragious beasts of all others, to know their affections by; for when the Lion stirs not his taile, he is in a good mood, gentle, mild, pleasantly disposed, and as if he were willing to be plaied withall; but in that fit he is seldom seen, for lightly he is alwaies angry.

OF PORKPENS

The Porkpens come out of India and Africke, kind of Urchin or hedge-hog they be, armed with prickes they be both; but the Porkpen hath the longer sharp-pointed quilles, and those, when he stretcheth his skin, he sendeth and shooteth from him; when the hounds presseth hard upon him, he flieth from their mouthes, and then takes vantage to launce at them somewhat farther off.

When the Hyaenaes flee before the hunter, and would not be taken, they wind with a cariere out of the way towards the

SOME EARLY NATURAL HISTORY

right hand, and wheele about until the man be gotten before them; and this they do because they would meet with his tracts and footing, which when they happen upon, and get behind him, you shall see the hunter incontinently to be so intoxicat in his brain, that he is not able to beare his head nor sit his horse, but fall from his back. But in case that they turn on the left hand, it is an evident signe that they be ready to faint, and then will they quickly be taken. The sooner also and with more ease be they caught (if we may believe art Magick) if the hunter tie his girdle about his middle with 7 knots, and the cord of his whip likewise, wherewith he ruleth and jerketh his horse with as many.

MEDICINES APPROPRIATE FOR DIVERS AND SUNDRY DISEASES WHICH POSSESS THE WHOLE BODY

But as I have made mention of the Cuckaw, there comes into my minde a strange and marvailous matter that the said Magitians report of this bird; namely, that if a man the first time that he heare her to sing, presently stay his right foot upon the very place where it was when he heard her, and withal marke out the print and just proportion of the sayd foot upon the ground as it stood, and then digge up the earth under it within the said compasse, looke what chamber or roome of the house is strewed with the said mould, there will no fleas breed there.

If any one will take up and put back again the sod that is struck from the ground by a horse's hoof, it is a remedy against the hiccough, so long as they bear in memory that place where they laid it back again.

Furthermore the little grub or worme which is found in the herb Tazill, called *Venus'* Laver, hath a wonderful operation to cure the toothache, if it be put into the hole of a faulty tooth; and no marvaile, for the caterpillars that breed in coleworts will presently fall off, if they be but touched with this worme.

As for the Phrensie, it seems that the lights of a mutton, applied hot round about the head, and so kept fast, is soveraigne to bring their heads again into temper, who are beside themselves. Say that true it were, that not only the brains of mice given in water to drink, or the ashes of a weazil, but also the flesh of an urchin kept in salt or dried, are very good for such as are bereft of their right wits; who will venture to give them these medicines, be they never so certain and assured?

In like manner, if a man carry a dog's tongue in his Shoe under his great toe, there will no Dogges bay or barke at him.

These may seem to some men strange things and monstrous; but less will they wonder hereat, when they shall heare and consider that a stone which a dog hath taken up in his mouth and bitten will cause debate and contention in the company where it is; and yet this is held for a certain truth, insomuch that it is growne into a common proverbe and byword.

OF THE STARS CALLED CASTOR AND POLLUX

I have seen myselfe in the campe, from the soldiers' sentinels in the night watch, the resemblance of lightning to stick upon the spears and pikes set before the rampart. They settle also upon the crosse sail-yards and other parts of the ship, as men do saile in the sea; making a kind of vocal sound, leaping to and fro, and shifting their places as birds doe which fly from bough to bough. Dangerous they be and unluckie, when they come out one by one and without a companion; and they drown those ships on which they light, and threaten shipwrack, yea and they set them on fire if haply they fall upon the bottome of the keel. But if they appear two and two together they bring comfort with them, and fortell a prosperous course in the voyage, as by whose coming, they say, that dreadful cursed and threatening Meteor called Helena is chased and driven away. And thereupon it is

that men assign this mighty power to *Castor* and *Pollux* and
invocate them at sea no lesse than gods. Men's heads also
in the eventide are seene many times to shine round about,
and to be of a light fire, which presageth some great matter.
Of all these things there is no certain reason to be given; but
secret these be, hidden with the majesty of Nature and reserved
within her Cabinet.

For while I contemplate the course of Nature, she hath
persuaded me to think nothing incredible concerning her.

LXV

THE GOLDEN IMAGE

NEBUCHADNEZZAR the king, made an image of
gold, whose height was threescore cubits, and the
breadth thereof six cubits: he set it up in the plain of
Dura, in the province of Babylon. Then Nebuchadnezzar
the king sent to gather together the princes, the governors, and
the captains, the judges, the treasurers, the counsellors, the
sheriffs, and all the rulers of the provinces, to come to the
dedication of the image which Nebuchadnezzar the king had
set up. Then the princes, the governors, and captains, the
judges, the treasurers, the counsellors, the sheriffs, and all
the rulers of the provinces, were gathered together unto the
dedication of the image that Nebuchadnezzar the king had
set up; and they stood before the image that Nebuchadnezzar
had set up.

Then an herald cried aloud, To you it is commanded, O
people, nations, and languages, That at what time ye hear
the sound of the cornet, flute, harp, sackbut, psaltery, dulcimer, and all kinds of musick, ye fall down and worship the
golden image that Nebuchadnezzar the king hath set up;
and whoso falleth not down and worshippeth shall the same
hour be cast into the midst of a burning fiery furnace.
Therefore at that time, when all the people heard the sound
of the cornet, flute, harp, sackbut, psaltery, and all kinds of

musick, all the people, the nations, and the languages, fell down and worshipped the golden image that Nebuchadnezzar the king had set up. Wherefore at that time certain Chaldeans came near, and accused the Jews. They spake and said to the king Nebuchadnezzar, O king, live for ever. Thou, O king, hast made a decree, that every man that shall hear the sound of the cornet, flute, harp, sackbut, psaltery, and dulcimer, and all kinds of musick, shall fall down and worship the golden image: and whoso falleth not down and worshippeth that he should be cast into the midst of a burning fiery furnace. There are certain Jews whom thou hast set over the affairs of the province of Babylon, Shadrach, Meshach, and Abed-nego; these men, O king, have not regarded thee: they serve not thy gods, nor worship the golden image which thou hast set up.

Then Nebuchadnezzar in his rage and fury commanded to bring Shadrach, Meshach, and Abed-nego. Then they brought these men before the king. Nebuchadnezzar spake and said unto them, Is it true, O Shadrach, Meshach, and Abed-nego, do not ye serve my gods, nor worship the golden image which I have set up? Now if ye be ready that at what time ye hear the sound of the cornet, flute, harp, sackbut, psaltery, and dulcimer, and all kinds of musick, ye fall down and worship the image which I have made, well: but if ye worship not, ye shall be cast the same hour into the midst of a burning fiery furnace; and who is that God that shall deliver you out of my hands? Shadrach, Meshach, and Abed-nego, answered and said to the king, O Nebuchadnezzar, we are not careful to answer thee in this matter. If it be so, our God whom we serve is able to deliver us from the burning fiery furnace, and he will deliver us out of thine hand, O king. But if not, be it known unto thee, O king, that we will not serve thy gods, nor worship the golden image which thou hast set up. Then was Nebuchadnezzar full of fury, and the form of his visage was changed against Shadrach, Meshach, and Abed-nego: therefore he spake, and commanded that they should heat the furnace one seven times more than it was wont to be heated. And he commanded the most mighty men that were in his army to bind Shadrach, Meshach, and Abed-nego, and to cast them into the burning fiery furnace. Then these men were bound in their coats, their hosen, and their hats, and their other garments, and were cast into the midst of the burning fiery furnace. Therefore because the king's commandment was urgent, and the furnace exceeding hot, the flame of the fire slew those men that took up Shadrach, Meshach, and Abed-nego. And these three men, Shadrach, Meshach, and Abed-nego, fell down bound into the midst of the burning fiery furnace. Then Nebuchadnezzar the king was astonied, and rose up in haste, and spake, and said unto his counsellors, Did not we cast three men bound into the midst of the fire? They answered and said unto the king, True, O king. He answered and said, Lo, I see four men loose, walking in the midst of the fire, and they have no hurt; and the form of the fourth is like the Son of God.

Then Nebuchadnezzar came near to the mouth of the burning fiery furnace, and spake, and said, Shadrach, Meshach, and Abed-nego, ye servants of the most high God, come forth, and come hither. Then Shadrach, Meshach, and Abed-nego, came forth of the midst of the fire. And the princes, governors, and captains, and the king's counsellors, being gathered together, saw these men, upon whose bodies the fire had no power, nor was an hair of their head singed, neither were their coats changed, nor the smell of fire had passed on them. Then Nebuchadnezzar spake, and said, Blessed be the God of Shadrach, Meshach, and Abed-nego, who hath sent his angel, and delivereth his servants that trusted in him, and have changed the king's word, and yielded their bodies, that they might not serve nor worship any god, except their own God. Therefore I make a decree, That every people, nation, and language, which speak any thing amiss against the God of Shadrach, Meshach, and Abed-nego, shall be cut in pieces, and their houses shall be made a dunghill: because there is no other God that can deliver after this sort. Then the king promoted Shadrach, Meshach, and Abed-nego, in the province of Babylon.

'AGAINST THE THREATS OF MALICE'

Against the threats
Of malice or of sorcery, or that power
Which erring men call Chance, this I hold firm:
Virtue may be assail'd, but never hurt,
Surpris'd by unjust force, but not enthrall'd;
Yea even that which Mischief meant most harm,
Shall in the happy trial prove most glory.
But evil on itself shall back recoil,
And mix no more with goodness, when at last
Gather'd like scum, and settl'd to itself,
It shall be in eternal restless change
Self-fed, and self-consumed; if this fail,
The pillar'd firmament is rottenness,
And earth's base built on stubble.

LXVI

HOW TO MANAGE A SEA-FIGHT

'FOR this master-peece of this worke, I confesse I might doe better to leave it to every particular man's conceit as it is, or those of longer practice or more experience; yet, because I have seene many bookes of the art of warre by land, and never any for the sea; seeing all men so silent in this most difficult service; and there are so many young captaines, and others that desire to be captaines, who know very little, or nothing at all to any purpose; for their better understanding I have proceeded thus farre. Now, for this that followes, what I have seene, done, and conceived by my small experience, I referre me to their friendly constructions and well-advised considerations.

'A saile! How beares she, or stands shee? to wind-ward or to lee-ward? Set him by the compasse. He stands right a-head; or on the weather-bow, or lee-bow. Let flie your colours, if you have a consort; else not. Out with all your sailes: a steady man to the helme: sit close, to keepe her steady. Give him chase, or fetch him up. Hee holds his owne; no, we gather on him.—Captaine, out goes his flags and pendants; also his waste-clothes and top-armings (which is a long red cloth about three quarters of a yard broad, edged on each side with calico, or white linnen cloth, that goeth round about the ship on the outsides of all her upper workes, fore and aft, and before the cubbridge heads; also about the fore and maine-tops, as well for the countenance and grace of the ship, as to cover the men from being seene).—He furles and slings his maine-yard; in goes his spret-sail. Thus they use to strip themselves into their short sailes, or *fighting sailes*, which is only the fore-saile, the maine and fore-top sailes; because the rest should not be fired nor spoiled; besides, they would be troublesome to handle, hinder our sight, and the using our armies.—He makes ready his close fights, fore and aft.

'Master! how stands the chase?—Right on head, I say. Well, we shall reach him by and by.—What! 's all ready? Yea, yea!—Every man to his charge: dowse your topsaile, to salute him for the sea: haile him with a noise of trumpets: "Whence is your ship?"—"Of Spaine; whence is yours?"—"Of England."—"Are you a merchant or a man-of-war?"—"We are of the sea!"——He waves us to lee-ward with his drawne sword; calls amaine for the King of Spaine, and springs his loufe.—Give him a chasepeece, with your broadside, and run a good berth a-head of him.—Done, done. We have the wind of him, and he tackes about. Tacke you about also, and keep your loufe. Be yare, at the helme; edge in with him; give him a volley of small shot; also your prow and broadside as before, and keep your loufe.—Hee pays us shot for shot. Well, wee shall requite him.—What! are you ready againe?—Yea, yea!—Try him once more as before.—Done, done.—Keepe your loufe, and lodge your ordnance againe. Is all ready?—Yea, yea! Edge in with him againe: begin with your bow peeces; proceed with your broadside, and let her fall off with the wind, to give her also your full chase, your weather broadside, and bring her round, that the sterne may also discharge; and your tackes close aboard againe.—Done, done.—The wind veeres; the sea goes too high to board her, and we are shot thorow and thorow, and betweene wind and water. Try the pump; beare up the helme.

'Master! let us breathe and refresh a little; and sling a man over board to stop the leakes, (that is, to trusse him up, about the middle, in a peece of canvas, and a rope to keepe him from sinking; and his armes at liberty, with a mallet in the one hand, and a plug tapped in oakum, and well tarred in a tarpawling clout, in the other, which he will quickly beat into the hole or holes the bullets made.) "What cheere, mates?" is all well?—"All well! all well! all well!"—"Then make ready to beare up with him againe, and with all your great and small shot charge him; and, in the smoke, board him thwart the hawse, on the bow, mid-ships, or, rather than faile, on his quarter; or make fast your grapplings, if you can, to his close fight, and sheere off.—Captaine! we are fowle on each other, and the ship is on fire. Cut any thing to get cleare, and smother the fire with wet cloathes.—In such a case, they will presently be such friends, as to help one the other all they can to get cleare, lest they both should burne together and sinke; and, if they be generous, the fire quenched, drinke kindly one to the other, heave their cans overboard, and then begin againe as before.

'Well, master, the day is spent, the night drawes on; let us consult. Chirurgion, looke to the wounded; and winde up the slaine, with each a weight or bullet at their heads and feet to make them sinke; and give them three gunnes for their funerals. Swabber, make cleane the ship. Purser, record their names. Watch, be vigilant to keepe your berth to wind-ward, that we lose him not in the night. Gunners, sponge your ordnance. Soldiers, scoure your peeces. Carpenters, about your leakes. Boatswaine and the rest, repair the sailes and shrouds; and, Cooke, see you observe your directions against the morning watch. "Boy, halla!"— "Master, halla!" "Is the kettle boiled?"—"Yea, yea!" Boatswaine, call up the men to prayer, and breakfast.

'Boy! fetch my cellar of bottels: a health to you all, fore and aft.—Courage, my hearts, for a fresh charge. Gunners, beat open the ports, and out with your lower tier; and bring me, from the weather side to the lee, so many peeces as we have ports to beare upon him. Master, lay him aboard, loufe for loufe. Midshipsmen, see the tops and yards well manned with stones, fire-pots, and brasse bales, to throw amongst them before we enter; or, if we be put off, charge them with all your great and small shot. In the smoke, let us enter them in the shrouds, and every squadron at his best advantage; so, sound drums and trumpets; and *Saint George for England*!

'They hang out a flag of truce; hale him amaine; abase (or take in) his flag: strike their sailes, and come aboard with their captaine, purser, and gunner; with their commission, cocket, or bills of loading.—Out goes the boat; they are lanched from the ship's side. Entertaine them with a general cry, "*God save the captaine and all the company*!" with the trumpets sounding. Examine them in particular; and then conclude your conditions, with feasting, freedome, or punishment, as you finde occasion; but always have as much care of their wounded as your owne. And, if there be either young women or aged men, use them nobly; which is ever the nature of a generous disposition. To conclude, if you surprise him, or enter perforce, you may stow the men, rifle, pillage, or sacke, and cry, "*a prise.*"'

How to call a Council of War

'To call a councell of warre in a fleet. There is your councell of warre, to manage all businesses of import; and the common counsell, for matters of small moment. When they would have a meeting, where the admirall doth appoint it; if in the admirall, they hang out a flag in the maine shrouds; if in the vice-admirall, in the fore-shrouds; if in the rear-admirall, in the mizen. If there bee many squadrons, the admirall of each squadron, upon sundry occasions, doth carry in their main-tops, flags of sundry colours; or else, they are distinguished by severall pendants from the yard's armes. Every night, or morning, they are to come under the lee of the admirall to salute him, and know his pleasure;

but no admirall, of any squadron, is to beare his flag in the main-top in the presence of the admirall-generall, except the admirall come aboard of him to councell, to dinner, or collation. And so, any ship else, where he so resideth during that time, is to weare his flag in the maine-top.'

To order a Navy at Sea

'They use to martiall or order those squadrons in rankes, like *maniples*, which is, foure-square; if the wind and sea permits a good berth or distance from each other, that they becalme not one another, nor come not fowle of each other; the Generall commonly in middest, his Vice-Admirall in the front, and his Rear-Admirall in the rear: or otherwise, in a *halfe-moone*, which is, two squadrons like two triangles, for the two hornes, and so the rest of the squadrons behinde each other a good distance; and the Generall in the middest of the halfe-circle, from whence he seeth all his fleet, and sendeth his directions, as he findes occasion, to whom he pleaseth.

'Now, betweene two navies they use often, especially in a harbour or road where they are at anchor, to fill old barkes with pitch, tar, traine-oile, lincet oile, brimstone, rosen, reeds, with dry wood, and such combustible things; sometimes they linke three or four together in the night, and put them adrift as they finde occasion. To passe a fort, some will make both ship and sailes all black; but if the fort keepe but a fire on the other side, and all the peeces point blanke with the fire, if they discharge (at) what is betwixt them and the fire, the shot will hit if the rule bee truly observed; for, when a ship is betwixt the fire and you, shee doth keepe you from seeing it till shee bee past it. To conclude, there is as many stratagems, advantages, and inventions to be used, as you finde occasions; and therefore, experience must be the best tutor.'

LXVII

SOME IRISH POEMS

DARK ROSALEEN

O MY dark Rosaleen,
    Do not sigh, do not weep!
    The priests are on the ocean green,
They march along the deep.
There's wine from the royal Pope,
    Upon the ocean green;
And Spanish ale shall give you hope,
    My dark Rosaleen!
    My own Rosaleen!
Shall glad your heart, shall give you hope,
Shall give you health and help, and hope,
    My dark Rosaleen.

Over hills, and through dales,
    Have I roamed for your sake;
All yesterday I sailed with sails
    On river and on lake.
The Erne, at its highest flood,
    I dashed across unseen,
For there was lightning in my blood,
    My dark Rosaleen!
    My own Rosaleen!
Oh! there was lightning in my blood,
Red lightning lightened through my blood,
    My dark Rosaleen!

All day long in unrest,
    To and fro do I move,
The very soul within my breast
    Is wasted for you, love!
The heart in my bosom faints
    To think of you, my Queen,

My life of life, my saint of saints,
  My dark Rosaleen!
  My own Rosaleen!
To hear your sweet and sad complaints,
My life, my love, my saint of saints,
  My dark Rosaleen!

Woe and pain, pain and woe,
  Are my lot, night and noon,
To see your bright face clouded so,
  Like to the mournful moon.
But yet will I rear your throne
  Again in golden sheen;
'Tis you shall reign, shall reign alone,
  My dark Rosaleen!
  My own Rosaleen!
'Tis you shall have the golden throne,
'Tis you shall reign, shall reign alone,
  My dark Rosaleen!

Over dews, over sands,
  Will I fly for your weal:
Your holy, delicate white hands
  Shall girdle me with steel.
At home in your emerald bowers,
  From morning's dawn till e'en,
You'll pray for me, my flower of flowers,
  My dark Rosaleen!
  My fond Rosaleen!
You'll think of me through daylight's hours,
My virgin flower, my flower of flowers,
  My dark Rosaleen!

I could scale the blue air,
  I could plough the high hills,
Oh, I could kneel all night in prayer,
  To heal your many ills!
And one beamy smile from you
  Would float like light between

My toils and me, my own, my true,
  My dark Rosaleen!
  My fond Rosaleen!
Would give me life and soul anew,
A second life, a soul anew,
  My dark Rosaleen!

O! the Erne shall run red
  With redundance of blood,
The earth shall rock beneath our tread,
  And flames wrap hill and wood,
And gun-peal, and slogan cry
  Wake many a glen serene,
Ere you shall fade, ere you shall die,
  My dark Rosaleen!
  My own Rosaleen!
The Judgment Hour must first be nigh
Ere you can fade, ere you can die,
  My dark Rosaleen!

A RETORT

Not hers your vast Imperial mart,
  Where myriad hopes on fears are hurled;
Where furious rivals meet and part
  To woo a world.

Not hers your vast Imperial town,
  Your mighty mammoth piles of grain,
Your loaded vessels sweeping down
  To glut the main.

Unused, unseen, her rivers flow
  From mountain tarn to ocean tide;
Wide vacant leagues the sunbeams show,
  The rain-clouds hide.

You swept them vacant! Your decree
  Bid all her budding commerce cease;
You drove her from your subject sea
  To starve in peace!

Well, be it peace! Resigned they flow,
   No laden fleet adown them glides,
But wheeling salmon sometimes show
   Their silvered sides;

And sometimes through the long still day
   The breeding herons slowly rise,
Lifting grey tranquil wings away
   To tranquil skies.

Stud all your shores with prosperous towns!
   Blacken your hill-sides, mile on mile!
Redden with bricks your patient downs!
   And proudly smile!

A day will come before you guess,
   A day when men with clearer light,
Will rue that deed beyond redress;
   Will loathe that sight.

And, loathing, fly the hateful place,
   And, shuddering, quit the hideous thing
For where unblackened rivers race
   And skylarks sing.

For where, remote from smoke and noise,
   Old Leisure sits knee-deep in grass;
Where simple days bring simple joys,
   And lovers pass.

I see her in those coming days,
   Still young, still gay; her unbound hair
Crowned with a crown of starlike rays,
   Serenely fair.

I see an envied haunt of peace,
   Calm and untouched, remote from roar;
Where wearied men may from their burdens cease
   On a still shore.

CORRYMEELA

Over here in England I'm helpin' wi' the hay,
And I wisht I was in Ireland the livelong day;
Weary on the English hay, an' sorra take the wheat!
Och! Corrymeela, an' the blue sky over it.

There's a deep dumb river flowin' by beyont the heavy trees,
This livin' air is moithered wi' the hummin' o' the bees;
I wisht I'd hear the Claddagh burn go runnin' through the heat,
Past Corrymeela, wi' the blue sky over it.

The people that's in England is richer nor the Jews,
There's not the smallest young gossoon but thravels in his shoes!
I'd give the pipe between me teeth to see a barefut child,
Och! Corrymeela, an' the low south wind.

Here's hands so full o' money an' hearts so full o' care,
By the luck o' love! I'd still go light for all I did go bare.
'God save ye, colleen dhas,' I said; the girl she thought me wild!
Far Corrymeela, an' the low south wind.

D'ye mind me now, the song at night is mortial hard to raise,
The girls are heavy goin' here, the boys are ill to plase;
When ones't I'm out this workin' hive, 'tis I'll be back again—
Aye, Corrymeela, in the same soft rain.

The puff o' smoke from one ould roof before an English town!
For a *shaugh* wid Andy Feelan here I'd give a silver crown,
For a curl o' hair like Mollie's ye'll ask the like in vain,
Sweet Corrymeela, an' the same soft rain.

LXVIII

A RIDE ON A BUFFALO

AT length the watch was told off, the lariats were shortened, the picket-pins driven home, and my comrades, rolling themselves up in their blankets, rested their heads in the hollow of their saddles, and went to sleep. There was a man named Hibbets in our party, who, from his habits of somnolency, had earned the 'soubriquet' of 'Sleepyhead.' For this reason the first watch had been assigned to him, being the least dangerous, as Indians seldom made their attacks until the hour of soundest sleep: that before daybreak. Hibbets had climbed to his post, the top of the bluff, where he could command a view of the surrounding prairie. Before night had set in, I had noticed a very beautiful spot on the bank of the arroyo, about two hundred yards from where my comrades lay. A sudden fancy came into my head to sleep there: and taking up my rifle, robe, and blanket, at the same time calling to 'Sleepyhead' to awake me in case of alarm, I proceeded thither. . . . I lay a good while awake, until my cigar burnt up to my lips (we smoke them close on the prairies); then, spitting out the stump, I turned over on my side, and was soon in the land of dreams.

I could not have been asleep many minutes when I felt sensible of a strange noise, like distant thunder or the roaring of a waterfall. The ground seemed to tremble beneath me. 'We are going to have a dash of a thunder-shower,' thought I, still half dreaming, half sensible to impressions from without; and I drew the folds of my blanket closer around me, and again slept. I was awakened by a noise like thunder—indeed, like the trampling of a thousand hoofs, and the lowing of a thousand oxen! The earth echoed and trembled, I could hear the shouts of my comrades: the voices of St. Vrain and Gode, the latter calling out,—'Sacr-r-re! monsieur; prenez garde des buffles!' I saw that they had drawn the horses, and were hurrying them under the bluff. I sprang to my feet, flinging aside my blanket. A fearful spectacle was before me. Away to the west, as far as the eye could reach, the prairie seemed in motion. Black waves rolled over its undulating outlines, as though some burning mountain were pouring down its lava upon the plains. A thousand bright spots flashed and flitted along the moving surface like jets of fire. The ground shook, men shouted, horses reared upon their ropes, neighing wildly. My dog barked, and howled, running around me! For a moment I thought I was dreaming; but no, the scene was too real to be mistaken for a vision. I saw the border of a black wave within ten paces of me, and still approaching! Then, and not till then did I recognize the shaggy crests and glaring eyeballs of the buffalo! 'Oh, God; I am in their track. I shall be trampled to death!'

It was too late to attempt an escape by running. I seized my rifle and fired at the foremost of the band. The effect of my shot was not perceptible. The water of the arroyo was dashed in my face. A huge bull, ahead of the rest, furious and snorting, plunged through the stream and up the slope. I was lifted and tossed high into the air. I was thrown rearwards, and fell upon a moving mass. I did not feel hurt or stunned. I felt myself carried onward upon the backs of several animals, that, in the dense drove, ran close together. These, frightened at their strange burden, bellowed loudly, and dashed on to the front. A sudden thought struck me, and, fixing on that which was most under me, I dropped my legs astride of him, embracing his hump, and clutching the long woolly hair that grew upon his neck. The animal 'routed' with extreme terror, and, plunging forward, soon headed the band. This was exactly what I wanted; and on we went over the prairie, the bull running at top speed, believing, no doubt, that he had a panther or a catamount between his shoulders. I had no desire to disabuse him of this belief, and, lest he should deem me altogether harmless, and come to a halt, I slipped out my bowie, which happened to be 'handy,' and pricked him up whenever he showed symptoms of lagging. At every fresh touch of the 'spur' he roared out, and ran forward at a redoubled pace. My danger was still extreme. The drove was coming on behind with the front of nearly a mile. I could not have cleared it had the bull stopped and left me on the prairie. Notwithstanding the peril I was in, I could not resist laughing at my ludicrous situation. I felt as one does when looking at a good comedy. We struck through a village of 'prairie dogs.' Here I fancied the animal was about to turn and run back. This brought my mirth to a sudden pause; but the buffalo usually runs in a 'bee-line,' and fortunately mine made no exception to the law. On he went, sinking to the knees, kicking the dust from the conical hills, snorting and bellowing with rage and terror. The 'Plum Buttes' were directly in the line of our course. I had seen this from the start, and knew that if I could reach them I would be safe. They were nearly three miles from the bluff where we had bivouacked, but in my ride I fancied them ten. A small one rose over the prairie, several hundred yards nearer than the main heights. Towards this I pricked the foaming bull in a last stretch, and he brought me cleverly within a hundred yards of its base. It was now time to take leave of my dusky companion. I could have slaughtered him as I leaned over his back. My knife rested upon the most vulnerable part of his huge body. No! I could not have slain that buffalo for the Koh-i-noor. Untwisting my fingers from his thick fleece, I slipped down over his tail, and without as much as saying 'Good night!' ran with all my speed towards the knoll. I climbed up; and sitting down upon a loose boulder of rock, looked over the prairie.

The moon was still shining brightly. My late companion had halted not far from where I had left him, and stood glaring back with an air of extreme bewilderment. There was something so comical in the sight that I yelled with laughter as I sat securely on my perch. I looked to the south-west. As far as the eye could see, the prairie was black, and moving. The living wave came rolling onward and toward me; but I could now observe it in safety. The myriads of glancing eyes, sparkling like phosphoric gleams, no longer flashed terror. The drove was still half a mile distant. I thought I saw quick gleams, and heard the report of fire-arms away over its left border; but I could not be certain. I had begun to think of the fate of my comrades, and this gave me hopes that they were safe. The buffaloes approached the butte on which I was seated; and, perceiving the obstacle, suddenly forked into two great belts, and swept right and left around it. What struck me at this moment as curious was, that my bull, my particular bull, instead of waiting till his comrades had come up and falling in among the foremost, suddenly tossed up his head, and galloped off as if a pack of wolves had been after him. He ran towards the outside of the band. When he had reached a point that placed him fairly beyond the flank, I could see him closing in, and moving on with the rest. This strange tactic of my late companion puzzled me at the time, but I afterwards learned that it was sound strategy on his part. Had he remained where I had parted with him, the foremost bulls coming up would have mistaken him for an individual of some other tribe, and would certainly have gored him to death. I sat upon the rock for nearly two hours, silently watching the sable stream as it poured past. I was on an island in the midst of a black and glittering sea. At one time I fancied I was moving, that the butte was sailing onward, and the buffaloes were standing still. My head swam with dizziness, and I leaped to my feet to drive away the strange illusion. The torrent rolled onward, and at length the hindmost went straggling past. I descended from the knoll, and commenced groping my way over the black, trodden earth. What was lately a green sward now presented the aspect of ground freshly ploughed and trampled by droves of oxen. A number of white animals, resembling a flock of sheep, passed near me. They were wolves hanging upon the skirts of the herd. I pushed on. . . .

At length I heard voices; and, in the clear moonlight, could see several horsemen galloping in circles over the plain. I shouted 'Halloa!' A voice answered mine, and one of the horsemen came galloping up; it was St. Vrain.

'Why, Lord bless me, Heller!' cried he, reining up, and bending from his saddle to get a better view of me, 'is it you or your ghost? As I sit here, it's the man himself, and alive!' 'Never in better condition,' I replied. 'But where did you come from? the clouds? the sky? where?' And his questions were echoed by the others, who at this moment were shaking me by the hand, as if they had not seen me for a twelvemonth. Gode seemed to be the most perplexed man of the party. 'Mon Dieu! run over; tramp by von million dam buffes, et ne pas mort! 'Cr-r-re matin!' 'We were hunting for your body, or rather, the fragments of it,' said St. Vrain. 'We had searched every foot of the prairie for a mile round, and had almost come to the conclusion that the fierce brutes had eaten you up.' 'Eat monsieur up! No! tre million buffles no him eat. Mon Dieu! Ha, Sleephead, pe dam!' This exclamation of the Canadian was addressed to Hibbets, who had failed to warn my comrades of where I lay, and thus placed me in such a dangerous predicament. 'We saw you tossed in the air,' continued St. Vrain, 'and fall right into the thick of them. Then, of course, we gave you up. But how, in heaven's name, have you got clear?' I related my adventure to my wondering comrades. 'Par Dieu!' cried Gode, 'un garcon tres bizarre: une aventure tres merveilleuse!'

LIX

SCROOGE'S VISITORS

THE GHOST OF CHRISTMAS PAST

THEY were now in the busy thoroughfares of a city where shadowy passengers passed and repassed; where shadowy carts and coaches battled for the way, and all the strife and tumult of a real city were. It was made plain enough, by the dressing of the shops, that here too it was Christmas time again; but it was evening, and the streets were lighted up. The Ghost stopped at a certain warehouse door, and asked Scrooge if he knew it.

'Know it!' said Scrooge. 'Was I apprenticed here!'

They went in. At the sight of an old gentleman in a Welsh wig, sitting behind such a high desk, that if he had been two inches taller he must have knocked his head against the ceiling, Scrooge cried in great excitement:

'Why, it's old Fezziwig! Bless his heart; it's Fezziwig alive again!'

Old Fezziwig laid down his pen, and looked up at the clock, which pointed to the hour of seven. He rubbed his hands, adjusted his capacious waistcoat; laughed all over himself, from his shoes to his organ of benevolence; and called out in a comfortable, oily, rich, fat, jovial voice:

'Yo ho, there! Ebenezer! Dick!'

Scrooge's former self, now grown a young man, came briskly in, accompanied by his fellow-'prentice.

'Dick Wilkins, to be sure!' said Scrooge to the Ghost. 'Bless me, yes. There he is. He was very much attached to me, was Dick. Poor Dick! Dear, dear!'

'Yo ho, my boys!' said Fezziwig. 'No more work to-night. Christmas Eve, Dick. Christmas, Ebenezer! Let's have the shutters up,' cried old Fezziwig, with a sharp clap of his hands, 'before a man can say Jack Robinson!'

You wouldn't believe how those two fellows went at it! Clear away! There was nothing they wouldn't have cleared away, or couldn't have cleared away, with old Fezziwig looking on. It was done in a minute. Every movable was packed off . . . the floor was swept and watered, the lamps were trimmed, fuel was heaped upon the fire; and the ware-house was as snug, and warm, and dry, and bright a ball-room, as you would desire to see upon a winter's night.

In came a fiddler with a music-book, and went up to the lofty desk, and made an orchestra of it, and tuned like fifty stomach-aches. In came Mrs. Fezziwig, one vast sub-stantial smile. In came the three Miss Fezziwigs, beaming and lovable. In came the six young followers whose hearts they broke. In came all the young men and women employed in the business. . . . Away they all went, twenty couple at once; hands half round and back again the other way; down the middle and up again; round and round in various stages of affectionate grouping; old top couple always turning up in the wrong place; new top couple starting off again, as soon as they got there; all top couples at last, and not a bottom one to help them! When this result was brought about, old Fezziwig, clapping his hands to stop the dance, cried out, 'Well done!' and the fiddler plunged his hot face into a pot of porter, especially provided for that purpose. But scorning rest, upon his reappearance he instantly began again, though there were no dancers yet, as if the other fiddler had been carried home, exhausted, on a shutter, and he were a bran new man resolved to beat him out of sight, or perish.

There were more dances, and there were forfeits, and more dances, and there was cake, and there was negus, and there was a great piece of Cold Roast, and there was a great piece of Cold Boiled, and there were mince-pies, and plenty of beer. But the great effect of the evening came after the Roast and Boiled, when the fiddler (an artful dog, mind! The sort of man who knew his business better than you or I could have told it him!) struck up 'Sir Roger de Coverley.' Then old Fezziwig stood out to dance with Mrs. Fezziwig. Top couple, too; with a good stiff piece of work cut out for them; three or four and twenty pair of partners; people who were not to be trifled with; people who *would* dance, and had no notion of walking.

But if they had been twice as many—ah, four times—old Fezziwig would have been a match for them, and so would Mrs. Fezziwig. As to *her*, she was worthy to be his partner in every sense of the term. If that's not high praise, tell me higher, and I'll use it. A positive light appeared to issue from Fezziwig's calves. They shone in every part of the dance like moons. You couldn't have predicted, at any given time, what would have become of them next. And when old Fezziwig and Mrs. Fezziwig had gone all through the dance; advance and retire, both hands to your partner, bow and curtsey, corkscrew, thread-the-needle, and back again to your place; Fezziwig 'cut'—cut so deftly, that he appeared to wink with his legs, and came upon his feet again without a stagger.

When the clock struck eleven, this domestic ball broke up. Mr. and Mrs. Fezziwig took their stations, one on either side of the door, and shaking hands with every person individually as he or she went out, wished him or her a Merry Christmas. When everybody had retired but the two 'prentices, they did the same to them; and thus the cheerful voices died away, and the lads were left to their beds; which were under a counter in the back-shop.

During the whole of this time, Scrooge had acted like a man out of his wits. His heart and soul were in the scene, and with his former self. He corroborated everything, remembered everything, enjoyed everything, and underwent the strangest agitation. It was not until now, when the bright faces of his former self and Dick were turned from them, that he remembered the Ghost, and became conscious that it was looking full upon him, while the light upon its head burnt very clear.

'A small matter,' said the Ghost, 'to make these silly folks so full of gratitude.'

'Small!' echoed Scrooge.

The Spirit signed to him to listen to the two apprentices, who were pouring out their hearts in praise of Fezziwig: and when he had done so, said, 'Why! Is it not? He has spent but a few pounds of your mortal money: three or four perhaps. Is that so much that he deserves this praise?'

'It isn't that,' said Scrooge, heated by the remark, and speaking unconsciously like his former, not his latter, self. 'It isn't that, Spirit. He has the power to render us happy or unhappy; to make our service light or burdensome; a pleasure or a toil. Say that his power lies in words and looks; in things so slight and insignificant that it is impossible to add and count 'em up: what then? The happiness he gives, is quite as great as if it cost a fortune.'

He felt the Spirit's glance, and stopped.

'What is the matter?' asked the Ghost.

'Nothing particular,' said Scrooge.

'Something, I think?' the Ghost insisted.

'No,' said Scrooge. 'No. I should like to be able to say a word or two to my clerk just now. That's all.'

His former self turned down the lamps as he gave utterance to the wish; and Scrooge and the Ghost again stood side by side in the open air.

THE GHOST OF CHRISTMAS PRESENT

And now, without a word of warning from the Ghost, they stood upon a bleak and desert moor, where monstrous masses of rude stone were cast about, as though it were the burial place of giants: and water spread itself wheresoever it listed, or would have done so, but for the frost that held it prisoner; and nothing grew but moss and furze, and coarse rank grass. Down in the west the setting sun had left a streak of fiery red, which glared upon the desolation for an instant, like a sullen eye, and frowning lower, lower, lower yet, was lost in the thick bloom of darkest night.

'What place is this?' asked Scrooge.

'A place where Miners live, who labour in the bowels of the earth,' returned the Spirit. 'But they know me. See!'

A light shone from the window of a hut, and swiftly they advanced towards it. Passing through the wall of mud and stone, they found a cheerful company assembled round a glowing fire. An old, old man and woman, with their children and their children's children, and another generation beyond that, all decked out gaily in their holiday attire. The old man, in a voice that seldom rose above the howling of the wind upon the barren waste, was singing them a Christmas song—it had been a very old song when he was a boy—and from time to time they all joined in the chorus. So surely as they raised their voices, the old man got quite blithe and loud; and so surely as they stopped, his vigour sank again.

The Spirit did not tarry here, but bade Scrooge hold his robe, and passing on above the moor, sped—whither? Not to sea? To sea. To Scrooge's horror, looking back, he saw the last of the land, a frightful range of rocks, behind them; and his ears were deafened by the thundering of water, as it rolled and roared, and raged among the dreadful caverns it had worn, and fiercely tried to undermine the earth.

Built upon a dismal reef of sunken rocks, some league or so from shore, on which the waters chafed and dashed, the wild year through, there stood a solitary lighthouse. Great heaps of seaweed clung to its base, and storm-birds—born of the wind one might suppose, as seaweed of the water—rose and fell about it, like the waves they skimmed.

But even here, two men who watched the light had made a fire, that through the loophole in the thick stone wall shed out a ray of brightness on the awful sea. Joining their horny hands over the rough table at which they sat, they wished each other Merry Christmas in their can of grog; and one of them: the elder, too, with his face all damaged and scarred with hard weather, as the figurehead of an old ship might be: struck up a sturdy song that was like a Gale in itself.

Again the Ghost sped on, above the black and heaving sea —on, on—until, being far away, as he told Scrooge, from any shore, they lighted on a ship. They stood beside the helmsman at the wheel, the look-out in the bow, the officers who had the watch; dark, ghostly figures in their several stations; but every man among them hummed a Christmas tune, or had a Christmas thought, or spoke below his breath to his companion of some bygone Christmas Day, with homeward hopes belonging to it. And every man on board, waking or sleeping, good or bad, had had a kinder word for another on that day than on any day in the year; and had shared to some extent in its festivities; and had remembered those he cared for at a distance, and had known that they delighted to remember him.